the kitchen garden cookbook

the kitchen garden cookbook

EDITOR-IN-CHIEF
Caroline Bretherton

LONDON, NEW YORK, MUNICH,
MELBOURNE, DELHI

Senior Editor Alastair Laing
Project Art Editor William Hicks
Editorial Assistant Roxanne Benson-Mackey
US Editor Liza Kaplan
Managing Editor Dawn Henderson
Managing Art Editor Marianne Markham
Senior Creative Nicola Powling
Senior Presentations Creative Caroline de Souza
Production Editor Maria Elia
Production Controller Alice Sykes
Creative Technical Support Sonia Charbonnier

DK INDIA
Senior Editor Chitra Subramanyam
Editor Charis Bhagianathan
Senior Art Editor Neha Ahuja
Designer Heema Sabharwal
Managing Editor Glenda Fernandes
Senior Art Editor (Lead) Navidita Thapa
DTP Manager Sunil Sharma
DTP Designer Tarun Sharma
DTP Operator Sourabh Challariya
Editor Nicola Hodgson
New photography William Reavell

First American Edition, 2011

Published in the United States by
DK Publishing, 375 Hudson Street
New York, New York 10014

11 12 13 14 15 10 9 8 7 6 5 4 3 2 1
001—178300—Mar/2011

A catalog record for this book is available from the Library of Congress.

ISBN 978-0-7566-7188-4

DK books are available at special discounts when purchased in bulk
for sales promotions, premiums, fund-raising, or educational use.
For details, contact: DK Publishing Special Markets, 375 Hudson Street,
New York, New York 10014 or SpecialSales@dk.com

Color reproduction by Colourscan, Singapore
Printed and bound in Singapore by Tien Wah Press

Discover more at **www.dk.com**

CONTENTS

INTRODUCTION

As a child, I grew up in a house with a large vegetable garden. I would watch endless weekends pass as my parents disappeared down to the bottom of the garden, only to reappear hours later tired, dirty, but happy and, no doubt, clutching a few freshly harvested zucchinis or a handful of asparagus spears. Come suppertime in summer, I would be sent off with a colander to crawl, commando-style, under the anti-squirrel netting to pick some strawberries for snacks. Such things leave a mark on your character and I found, as I grew older, that I had in turn developed a hankering to grow my own.

Living in a city meant this wasn't necessarily going to be easy, but after a long wait I finally inherited an old, overgrown patch of ground that was soon to become my very own garden. It may be that you have a large or small kitchen garden, balcony, or even roof terrace, but whatever piece of soil you have available, there will be something you'll be able to grow on it.

Growing your own is satisfying in so many ways: the excitement of watching the first young seedlings appear; planting out fledgling plants in pleasingly straight rows; and that particular sense of peace that falls over a garden in the early evening, when you've gone out to water and sit down to survey all your work coming to fruition, the stresses of life a distant memory. You may feel tired and dirty after a long day spent planting potatoes, but it is a weariness filled with its own sweet sense of satisfaction at a job well done.

By far the most fulfilling part of growing your own is harvesting the crops. I'm never sure whether spring is my favorite season, arriving with its tender young peas and fava beans, first delicate lettuces, and early potatoes. But then there is the florid abundance of high summer, when, no matter how fast you pick them, you'll never be able to keep up with the green beans and zucchinis. Summer's swan song must be the tomatoes finally ripening into a myriad of shapes and colors, heralding the onset of autumn with its bulging pumpkins for hardening off and storing, before the taming of the plot really begins in winter. It is then that I pull up anything else worth preserving and finally set the garden to order, ready for next year. Brassicas, overwintering fava beans, leeks, garlic, and other hardy crops all wait patiently for the spring when the plot once more comes to life.

Finally, there is the cooking. Having invested so much time and energy in growing your own fruit and vegetables, you'll want to make the best of them. I have included in this book some of my favorite recipes for home-grown crops; whether they be simple, everyday supper dishes helping to use up a glut of produce, or more elaborate meals designed to showcase some treasured harvest. Vegetables can often be sidelined as a support act, but after you have grown them yourself you will want to give them a starring role. Tarts and casseroles, stews and salads can all be wonderful vehicles to allow the intense flavors of your freshly harvested crops to shine through.

Every gardener knows that a glut of a certain type of fruit or vegetable is inevitable. Depending on your particular climate, different crops will produce unnervingly high yields and you'll want to make the best of them, both in terms of flavor and lack of waste. Eating the same thing every day for a month could get repetitive, so here I hope you'll find inspiration to see your produce in a new light. Pickling, preserving, and freezing are all good ways to lock the goodness of our gardens away for the lean months of winter, and for that reason, you'll find many recipes that cover all aspects of preserving.

I can truthfully say there are few things in life that give me greater pleasure than growing, tending, harvesting, and cooking my own produce. Working with the rhythms of the seasons, both in the garden and the kitchen, and eating food that is grown locally, without the use of chemicals, and practically for free, are all things that I find intensely rewarding and I hope you will, too.

Caroline

SPRING

Asparagus

Peas

Fava beans

Swiss chard

Cauliflower

Spinach

Lettuce

Arugula

Radishes

Rhubarb

Such a regal vegetable as freshly picked asparagus needs only the simplest treatment, and this rich, classic hollandaise sauce is an ideal accompaniment.

Char-grilled asparagus
with hollandaise

Serves 4 • Prep 10 mins • Cooking 10 mins

INGREDIENTS

1 lb (500g) asparagus

1 tbsp olive oil

2 tbsp white wine vinegar

4 egg yolks

$1/2$ cup butter, melted

salt and freshly ground
    black pepper

juice of $1/2$ lemon

METHOD

1 Trim or snap off the woody ends of the asparagus spears. Working in batches if needed, heat a ridged cast-iron grill pan and brush with the oil. When very hot, add the asparagus and grill for 5–6 minutes, depending on the thickness of the spears, turning once, until lightly charred and just tender.

2 Meanwhile, to make the sauce, heat the vinegar in a small, nonreactive saucepan and allow to simmer until it reduces by half. Remove from the heat, add 2 tbsp water, then whisk in the egg yolks one at a time.

3 Return the pan to very low heat and whisk continuously until the mixture is thick and light. Remove from the heat and gradually whisk in the melted butter. Season to taste with salt and pepper and stir in the lemon juice.

4 Divide the asparagus between plates and serve with the sauce spooned over the spears.

ASPARAGUS

When to pick
Asparagus is best picked when 6in (15cm) high and no thicker than your index finger. Harvest with a sharp knife, cutting just below the soil's surface.

Use fresh
Asparagus can be steamed, boiled, roasted, stir-fried, or grilled. Refridgerate raw in a plastic bag up to 3 days with stems wrapped in damp paper towels.

How to preserve
Green asparagus can be preserved in oil, having been cooked lightly in advance of packing.

Freezing options
Flavor is best preserved if asparagus is grilled, but it can be blanched for 2–3 minutes, cooled in ice water, drained, and frozen for up to 9 months.

As much as I love steamed asparagus, grilling is a good alternative, producing a meatier result. Here, the stronger taste of the asparagus is a great match for a sharp, tangy sheep's milk cheese or Parmesan.

Char-grilled asparagus
with olive oil and cheese

Serves 4 • **Prep** 5 mins • **Cooking** 10 mins

INGREDIENTS

1lb (500g) asparagus

4 tbsp olive oil

2 tbsp balsamic vinegar
   or balsamic glaze

coarse sea salt

hard sheep's milk cheese or
   Parmesan cheese, shaved
   with a vegetable peeler, to
   garnish before serving

METHOD

1 Trim or snap the woody ends from the asparagus spears. Heat a ridged cast-iron grill pan and brush lightly with some of the oil. When very hot, add the asparagus and grill for 5–6 minutes, depending on the thickness of the spears, turning once, until tender and bright green.

2 Divide the asparagus between serving plates and drizzle with the remaining olive oil and balsamic vinegar or balsamic glaze. To serve, sprinkle with a few grains of salt and scatter freshly shaved cheese over.

The delicate color of white asparagus is produced by growing it in the dark, a method known as forcing. Served with subtly flavored mayonnaise, it makes a glorious spring dish.

White asparagus with
garlic and herb mayonnaise dip

Serves 4 as a dip • **Prep** 5 mins • **Cooking** 10 mins

INGREDIENTS

1lb 2oz (500g) white or thick
    green asparagus spears,
    woody ends removed
2 egg yolks
2 tbsp white wine vinegar
1 tsp Dijon mustard
1 1/4 cups light olive oil
juice of 1/2 lemon
sea salt and freshly ground
    black pepper
1 garlic clove, crushed
1 tbsp chopped parsley
1 tbsp chopped tarragon

METHOD

1 Trim or snap off the woody ends of the asparagus spears. The spears can be tied in bundles, if preferred, then steamed upright in a deep pot, just until tender. Cover the pot with a lid, or make a loose tent with foil to cover, but not damage, the asparagus tips.

2 Place the egg yolks, vinegar, and mustard in a food processor, and blend for 1–2 minutes, or until pale and creamy. Alternatively, whisk by hand in a large bowl, using a balloon whisk.

3 With the motor still running, or still whisking by hand, slowly pour in the olive oil. Blend the mixture until it is thick, creamy, and smooth.

4 Spoon into a bowl and stir in the lemon juice. Season to taste with salt and pepper. Flavor the mayonnaise with the garlic, parsley, and tarragon. Season to taste. Use as a dip.

Caution: Because of the possible threat of salmonella, the USDA recommends that everyone should avoid raw or lightly cooked eggs; especially the very young, the elderly, pregnant women, and other people with compromised immune systems.

A simple way to turn a bunch of asparagus into a main course, this recipe sings with the freshness of the lemon zest, capers, and fresh Parmesan used.

Pasta with asparagus
and zucchini

Serves 4 • **Prep** 10 mins • **Cooking** 20 mins

INGREDIENTS

1 tbsp olive oil

1 onion, finely chopped

sea salt

4 small zucchini, 2 diced
  and 2 grated

3 garlic cloves, grated
  or finely chopped

1 bunch thin asparagus spears,
  trimmed and stalks cut into
  3 pieces each

¼ cup dry white wine

1–2 tsp capers, rinsed and
  chopped

zest of 1 lemon

12oz (350g) dry penne or other
  tube-shaped pasta

handful of flat-leaf parsley,
  finely chopped

Parmesan cheese, grated,
  to serve

METHOD

1 Heat the oil in a large frying pan, add the onion and a pinch of salt, and cook over low heat for 5 minutes or until soft and translucent. Add all the zucchini and cook, stirring occasionally, for 10 minutes or until it has cooked down and softened. Don't allow it to brown.

2 Stir in the garlic and asparagus. Add the wine, raise the heat, and allow to boil for 2–3 minutes, then return to a simmer. Cook for 2–3 minutes, or until the asparagus softens, then remove from the heat and stir in the capers and lemon zest. For a creamier sauce, add a splash of cream once the wine cooks down, during the final minutes of cooking.

3 Meanwhile, cook the pasta in a large pot of boiling, salted water for 10 minutes or until it is tender but still has a bit of bite to it. Drain, reserving a tiny amount of the cooking water. Return the pasta to the pot with the reserved cooking water and toss together. Add the zucchini mixture and parsley, then toss again. Sprinkle with Parmesan and serve.

Serve this light, fragrant quiche warm. It is the perfect way to spotlight homegrown asparagus. A few stems treated this way take center stage as part of an elegant lunch or supper dish.

Asparagus quiche

Serves 4–6 • **Prep** 20 mins, plus chilling • **Cooking** 45 mins

INGREDIENTS

For the pastry

1 ½ cups all-purpose flour

pinch of sea salt

3 tbsp cold lard or vegetable shortening, diced

3 tbsp cold butter, diced

2 tbsp cold water

For the filling

8oz (175g) asparagus

a little olive oil

4oz (115g) cream cheese, cut into pieces, at room temperature

2 tsp chopped fresh thyme

freshly ground black pepper

3/4 cup shredded, aged Cheddar cheese

2 eggs

1/2 cup half-and-half

METHOD

1 Sift the flour and salt into a bowl. Add lard and butter and rub in with the fingertips until the mixture resembles breadcrumbs. Mix in cold water to form a firm dough. Knead on a lightly floured surface. Roll out and use to line an 8in (20cm) tart pan with removable bottom, set on a baking sheet. Chill for 30 minutes.

2 Preheat the oven to 400°F (200°C). Line the pastry-lined tart pan with parchment paper and fill with baking beans. Bake for 10 minutes. Remove the paper and beans, and bake another 5 minutes. Remove from the oven. Lower the oven temperature to 350°F (180°C).

3 Toss the asparagus in a little olive oil. Cook on a hot grill pan for 4 minutes, turning once or twice, until bright green and just tender.

4 Spread the cream cheese over the bottom of the pastry shell. Sprinkle with thyme, pepper, and Cheddar. Trim the asparagus to fit the tart. Scatter in trimmings and lay the spears attractively on top. Beat the eggs and half-and-half together with a little salt and pepper. Pour into the shell. Bake until the custard is golden and set, about 30 minutes. Cool on a wire rack 10 minutes before removing the fluted ring. Serve warm or cold.

PEAS

When to pick
Pick frequently to encourage regrowth. Choose small peas if eating the pod. Allow pods to swell if harvesting peas. Pick from the bottom up.

Eat and store fresh
Peas should be eaten as soon as possible after picking, because the natural sugars in the vegetable soon turn to starch.

How to preserve
Larger peas can be dried for winter cooking, or the whole pods used to make pea pod wine.

Freezing options
Peas freeze well. Blanch for 1–2 minutes, leave to cool, then open freeze on trays, bag up, and store in the freezer for up to 12 months.

Growing peas is a pleasure, but discarding the pods can seem a waste. Here pods as well as peas can be used to make this vibrant spring soup. A cheats' version could use frozen peas!

Pea soup
with mint gremolata

Serves 6 • **Prep** 10 mins • **Cooking** 35 mins

INGREDIENTS

For the soup

1 onion, finely chopped

2 tbsp butter

1 potato, coarsely chopped

1lb (550g) peas in their pods, coarsely cut up

5 cups chicken or vegetable stock

1 tsp superfine sugar

1 sprig of fresh mint

salt and freshly ground black pepper

a little half-and-half, to serve

For the gremolata

2 tbsp finely chopped flat-leaf parsley

2 tbsp finely chopped fresh mint

2 tsp finely grated lemon zest

1 garlic clove, finely chopped

METHOD

1 Cook the onion gently in the butter for 7–10 minutes, stirring until soft. Add the remaining soup ingredients, except the half-and-half. Bring to a boil, reduce the heat, partially cover, and simmer gently for 20 minutes, or until the peas and potato are very soft. Discard mint.

2 Working in batches if necessary, purée the soup in a blender or food processor. Pass through a sieve to remove the pods and pea skins. Taste and adjust the seasoning. To serve, either reheat or chill.

3 Meanwhile, thoroughly mix together the gremolata ingredients. Ladle the soup into bowls. Before serving, add a swirl of half-and-half and sprinkle with a little of the gremolata.

This classic Spanish tapas dish is a good way to use peas that grew a little too large. Their slightly mealy texture stands up to the strong flavors of Serrano ham and smoked paprika.

Peas with ham

Serves 4 • **Prep** 5 mins • **Cooking** 15 mins

INGREDIENTS

2 tbsp olive oil

1 onion, finely chopped

8oz (200g) Serrano ham, diced

1 cup canned tomato puree

1 tsp smoked paprika

1 cup shelled peas

1 garlic clove, crushed

1 tbsp finely chopped fresh
    parsley

salt and freshly ground black
    pepper

$^{1}/_{2}$ cup dry white wine

METHOD

1 Heat the oil in a frying pan and add the onion. Cook for 5 minutes, stirring frequently, until soft.

2 Increase the heat, add the ham and cook until it begins to brown, then add the tomatoes and paprika. Bring to a boil, reduce the heat, and simmer for 3 minutes, stirring frequently. Stir in the peas.

3 Mix the garlic, chopped parsley, and about $^{1}/_{2}$ tsp salt together, then stir in the wine. Pour this mixture into the pan, and season to taste with pepper. Simmer for 5 minutes, transfer to a heated serving dish, and serve hot.

Baby peas are at their absolute best, added raw to this delicate salad. For a main course, omit the feta and substitute fillets of hot or cold grilled salmon for a classic taste of British summer.

Feta and pea salad
with watercress mayonnaise

Serves 4 • **Prep** 15 mins

INGREDIENTS

handful of fresh watercress, coarsely chopped

3–4 tbsp prepared mayonnaise

1 tsp cream-style, prepared white horseradish

salt and freshly ground black pepper

6 oz (175g) feta cheese, cut into small cubes

1 cup shelled peas

2 handsful of fresh baby spinach leaves

small handful of fresh mint leaves

lemon wedges, to serve

METHOD

1 Using a food processor, process the watercress, mayonnaise, and horseradish until well combined. Taste, and season with salt and black pepper.

2 Put the feta, peas, spinach, and mint leaves in a bowl, and gently mix through. Season with a little black pepper if you wish. Transfer to a serving bowl, and serve with the mayonnaise and lemon wedges on the side.

Note: If it is not the season for fresh peas, frozen ones make an ideal substitute. Leave them to defrost in a colander. You could use a good-quality fresh ricotta instead of the feta; if you do, omit the mayonnaise.

A deceptively simple dish to prepare, this recipe showcases late spring produce. The bright colors of the peas and asparagus contrast beautifully with the golden yolk of the poached egg.

Warm pea pancakes
with grilled asparagus

Serves 4 (makes 8 pancakes) • **Prep** 10 mins • **Cooking** 30 mins

INGREDIENTS

3 cups shelled peas

1 large handful fresh
    mint leaves, chopped

3¹/₂ tbsp melted butter, plus
    extra for frying

¹/₄ cup all-purpose flour

¹/₄ cup heavy cream

2 tbsp freshly grated
    Parmesan cheese

6 large eggs

sea salt and freshly ground
    black pepper

1 large bunch asparagus,
    woody ends removed

1 tsp extra virgin olive oil

METHOD

1 Bring a pan of salted water to a boil and add the peas. Cook for 1–2 minutes, and then drain and cool.

2 Put peas and mint into a food processor and process, pulsing the machine on and off, to get a coarse texture. Add the melted butter, flour, cream, Parmesan, two of the eggs, and season with salt and pepper. Process to a stiff paste.

3 Heat some butter or oil in a large frying pan and, working in batches, add a couple of tablespoonfuls of the mixture for each pancake. Cook on medium heat, and use the back of a spoon to smooth them. After 3–4 minutes, the edges of the pancakes will change color. Carefully turn them over and cook another couple of minutes.

4 Bring a large saucepan of water to a boil and lightly poach the remaining 4 eggs until just set. Remove them with a slotted spoon.

5 Meanwhile, cook the asparagus on a hot grill pan with a little olive oil, seasoning while they cook, until golden. Serve immediately.

FAVA BEANS

When to pick
Harvest beans when the pods are firm and swollen. Pick from the bottom of the plant upward. Young bean pods can be picked and eaten whole.

Eat and store fresh
Eat as soon as possible if eating raw or whole. The podded beans will keep for 2–3 days in a plastic bag in the fridge.

How to preserve
The beans can be dried for winter use. Remove from the pod and air dry on a rack (see page 93).

Freezing options
Blanch the beans for 2 minutes and cool. Peel them and freeze in small portions for up to 12 months.

Inspired by the classic Italian bread salad, panzanella, this unusual green version is redolent of the fresh colors and flavors of spring, cut with the salty tang of crumbled feta.

Fava bean
and feta panzanella

Serves 4 • **Prep** 25 mins, plus standing • **Cooking** 10 mins

INGREDIENTS

4 cups shelled fava beans

6oz (150g) ciabatta or other crusty Italian bread, cut into $3/4$in (2cm) cubes (about 3 cups)

$3/4$ cup extra virgin olive oil

sea salt and freshly ground black pepper

2 tbsp white wine vinegar

1 large garlic clove, crushed

4 scallions, greens removed, whites finely chopped

8oz (200g) feta cheese, cut into $1/2$in (1cm) cubes or coarsely crumbled

1 handful of fresh mint, chopped

2 tbsp chopped fresh dill (optional)

4 handsful arugula, watercress, or baby lettuce leaves

juice of 1 lemon

METHOD

1 Place the oven rack in the upper third of the oven and preheat to 425°F (220°C). Cook the beans in boiling salted water for 2–3 minutes until just cooked, then plunge into cold water to cool, and peel off the skins.

2 Meanwhile toss the bread cubes in $1/4$ cup of olive oil, sprinkle with a little salt and pepper, and spread in an even layer on a baking sheet. Bake for 8 minutes, turning once, until the bread is golden and crispy.

3 In a large serving bowl, whisk together the remaining $1/2$ cup olive oil, the vinegar and garlic, and then season with plenty of black pepper and just a little salt (the feta is salty). Add the fava beans, bread cubes, scallions, feta, mint, and dill, and toss well to coat.

4 Leave the salad for 30 minutes to develop the flavors and soften the bread. To serve, add the arugula, squeeze the lemon over, and check again for seasoning.

Tiny fava beans can be eaten without their outer skins being removed. Larger beans need to be peeled first, then used to make this vividly colored topping for bruschetta or crostini.

Fava bean, garlic
and herb crostini

Serves 4 (makes 12) • **Prep** 15 mins • **Cooking** 15 mins

INGREDIENTS

½ baguette

3 tbsp extra virgin olive oil

salt and freshly ground
    black pepper

1 cup shelled fava beans

1 small shallot

1 garlic clove

small sprig of fresh tarragon
    leaves, chopped

METHOD

1 Preheat the oven to 300°F (150°C). Slice the baguette into 12 thin slices and use 2 tbsp of the olive oil to brush both sides of slices. Season with salt and pepper. Place the slices on a baking sheet and bake for 15 minutes, or until crisp all the way through.

2 Meanwhile, blanch the beans in a pan of boiling water for 2 minutes, drain, and refresh in cold water. Remove the tough outer skins and discard. Remove a few beans for garnish and place the remainder in a food processor with the shallot, garlic, the remaining 1 tbsp olive oil, and the tarragon. Process to form a thick paste. Season to taste with salt and pepper.

3 Spread on the prepared crostini just before serving. Garnish with the reserved beans and a sprinkling of black pepper.

Swiss chard is a marvelous plant that will reward you with months of green leaves once established. In recipes it can be substituted for spinach, but remove the tough central ribs.

Swiss chard cheese tart

Serves 6 • **Prep** 15 mins plus cooling • **Cooking** 1 hour

INGREDIENTS

1 sheet of prepared pie dough
for a 9in (23cm) pie

plain flour, for dusting

2 eggs, plus 1 extra, beaten
lightly, for egg wash

1 tbsp olive oil

1 onion, chopped finely

salt and freshly ground
black pepper

2 garlic cloves, grated
or chopped finely

sprig of rosemary, leaves picked
and chopped finely

8oz (250g) Swiss chard, stalks
removed, and leaves
chopped coarsely

1 cup shredded Gruyère cheese

4oz (125g) feta cheese, cut into
small cubes

1 cup heavy cream

METHOD

1 Preheat the oven to 400°F (200°C). Roll out the pastry on a floured work surface and use to line an 8 in (20 cm) tart pan with a removable bottom. Trim away the excess, line the pastry shell with parchment paper, and fill with baking beans. Bake in the oven for 15–20 minutes until the edges are golden. Remove the beans and paper, and brush the bottom of the shell with a little of the egg wash. Return to the oven for 1–2 minutes to crisp. Remove from the oven, and set aside. Reduce the oven temperature to 350°F (180°C).

2 Heat the oil in a pan over low heat. Add the onion and a pinch of salt, and cook gently for about 5 minutes until soft and translucent. Add the garlic and rosemary, and cook for a few seconds, then add the Swiss chard. Cook, stirring, for about 5 minutes until it wilts.

3 Spoon the onion and chard mixture into the shell. Sprinkle over the Gruyère cheese, and scatter with the feta. Season well with salt and pepper. Mix together the cream and 2 eggs until well combined, and carefully pour over the tart filling. Bake for 30–40 minutes until set and golden. Cool for 10 minutes before removing the pan ring. Serve warm or at room temperature.

SWISS CHARD

When to pick
Pick Swiss chard at any stage: the tiny leaves can be used raw, the bigger ones cooked. Cut the leaves $3/4$–$1 1/4$in (2–3cm) above the base to encourage regrowth.

Eat and store fresh
Baby chard is best eaten immediately if used raw in a salad. Bigger leaves can be rinsed, dried, and kept in a plastic bag in the fridge for up to 3 days.

Freezing options
Rinse and shred the leaves, blanch for 1–2 minutes, cool in ice water, squeeze out excess water and freeze for up to 12 months.

This rich, warming dish uses only the dark green leaves of chard, but rather than simply discarding the often colorful stems, cut them into lengths, steam for a few minutes, and serve alongside.

Gratin of Swiss chard
with beans and pancetta

Serves 4–6 • **Prep** 10 mins, plus soaking • **Cooking** 1 hour 20 mins, plus resting

INGREDIENTS

$2^1/_2$ cups dried navy beans or
    cannellini beans, soaked
    overnight
8oz (200g) pancetta, diced
2 tbsp extra virgin olive oil
4 garlic cloves, crushed
1lb (400g) Swiss chard,
    stemmed and finely
    shredded
$2^1/_2$ cups heavy cream
sea salt and freshly ground
    black pepper
3 slices firm white bread,
    torn into pieces
$^1/_2$ cup freshly grated
    Parmesan cheese
8 fresh basil leaves

METHOD

1 Place the oven rack in the upper third of the oven and preheat to 400°F (200°C). Drain the soaked beans, put them into a large pot of cold water, and bring to a boil. Reduce heat to medium-low and skim off foam at the surface. Cook about 40 minutes until tender. Drain.

2 In a large frying pan, cook the pancetta in the olive oil for 3–4 minutes, stirring occasionally, until golden brown. Add garlic and continue to cook for up to 30 seconds, being careful not to let the garlic burn. Remove garlic and pancetta with a slotted spoon and set aside. Add the chard to the oil and cook, stirring, for about 1 minute until it has wilted, but is still firm to the bite.

3 Add the pancetta, garlic, and beans to the chard. Mix well, stir in the cream, and season with salt and pepper.

4 Tip everything into a $1^1/_2$ quart (1.5 liter) gratin dish. Top with crumbs made by processing the bread, Parmesan, and basil in a food processor. Bake for 30 minutes or until bubbly-hot inside and golden brown on top. Allow to rest for 10 minutes before serving.

CAULIFLOWER

When to pick

Pick when the heads are 6–8in (15–20cm) across, and florets are firm. Cut the stem 2in (5cm) below the head, leaving a few leaves to protect the interior.

Eat and store fresh

Young cauliflower to be eaten raw should be used as soon as possible after harvesting. Refrigerate larger heads, inner leaves intact, for up to 5 days.

How to preserve

Use cauliflower in chutneys, pickles, and relishes like piccalilli (page 36), or preserve them in oil (pages 38–9).

Freezing options

Separate heads into florets, blanch for 3 minutes, cool in ice water, drain, then freeze in sealed plastic bags for up to 12 months.

The blandness of cauliflower here works as a foil to the subtle spiciness of toasted coriander seeds. The bacon adds a welcome depth of flavor, but can be omitted for a vegetarian version.

Cauliflower soup
with toasted coriander

Serves 4–6 • **Prep** 15–20 mins • **Cooking** 40 mins

INGREDIENTS

2 tsp coriander seeds

3 tbsp unsalted butter

1 onion, diced

1 potato, diced

1 head of cauliflower, finely chopped

2 cups vegetable stock

1 bay leaf

8 bacon slices

1 cup whole milk

$\frac{1}{2}$ cup half-and-half

salt and freshly ground black pepper

METHOD

1 Heat a heavy frying pan and lightly toast the coriander seeds, stirring all the time, for about 1 minute. Grind the seeds to a coarse powder using a mortar and pestle and set them aside.

2 Melt the butter in a large saucepan over low heat. Add the onion and potato, cover the pan and leave to soften for 10 minutes. Add the cauliflower and ground coriander, season well, cover and continue cooking for another 10 minutes.

3 Pour over the stock, add the bay leaf, cover, and simmer for about 15 minutes, until the cauliflower has softened. Meanwhile, cook the bacon under a hot broiler until crisp. Drain on paper towels, chop coarsely, and set aside to cool.

4 Remove the bay leaf and purée soup, using a stick blender. Or cool and puree batches in a blender. In the pan, stir in the milk and the cream, reheat and season as necessary. Ladle into bowls and scatter with bacon to serve. Freeze up to a month without cream or bacon.

Nothing is more comforting than baked cauliflower with cheese sauce. The secret is to boil or steam the cauliflower until barely tender and finish cooking the dish in the oven.

Cauliflower and cheese

Serves 4–6 • **Prep** 15 mins • **Cooking** 15 mins

INGREDIENTS

1 head of cauliflower, outer
    leaves removed, separated
    into large florets
salt and freshly ground
    black pepper
1 cup fresh breadcrumbs
2 tbsp butter, diced, plus extra
    for greasing the baking dish
3 tbsp all-purpose or whole
    wheat flour
$1^1/_2$ tsp mustard powder
2 cups whole milk
1 cup shredded, aged,
    Cheddar cheese

METHOD

1 Bring a large saucepan of salted water to a boil. Add the cauliflower florets and boil for 5 to 7 minutes, or until just tender. Drain and rinse with cold water to stop the cooking. Drain well. Arrange the florets in a buttered, ovenproof serving dish.

2 Preheat the broiler to its highest setting. To make the cheese sauce, melt the butter in a saucepan over low heat, add the flour and mustard powder, and stir to combine. Cook for 2 minutes, stirring all the time. Remove from the heat, add the milk, and whisk constantly until smooth. Return to the heat and bring slowly to a boil, then reduce the heat and simmer to thicken for 1–2 minutes. Remove the pan from the heat and stir in three-quarters of the cheese until melted. Season to taste with salt and pepper, then pour the sauce over the florets.

3 Toss the remaining cheese with the breadcrumbs and sprinkle over the florets. Place the dish 6in (15cm) from the broiler for 5 to 10 minutes, or until the sauce bubbles and the top is golden. Serve hot.

A few spices can turn the humble cauliflower into something far more interesting. This dish can be served simply with some buttery basmati rice, or as part of an Indian meal.

Braised cauliflower
with chiles and cilantro

Serves 4 • **Prep** 10 mins • **Cooking** 10 mins

INGREDIENTS

1 head cauliflower, about 1lb
   (400g), outer leaves
   removed, cut into
   small florets
2 dried red chiles
1 tsp cumin seeds
2 tbsp sunflower or vegetable
   oil
1 tsp black mustard seeds
$\frac{1}{2}$ tsp turmeric
2 garlic cloves, crushed
$1\frac{1}{2}$ tbsp butter, cut into pieces
sea salt
2 tbsp finely chopped cilantro

METHOD

1 Cook the cauliflower in salted boiling water for 1–2 minutes, drain, and rinse under cold water.

2 Grind together the chiles and cumin seeds in a mortar and pestle, until coarsely broken. Heat the oil in a large, deep-sided frying pan or wok, and add the chiles and cumin seeds, mustard seeds, turmeric, and garlic. Cook gently, stirring, for 1 minute until the mustard seeds start to pop.

3 Add the cauliflower and enough water to cover the bottom of the pan (about $\frac{1}{3}$ cup). Bring the water to a boil and cover. Turn the heat down and simmer the cauliflower for 3–5 minutes, until almost cooked through.

4. Uncover the pan and turn up the heat. Allow the water to cook down, turning the cauliflower all the time. When all the water has evaporated (about 4–5 minutes), add the butter and mix well until it melts. Season with salt and sprinkle with cilantro, before serving.

This vibrant yellow pickle is given its color by a combination of turmeric and mustard powder. It is a classic accompaniment to cold, cooked ham or cheeses, such as mature Cheddar.

Piccalilli

Makes 5lb (2.25kg) or 3 medium jars • **Prep** 15 mins, plus soaking • **Cooking** 20 mins

INGREDIENTS

1 head of cauliflower, outer leaves removed, separated into small florets

2 large onions, quartered, and thinly sliced, or 1lb (450g) small boiling onions

2lb (900g) mixed vegetables, such as zucchini , carrots, and green beans cut into bite-sized pieces

2oz (60g) sea salt

2 tbsp all-purpose flour

1 cup plus 2 tbsp granulated sugar (increase this quantity slightly if you don't like sharp pickles)

1 tbsp turmeric

1 x 2oz tin of English mustard powder

4 cups cider vinegar or distilled white vinegar

METHOD

1 Put all the vegetables into a large, nonmetallic bowl. Dissolve the salt in 4 cups of water and pour this brine over the vegetables. Put a plate on top and keep the vegetables submerged for 24 hours.

2 The next day, drain the vegetables in a colander, and rinse in cold water. Bring a large pan of water to a boil, add the vegetables, and blanch for about 2 minutes. Do not overcook them, as they should be crunchy. Drain and refresh in cold water to halt the cooking process.

3 Put the flour, sugar, turmeric, and mustard powder in a small, nonmetallic bowl and mix in a little of the vinegar to make a paste. Put it in a large stainless steel saucepan along with the remaining vinegar, bring to a boil, and stir continuously so no lumps appear. Reduce the heat and simmer for about 15 minutes.

4 Add the vegetables to the sauce and stir well to coat. Ladle into warm, sterilized jars with nonmetallic or vinegar-proof lids, making sure there are no air gaps, before sealing and labeling. Store in a cool, dark place. Allow the flavors to mature for 1 month, and refrigerate after opening. Unopened it will keep for up to 6 months.

Preserve vegetables in oil

Traditionally, many vegetables, olives, and cheeses were stored under olive oil. These days, this technique is considered a short-term method of preservation, and produce stored in this way should always be refrigerated. When preserving vegetables in oil, they are first cooked in vinegar to acidify them, before being covered in oil and refrigerated. Once opened, top up with extra oil, to keep the vegetables covered. Serve with torn basil leaves or chopped parsley, and bread.

1 **Dice or slice each vegetable** Wash and peel the vegetables as necessary and cut into even-sized pieces about ¹/₂in (1cm) thick. Leave small shallots and mushrooms whole.

2 **Boil the vegetables** Put the vegetables in batches in a stainless steel saucepan and add enough vinegar to just cover them. Add the sugar and salt and bring to a boil.

Recipe Mixed vegetables

Makes approx. 1½lb (675g) or 2 medium jars
Prep 20 mins • **Cooking** 10 mins • **Keeps** 1–2 months

INGREDIENTS

1lb 5oz (600g) vegetables
white wine vinegar
2 tsp sugar
2 tsp sea salt
²/₃ cup extra virgin olive oil

to season, choose from:
1 tsp dried fennel seeds,
1 tsp dried oregano, 1 bay
leaf, 1 sprig rosemary,
1 sprig lemon thyme,
a pinch hot pepper flakes

Other vegetables to try

Mediterranean vegetables are particularly suited to this method of preservation, but other vegetables work well too.

Tomatoes Oven-dry first (see pages 92–3).
Garlic Cook and store as whole cloves or purée.
Globe artichokes Griddled baby artichokes are particularly good (see page 81).
Peppers Choose ripe, firm, unblemished peppers.
Eggplants Cook first, choose firm eggplants.
Zucchinis Pick small and firm zucchinis.

3 **Pat the vegetables dry** When the soft vegetables have boiled for 2–3 minutes and firmer vegetables until al dente, pat dry on paper towels and allow to cool.

4 **Pack the vegetables loosely** Pack the vegetables into sterilized jars, add the seasonings, cover with olive oil, and press down lightly. Top up with olive oil, seal, and store.

When to pick
Pick spinach at any time, cutting the leaves ³/₄–1¹/₄in (2–3cm) above the base. Used as a "cut and come again" vegetable, a few plants should last until the first frost.

Eat and store fresh
Baby spinach is lovely when eaten raw in salads straight from picking. Wash and dry larger leaves and keep in a plastic bag in the fridge for up to 3 days.

Freezing options
Wash and shred the leaves, blanch for 1–2 minutes, leave to cool, squeeze out excess water, and then freeze for up to 12 months.

With this fragrant and vividly colored soup, the spinach is added at the last moment so that it does not overcook and lose any of the color or flavor that are such vital parts of the dish.

Creamy spinach
and rosemary soup

Serves 6 • **Prep** 15 mins • **Cooking** 25 mins

INGREDIENTS

3¹/₂ tbsp butter
¹/₂ cup finely chopped onion
³/₄ cup diced, peeled potato
sea salt and freshly ground
    black pepper
2 cups hot vegetable stock,
    chicken stock, or water
1¹/₂ cups whole milk
¹/₂ cup half-and-half
    plus 2 tbsp, to garnish
12oz (350g) spinach with
    stalks removed and
    discarded; leaves rinsed and
    roughly chopped
1 tbsp chopped fresh rosemary
sprig of rosemary and
    rosemary flowers, to garnish

METHOD

1 Melt the butter in a heavy pan. When it starts to foam, add the onion and potato, and stir to coat. Season well with salt and freshly ground black pepper, and then cover the pan with a lid and cook the vegetables over low heat for 10 minutes.

2 Add the stock, milk, and ¹/₂ cup half-and-half, bring to a boil, and then simmer for 5 minutes or until the potato and onion are completely cooked. Add the spinach and boil the soup with the lid removed for 2–3 minutes or until tender. Do not overcook. Add the chopped rosemary, and then process the soup in a blender, in batches if necessary , or using a hand-held blender, until smooth. Return to the pan and reheat gently.

3 Serve in warm bowls garnished with a swirl of half-and-half and a sprig of rosemary. If you have rosemary in bloom, add a few flowers for extra pizzazz.

This sauce is a great way to use up a glut of spinach, and is especially useful frozen in batches. Once defrosted it can be stirred into pasta or gnocchi or used to top smoked fish or salmon.

Spinach sauce

Serves 4 • **Prep** 15 mins • **Cooking** 20 mins

INGREDIENTS

4 tbsp extra virgin olive oil

2 large onions, finely diced

4 garlic cloves, thinly sliced

2 fresh, hot, red chilies, seeded
    and finely chopped

1¼lb (550g) baby spinach
    leaves, rinsed and coarsely
    chopped

1 cup dry white wine

2 tbsp all-purpose flour

4 cups whole milk

sea salt and freshly ground
    black pepper

METHOD

1 Heat the oil in a large, heavy pan, add the onions, and cook over medium heat, stirring frequently, for 5 minutes or until soft and translucent.

2 Stir in the garlic and chiles and cook for 2 minutes. Add the spinach and cook, stirring constantly for another 3 minutes, or until wilted. Add the wine and simmer for 5 minutes, or until reduced by half. Add the flour and combine well. Cook, stirring, for 2 minutes longer.

3 Pour in half the milk and stir well to blend. Add the rest of the milk a little at a time, stirring constantly, and cook for 5 minutes, or until you have a creamy sauce. Season well with salt and freshly ground pepper.

Spinach is a very productive plant, and it's good to add variety with a few more unusual side dishes. Here spinach is given a slightly Moorish feel, with the addition of pine nuts and raisins.

Spinach
with pine nuts and raisins

Serves 4 • **Prep** 5 mins • **Cooking** 10 mins

INGREDIENTS

1 tbsp extra virgin olive oil

3 tbsp dark raisins

3 tbsp pine nuts

3 tbsp dry sherry

8oz (200g) spinach, rinsed and
    coarsely chopped

1 tsp paprika

sea salt and freshly ground
    black pepper

METHOD

1 Put the oil, raisins, and pine nuts in a large, shallow frying pan over medium heat. When the raisins and pine nuts start to sizzle, cook for 2 minutes, stirring constantly. Carefully add the sherry and cook until the liquid has reduced by half.

2 Add the spinach and paprika, stirring constantly for 5 minutes, or until the spinach has wilted. Season with salt and freshly ground black pepper, and serve hot or cold.

43

This mild, creamy curry, flavored with coconut, is perfect for using up a glut of tomatoes and spinach from your garden. It makes a light and fragrant supper dish that is easy to prepare.

Spinach and coconut
shrimp curry

Serves 4 • **Prep** 15 mins • **Cooking** 20 mins

INGREDIENTS

2 tbsp vegetable oil

2 red onions, finely chopped

4 garlic cloves, finely chopped

large thumb-sized knob of fresh
    ginger, grated

2 tsp ground cumin

1 tsp ground coriander

$^1/_2$ tsp turmeric

$^1/_4$ – $^1/_2$ tsp chili powder

4 tomatoes, peeled and
    chopped

14oz (400ml) can coconut milk

10 curry leaves (optional)

$5^1/_2$oz (150g) spinach,
    stemmed and rinsed, finely
    shredded

1lb (400g) peeled and deveined
    large shrimp

$^1/_2$ tsp granulated sugar

sea salt

METHOD

1 Heat the oil in a large, deep-sided frying pan or wok. Add the onions, garlic, and ginger and cook for 2–3 minutes over low heat, stirring often, until softened, but not brown. Add the spices and cook for a further 1–2 minutes to release the flavors.

2 Add the tomatoes and continue to cook over low heat for another 2 minutes, until the flesh starts to break down. Add the coconut milk and curry leaves (if using), and bring to a boil. Mix in the spinach and lower the heat, continuing to cook until the leaves have wilted. Baby spinach will take 1–2 minutes; larger leaves will take up to 4 minutes.

3 Add the shrimp, sugar, and a pinch of salt, and cook for a further 2 minutes over high heat, or until the shrimp turn pink on the outside and opaque throughout. Serve with basmati rice, naan bread, and lime wedges on the side.

Growing spinach is both easy and rewarding. If you tire of eating it simply wilted down in olive oil, butter, and garlic, try making these delightful little soufflés instead.

Spinach soufflés

Serves 4 • **Prep** 20 mins • **Cooking** 25–30 mins

INGREDIENTS

(8oz) 225g spinach, chopped
(1^{1}/$_{2}$oz) 45g butter, plus extra
(1^{1}/$_{2}$oz) 45g plain flour
(12fl oz) 360ml whole milk
(2^{1}/$_{2}$oz) 75g Parmesan
    cheese, grated
pinch of grated nutmeg
sea salt and freshly ground
    black pepper
4 large eggs, separated

METHOD

1 Preheat the oven to 400°F (200°C). Cook the spinach, covered, in a large saucepan over medium heat for 2–3 minutes or until wilted. Drain, squeezing out as much excess water as possible.

2 Butter 4 x 8oz (200ml) ramekins. Melt the rest of the butter in a saucepan and add the flour. Cook gently, stirring for 2 minutes, and then gradually add the milk, whisking all the time. Bring to a boil, and then reduce the heat and leave to simmer for 3–4 minutes. Reserve 2 tbsp of the Parmesan and add the rest to the pan, along with the nutmeg, and season to taste with salt and pepper. Transfer the cheese sauce to a large bowl.

3 Stir the spinach into the mixture. Leave it to cool, and then stir in the egg yolks. Place the prepared ramekins on a baking sheet in the oven to heat. Beat the egg whites until stiff and stir 2 tbsp of these into the sauce, before gently folding in the remainder.

4 Carefully spoon the mixture into the preheated ramekins. Run a knife around the edge of the mixture to help the soufflés rise neatly. Sprinkle with the reserved Parmesan and bake in the preheated oven for 20–25 minutes, or until well-risen and golden. Serve immediately.

Here the bitter taste of frisée lettuce is offset by the saltiness of smoked bacon and the unctuous texture of a perfectly poached egg. Other firm-leaved and crunchy lettuces may be used.

Bistro salad
with egg and bacon bits

Serves 4 • **Prep** 5 mins • **Cooking** 10 mins

INGREDIENTS

4 eggs

1 tbsp lemon juice

6 tbsp extra virgin olive oil

2 thick slices of bread

1 garlic clove, halved

1/4in (5mm) slice fresh ginger

4 thick slices of bacon, cut into
    1/2in (1cm) pieces (lardons)

1/2–1 head frisée lettuce, torn

3 sprigs of thyme, leaves picked

small handful of flat-leaf parsley

small handful of cilantro

1 small red onion, thinly sliced

For the dressing

2 tbsp red wine vinegar

1/4 tsp crushed chili flakes

2 tsp Worcestershire sauce

1/4 tsp granulated sugar

sea salt and freshly ground
    black pepper

METHOD

1 Crack open the eggs and poach in gently simmering water with the lemon juice for about 3 minutes. Remove with a slotted spoon and immediately plunge the eggs into cold water to stop the cooking.

2 Remove the crusts from the bread and discard them. Dice the bread. Heat 1 tbsp olive oil in a nonstick frying pan. Add the bread, garlic, and ginger, and cook, tossing and stirring, until golden. Drain the croutons on paper towels. Discard the garlic and ginger.

3 In the same pan, cook the bacon pieces until crisp and golden. Drain on paper towels.

4 Put the lettuce in a salad bowl, and tear in the herbs. Add the onion, separated into rings, the bacon pieces, and the croutons.

5 Add the remaining 5 tbsp olive oil to a saucepan with the dressing ingredients. Heat gently, stirring. Pour over the salad and toss. Arrange the salad into individual bowls and top each with a poached egg.

LETTUCE

When to pick
Pick leaves when young, glossy, and crisp-looking, picking the outer leaves first. Harvest when the heart is large but firm. "Cut and come again" varieties can be harvested as needed.

Eat and store fresh
Eat as soon as possible for the sweetest flavor. Keep individual heads, unwashed, in the fridge for up to 3 days. "Cut and come again" leaves can be washed, dried, and stored in a plastic bag for up to 3 days in the fridge.

This chilled soup recipe is a wonderful way to use up excess lettuce, but remember to use only the sweetest lettuces to emphasize the flavor of this delicate vegetable.

Lettuce soup
with peas

Serves 4 • **Prep** 20 mins, plus 30 mins chilling

INGREDIENTS

1 cup shelled peas

1 small garlic clove

pinch of coarse salt

2 medium round lettuces, such as iceberg, about 1lb (500g) total, cleaned, torn into pieces, and solid cores discarded

1 cup plain yogurt

³/₄in (2cm) piece fresh ginger, peeled and finely grated

handful of fresh mint leaves

juice of ¹/₂ lemon

sea salt and freshly ground black pepper

METHOD

1 Bring a small amount of water to a boil in a saucepan, add the peas, and cook for 1 minute. Drain, reserving the cooking water. Cool the peas in a colander under cold running water, and refrigerate.

2 Cut the garlic in half, remove any green at the center and discard. Crush with the salt.

3 Combine the garlic with all the other ingredients (except the peas) in a food processor or blender, adding just enough of the reserved cooking water to get the blades moving or until the desired consistency is achieved. This will vary according to the type of lettuce and the kind of machine you are using, but aim to get it fairly smooth, with only a bit of texture.

4 Transfer the soup to a large bowl and chill for 30 minutes. When ready to serve, stir through the cooked peas, leaving a few to garnish.

A mix of lettuce varieties and spicy leaves, such as arugula or mizuna, really lifts this salad. If you have been preserving your artichoke hearts in oil (see p81), this is an ideal time to use them.

Antipasti salad

Serves 4 • **Prep** 30 mins • **Cooking** 10 mins

INGREDIENTS

1lb (450g) green beans
sea salt and freshly ground
    black pepper
3 tbsp chopped fresh parsley
2 tsp fresh lemon thyme leaves
1 tbsp chopped fresh fennel
2 tbsp extra virgin olive oil
5oz (125g) mixed lettuce
and spicy salad leaves
1 x 14oz can of artichoke
    hearts, drained and halved
4 slices Parma ham, shredded
16 black olives, pitted, chopped
$3/4$ cup cherry tomatoes, halved
2 scallions , chopped
3 tbsp chopped fresh chervil

For the dressing

5 tbsp extra virgin olive oil
sea salt and freshly ground
    black pepper
$1/2$ garlic clove, crushed
$1^{1}/_2$ tbsp balsamic vinegar

METHOD

1 Bring a pot of lightly salted water to a boil. Trim the green beans and blanch in the boiling water for 5–7 minutes. Refresh in cold water and drain.

2 Place the beans in a wide, shallow salad bowl. Season lightly with salt and pepper and scatter over half the parsley, lemon thyme, and fennel. Drizzle over half of the olive oil, toss, and set aside.

3 Make the dressing by pouring the remaining olive oil into a small jug. Season with salt and pepper, and then whisk in the garlic and balsamic vinegar.

4 Scatter the salad leaves over the beans, and then the drained and halved artichoke hearts, shredded ham, olives, tomatoes, and scallions. Whisk the dressing and drizzle it over the salad. Toss, sprinkle with the chervil, and serve.

This is a wonderfully light and zesty salad. Fresh crabmeat is combined with the sweet and sour flavor of pink grapefruit and finished with cilantro leaves.

Crab salad
with grapefruit

Serves 4 • **Prep** 10 mins

INGREDIENTS

12oz (350g) cooked fresh or
   canned white crabmeat,
   drained and picked over to
   remove any bits of shell or
   cartilage
handful of baby salad leaves
handful of fresh cilantro leaves
2 pink grapefruits, peeled,
   segmented, pith removed

For the dressing
3 tbsp extra virgin olive oil
1 tbsp white wine vinegar
pinch of caster sugar
sea salt and freshly ground
   black pepper

METHOD

1 In a small bowl or jug, whisk together the dressing ingredients. Season with salt and pepper.

2 Mix the crabmeat with a drizzle of the dressing. Divide the salad leaves and half of the cilantro leaves between 4 serving plates, and scatter over the grapefruit segments.

3 When ready to serve, drizzle the salad with the remaining dressing. Divide the crabmeat between the plates, spooning it neatly on top of the leaves. Scatter over the remaining cilantro and serve immediately.

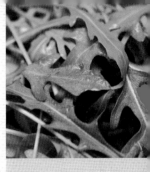

Arugula is a prolific and easy crop to grow. Here, its spicy leaves are combined with salty pancetta and Parmesan to make a quick pasta dish. Add the arugula only at the last minute.

Pasta with arugula
and pancetta

Serves 4 • **Prep** 5 mins • **Cooking** 15 mins

INGREDIENTS

1 tbsp extra virgin olive oil

1 onion, finely chopped

1 fresh hot red chile , seeded
    and finely chopped

8oz (250g) pancetta, cut into
    $^1/_4$in (5mm) cubes

2 garlic cloves, grated or
    finely chopped

12oz (350g) dried spaghetti

7oz (200g) wild arugula leaves

sea salt and freshly ground
    black pepper

Parmesan cheese,
    grated, to serve

METHOD

1 Heat the oil in a large frying pan, add the onion, and cook over low heat for 5 minutes, until softened.

2 Add the chile and cook for a few minutes more. Add the pancetta and cook for 5 minutes, or until crisp and golden, and then stir in the garlic and cook them for a few more seconds.

3 Meanwhile, cook the pasta in a large pot of boiling, salted water for 8–10 minutes, or until it is cooked but still has a bit of bite to it. Drain, keeping back a tiny amount of the cooking water.

4 Return the pasta to the pot and toss with the pancetta mixture. Add the arugula, season to taste with salt and freshly ground pepper and toss gently. Sprinkle with Parmesan and serve.

ARUGULA

When to pick
Pick arugula leaves before they grow larger than 3–4in (8–10cm), as they can become very hot or bitter. Always pick leaves before the plant begins to bolt (run to seed).

Eat and store fresh
Young arugula can be washed, dried, and stored in a plastic bag in the fridge for up to 3 days.

How to preserve
Excess arugula can be made into arugula pesto (see page 55) and stored in the fridge for up to 1 week.

Arugula is one of the fastest growing salad crops. To keep on top of it, I like to make batches of this pesto to freeze. You can grow cultivated and wild types, but wild arugula can be bitter for cooking.

Arugula pesto

Makes approx. 1 cup • **Prep** 10 mins • **Cooking** 2–3 mins

INGREDIENTS

$^{1}/_{4}$ cup pine nuts

2 cups arugula leaves

$^{1}/_{2}$ cup fresh basil
leaves (optional)

about $^{1}/_{4}$ cup freshly grated
Parmesan cheese

1 small garlic clove, crushed

sea salt and freshly ground
black pepper

$^{1}/_{2}$ cup extra virgin olive oil

METHOD

1 In a dry frying pan, over low heat, gently toast the pine nuts for 2–3 minutes, shaking the pan constantly, until they are golden brown all over. Set aside to cool.

2 Put the arugula and basil leaves (if using), the pine nuts, Parmesan, garlic, a generous dash of salt, and a good grinding of pepper into a food processor. Add 2–3 tbsp of the olive oil and process to a thick paste. (If you are serving it with pasta, you can add a little more garlic and Parmesan; or less if you are using it as an accompaniment to grilled chicken or fish.)

3 With the motor running, continue to add the oil, in a thin stream, until the pesto becomes a thin paste. Taste the pesto and adjust the seasonings if needed.

Note If you prefer a coarser texture, pulse the ingredients in the food processor until the mixture reaches the desired consistency. This will store in an airtight container for up to 5 days in the fridge and up to 2 weeks in the freezer.

Quickly char-grilling some squid and tossing it with chile and lemon is a simple, yet delicious, way to enhance the spicy flavor of arugula leaves for a substantial lunch or supper.

Squid and arugula salad

Serves 4 • **Prep** 15 mins • **Cooking** 2 mins

INGREDIENTS

1¼lbs (600g) whole calamari
(several small young squid,
rather than one large one)
4 tbsp extra virgin olive oil
2 small hot red chiles, seeded
and finely chopped
1 garlic clove, crushed
finely grated zest and juice
of 1 lemon, plus extra
lemon wedges, to serve
sea salt and freshly ground
black pepper

For the arugula salad

3½oz (100g) arugula leaves
large handful of flat-leaf
parsley, roughly chopped
2 tbsp extra virgin olive oil
juice of ½ lemon

METHOD

1 Clean the squid by grabbing the head and tentacles together in one hand, and pulling them out of the body. Cut the head from the tentacles and discard, making sure that the tentacles remain attached as one. Cut or pull out the small beak from inside the tentacles. Pull out and discard the transparent cartilage from inside the body, and rinse the body (the thin outer skin should peel away) and tentacles well. Pat dry with paper towels.

2 Put the tentacles and bodies (tubes and wings attached) in a bowl with the olive oil, chiles, garlic, and lemon zest and juice. Season with salt and pepper.

3 Heat a gas barbecue, charcoal grill, or grill pan until hot. Cook the squid bodies and tentacles over high heat for 1–2 minutes, turning halfway through cooking until lightly charred on all sides. Remove to a chopping board. Cut the tentacle clusters in half crosswise, and put in a bowl. Slice the tubes into ⅛ in (3mm) rings, slicing through the wings as you go, and put in the bowl with the tentacles.

4 Add all of the salad ingredients to the bowl with the squid, and gently toss through. Serve immediately along with lemon wedges.

The hot, spicy taste and crunchy texture of radishes are always a welcome addition to a bowl of salad. Here they take a leading role when combined with smoked salmon and spiced yogurt.

Smoked salmon
with radishes and yogurt

Serves 4 • **Prep** 15 mins

INGREDIENTS

3 tomatoes

1 tbsp capers, rinsed, gently squeezed dry, and chopped

handful of radishes, diced

1 orange bell pepper, seeded and diced

4 scallions, finely chopped

1 hot red chile, seeded and finely chopped

juice of 1 large orange

juice of 1 lime

sea salt and freshly ground black pepper

8oz (250g) smoked salmon, chopped

For the spiced yogurt dressing

4–6 tbsp Greek-style yogurt

juice of 1 lemon

pinch Asian five-spice powder

METHOD

1 Skin the tomatoes by leaving them covered in boiling water for 1 minute. Drain, cool under running water, and peel. Seed the skinned tomatoes and dice them.

2 In a bowl, mix together the tomatoes, capers, radishes, pepper, scallions , and chile . Add the orange and lime juice, and season with salt and black pepper. Toss together, and let stand for about 10 minutes, to allow the flavors to develop.

3 To make the spiced yogurt dressing, mix together the yogurt, lemon juice, and five-spice powder in a small bowl. Season to taste.

4 When ready to serve, add the smoked salmon pieces to the salad mixture, and stir through well. Serve with the yogurt dressing on the side.

RADISHES

When to pick
Radishes can be ready to harvest within 4 weeks of planting. The larger they grow, the hotter they taste. Pick them small, firm, and before they turn woody.

Eat and store fresh
Best eaten washed and trimmed, the day they are picked. Store in a fridge for up to 3 days, and refresh in cold water before eating, to crisp them up.

How to preserve
Radishes can be used as an ingredient in pickles and relishes.

RHUBARB

When to pick
Young, forced rhubarb can be picked early, the main crop picked when the stalks are still pink or red. After midsummer, leave the plant to rebuild its energy stocks.

Eat and store fresh
Although it may be eaten raw, rhubarb is usually cooked before eating. It will store in the fridge, washed and wrapped in newspaper, for up to 1 week.

How to preserve
Although low in pectin, rhubarb is delicious made into jam with fresh root ginger. It can also be used in chutneys, cordials, and syrups (see page 64).

Freezing options
Best frozen poached in syrup, or cooked and puréed (see pages 194–5).

In my garden, there is always an abundance of rhubarb in early summer. This ice cream, which gives a new twist to the traditional pairing of rhubarb and custard, is a lovely way to preserve it.

Rhubarb and custard
ice cream

Serves 4–6 • **Prep** 30 mins, plus chilling and freezing • **Cooking** 20 mins

INGREDIENTS

1lb (450g) rhubarb, cut into chunks

2 cups granulated sugar

5 egg yolks

pinch of salt

2 cups whole milk

$1/2$ cup half-and-half

1 tsp vanilla extract

METHOD

1 Gently cook the rhubarb with $1/4$ cup of the sugar and 2 tbsp water in a covered saucepan for about 10 minutes, or until really tender, stirring occasionally. Purée in a blender or food processor. Leave to cool.

2 Beat the egg yolks, remaining sugar, and salt in a large heatproof bowl with an electric mixer or balloon whisk, until thick and pale. Gently heat the milk and half-and-half until hot to the touch, and stir into the egg mixture with the vanilla. Put the bowl over a pot of gently simmering water and stir with a wooden spoon until the custard just coats the back of the spoon. Remove the bowl from the pan, place in a bowl, cover, and refrigerate.

3 When the custard is cold, mix with the rhubarb purée and freeze in an ice cream maker, following the manufacturer's directions; or pour into a shallow, freezer-proof container with a lid, and freeze for about 2 hours until frozen around the edges. Break up ice crystals with a fork, freeze for another 2 hours, beat with the fork again, and store in the freezer for up to 1 week.

Rhubarb and ginger is a classic combination, the spicy warmth of ginger cutting through the sweet and sour flavor of rhubarb. Here, the rhubarb gives a new twist to a classic pavlova.

Rhubarb and ginger
meringue cake

Serves 4–6 • **Prep** 30 mins, plus cooling • **Cooking** 1 hour

INGREDIENTS

4 egg whites, at
    room temperature
pinch of salt
1 cup plus 2 tbsp
    superfine sugar

For the filling

1¼lbs. (600g) rhubarb, cut
    into chunks
⅓ cup superfine or
    granulated sugar
4 pieces of stem ginger in
    syrup, drained and chopped
½ tsp ground ginger
1 cup heavy cream
confectioners' sugar, to dust

METHOD

1 Preheat the oven to 350°F (180°C). Place parchment paper on 2 baking sheets.

2 Using a mixer or whisk, beat the egg whites, salt, and ½ cup of the sugar in a dry bowl until stiff, glossy peaks form. Fold in remaining sugar, a spoonful at a time.

3 Spread a mound of meringue into a 7in (18cm) circle on each baking sheet. Bake in the upper and lower thirds of the oven for 5 minutes, then reduce the temperature to 250°F (130°C), and bake for 1 hour, switching the positions of the sheets after 30 minutes. Open the oven door and leave the meringues to cool completely.

4 Meanwhile, cook rhubarb, sugar, stem and ground ginger, and 1 tbsp water in a covered saucepan over low heat 20 minutes, until soft. Drain excess liquid and chill.

5 Whip cream until stiff peaks form, then fold in the rhubarb mixture. Place a meringue on a plate, spread it with filling, and top with the remaining meringue. Dust with confectioners' sugar and serve.

Preserving rhubarb as a purée ensures a ready supply for a quick dessert all year. Fold into a combination of half whipped cream and half cold custard to make a delicious rhubarb fool.

Rhubarb and vanilla
freezer purée

Makes approx. 2 cups • **Prep** 5 mins • **Cooking** 30 mins

INGREDIENTS

1lb (450g) rhubarb,
    cut into chunks
$^1/_2$ cup granulated or
    light brown sugar
1 vanilla bean, split
    in half lengthwise

METHOD

1 Place the rhubarb chunks in a saucepan. Add the sugar, $^1/_2$ cup water, and the vanilla bean.

2 Bring the ingredients to a boil, and then simmer for 25–30 minutes or until the rhubarb reduces and thickens. Stir occasionally to prevent the mixture from sticking to the bottom of the pan.

3 When the rhubarb is the consistency of a purée, take out the vanilla bean and put the purée into clean freezer-safe containers, leaving $^1/_2$ in (1cm) space at the top. Leave to cool, and then seal and freeze.

This syrup has a heady, aromatic kick. Enjoy it diluted with water, or serve drizzled over ice cream. Pick your rose petals before they start to fade and use them quickly.

Rhubarb syrup
with rose petals

Makes approx. 2 cups or 2 small bottles • **Prep** 20 • **Cooking** 40–50 mins

INGREDIENTS

1lb (450g) rhubarb, cut into
    short lengths

$1^2/_3$ cup granulated sugar

8 fragrant pink or red rose
    petals (grown
    organically without
    sprays or pesticides)

2 tbsp rose water

1 tsp citric acid

METHOD

1 Put enough water in a heavy saucepan to just cover the bottom. Add the rhubarb, sugar, and rose petals. Bring to a boil, stir gently, cover, reduce the heat, and cook for 20–30 minutes, stirring once or twice, until really pulpy.

2 Strain the pulp in a jelly bag or a muslin-lined sieve set over a measuring cup or bowl. Press the pulp to extract the maximum juice. Return the juice to the pan and bring back to a boil.

3 Remove from the heat and stir in the rose water and citric acid. Pour immediately into warm, sterilized bottles using a sterilized funnel. Seal, label, leave to cool, and then store in the fridge. Shake before use.

Note The syrup will keep for 1 month, refrigerated.

SUMMER

Green beans

Runner beans

Artichokes

Tomatoes

Peppers

Chile peppers

Eggplant

Okra

Cucumbers

Zucchini

Corn

Fennel

Potatoes

Herbs

Gooseberries

Strawberries

Raspberries

Blackberries

Blueberries

Black currants

Red currants

Melons

Cherries

Peaches

Apricots

GREEN BEANS

When to pick
Harvest when no more than 4–6in (10–15cm) long, picking from the bottom up to encourage regrowth. Leave some to grow larger and use the fresh beans inside.

Eat and store fresh
Best eaten as soon as they are harvested, Green beans will keep for up to 3 days in the fridge. Eat tiny beans raw in salads, bigger ones cooked.

How to preserve
Can be used as an ingredient in pickles, relishes, or chutneys. The last of the beans can be left on the plant to dry and the pulses harvested for winter use.

Freezing options
Trim and slice, blanch for 2–3 minutes, cool, and freeze for up to 12 months.

Green beans provide almost daily yields once they get into their stride. Here, some butter and a scattering of toasted hazelnuts turn them into an interesting side dish for most meats and fish.

Green beans
with toasted hazelnuts

Serves 4 • **Prep** 5 mins • **Cooking** 5 mins

INGREDIENTS

8oz (250g) green
    beans, trimmed

sea salt

2 tbsp butter, cut into bits

$1/2$ cup hazelnuts, toasted,
    skinned, and coarsely
    chopped

METHOD

1 Put the beans in a pot of salted water and boil for 5–6 minutes, or until they are cooked but still have a bit of bite to them. Drain, and then refresh under cold water so that they stop cooking and retain their color.

2 Transfer to a serving dish, top with the butter and toasted hazelnuts. This dish is particularly good served with roasted chicken or lamb.

This delicious, Asian-inspired warm salad makes a great side dish for salmon or chicken grilled with a teriyaki glaze. It works with any combination of green beans, sugar snaps, or baby peas.

Warm green bean salad

Serves 6 • **Prep** 15 mins • **Cooking** 10 mins

INGREDIENTS

3 tbsp sesame seeds

1lb (450g) green beans, trimmed

8oz (250g) sugar snap peas, trimmed

3 shallots or scallions, chopped

1 garlic clove, chopped

1 tbsp soy sauce

$\frac{1}{2}$ tbsp Asian sesame oil

$\frac{1}{2}$ tbsp honey

1in (2.5cm) piece of fresh ginger, peeled and finely grated

sea salt and freshly ground black pepper

METHOD

1 Preheat the oven to 350°F (180°C). Place the sesame seeds in a small pan and bake, stirring once or twice, for 8 minutes, or until the seeds are nicely browned; watch closely, because they burn easily.

2 Bring a large saucepan of salted water to a boil. Cook the green beans for 3 minutes, and then add the sugar snap peas and blanch for another minute.

3 Drain the beans and sugar snap peas in a colander, and shake off any excess water. Combine all the remaining ingredients in a large serving bowl. Add the beans and sugar snap peas, and toss to coat well. Sprinkle with the sesame seeds and serve.

This soup can be made using fresh or dried beans. Use fresh cranberry and navy beans (found inside overgrown green beans) for an authentic take on this Mediterranean classic.

Soupe au pistou

Serves 6–8 • **Prep** 30 mins • **Cooking** 1½ hours

INGREDIENTS

3 garlic cloves

coarse sea salt

large handful of basil leaves

5 tomatoes, peeled,
    seeded, and chopped

freshly ground black pepper

¼ cup grated Mimolette
    cheese

3 tbsp extra virgin olive oil

1 ham hock or about 6oz
    (150g), or 3oz (75g)
    slab bacon

1 cup shelled fresh
    navy beans

1 cup shelled fresh
    cranberry beans

8oz (250g) Romano
    (or green) beans, sliced

2 medium floury
    potatoes, diced

4 medium zucchini, chopped

3½oz (100g) dried macaroni

METHOD

1 To make the pistou, pound the garlic in a large mortar with a pestle, and then add a little salt and the basil, and pound to a paste. Add 2 of the tomatoes, and continue pounding and mixing until you have a thick sauce. Add pepper, cheese, and oil. Mix well and adjust seasonings.

2 For the soup, put 8 cups cold water in a large soup pot. Add the ham hock. Bring to a simmer, and then partially cover and leave to simmer gently for 30 minutes, occasionally skimming off any foam that rises.

3 Meanwhile, put the cranberry and navy beans in a saucepan, cover with plenty of cold water, and bring to a boil. Simmer for 10 minutes, drain, and refresh. Add the rest of the vegetables with enough water to cover. Season lightly. Return to a simmer, then partially cover and simmer gently for 1 hour, skimming occasionally.

4 Remove the ham hock and shred the meat, discarding the fat. Lift half of the ingredients out of the pot, mash with a fork, and then return to the soup with the ham. Add the macaroni and cook until just tender. Stir in the pistou, and serve.

If you have a glut of green beans, leave the whole beans to dry on the stalk, harvest, and pod them for your own source of navy beans to be kept and used in recipes like this warming soup.

Herbed bean
and chorizo soup

Serves 4 • **Prep** 15 mins, plus soaking • **Cooking** 1 hour

INGREDIENTS

1¹/₄ cups dried navy beans, or
cannellini beans, soaked
overnight

1 tbsp sunflower, peanut, or
mild olive oil

1 onion, finely chopped

2 garlic cloves, crushed

1 fennel bulb, trimmed and
finely chopped

2 tsp dried fennel seeds

1 tbsp finely chopped
fresh parsley

2 tsp chopped, fresh
thyme leaves

sea salt and freshly ground
black pepper

4oz (100g) Spanish chorizo,
diced

METHOD

1 Drain and rinse the soaked beans. Heat the oil in a large heavy soup pot over medium heat, add the onion and cook, stirring. Add the garlic, chopped fennel, fennel seeds, parsley, and half the thyme, and cook for 3–5 minutes until slightly softened. Tip in the beans. Stir, pour in 8 cups of fresh, cold water, and season lightly.

2 Bring to a simmer and cook for 40 minutes, or until the beans are tender, skimming from time to time to remove any foam that rises to the surface. Remove from the heat and leave to cool a little. Transfer to a blender or food processor and process briefly until mixed but only partially puréed. Return to the pot, taste, and adjust the seasoning.

3 Gently reheat the soup. Meanwhile, place a small non-stick pan over medium-high heat and cook the chorizo for 2–3 minutes until crisp and browned, stirring frequently. Drain on a plate lined with paper towels.

4 Ladle the soup into bowls, add a little chorizo to each and finish with a scattering of thyme. Serve immediately.

Climbing, or pole, beans are prolific and in summer you can pick and eat them daily. This recipe was inspired by a meal eaten on holiday, but similar dishes are enjoyed all over southern Europe.

Greek beans

Serves 4 • **Prep** 10 mins • **Cooking** 25 mins

INGREDIENTS

2 tbsp extra virgin olive oil

2 onions, thinly sliced

2 garlic cloves, crushed

4 large overripe tomatoes, peeled and coarsely chopped

1lb (400g) green beans, trimmed

sea salt and freshly ground black pepper

$1/2$ tsp granulated sugar

METHOD

1 Heat the oil in a large saucepan over medium heat, and cook the onions for 5-7 minutes, stirring constantly, until soft and golden brown.

2 Add the garlic and continue to cook for 1 minute. Add the tomatoes and 2 tablespoons of water. Cook the tomatoes for a couple of minutes until slightly thickened, then add the green beans and another 1 tablespoon of water. Season well with salt, pepper, and sugar, and cover. Turn down the heat and leave to simmer slowly for 15–20 minutes until the beans are well cooked.

3 A couple of minutes before the beans are ready, uncover the pan, and turn up the heat to boil away any excess liquid. Stir in a splash of olive oil just before serving to emulsify the mixture. These beans are best served warm or at room temperature.

The red stripy pods of cranberry (borlotti) beans are a beautiful sight. The cream and purple dappled beans inside are ideal for this slow-cooked dish, which tastes wonderful with grilled meats.

Cranberry beans
with tomatoes and capers

Serves 4–6 • **Prep** 10 mins • **Cooking** 1½ hours

INGREDIENTS

1 onion, finely chopped

2 garlic cloves, crushed

6 tbsp extra virgin olive oil

1 x 14.5oz can diced tomatoes

½ cup dry white wine

1 tsp granulated sugar

sea salt and freshly ground
   black pepper

4 cups (1lb/450g) shelled fresh
   cranberry (borlotti) beans

2 tbsp capers, rinsed gently,
   dried, and chopped

handful of fresh basil leaves,
   finely chopped

1 tbsp balsamic vinegar

METHOD

1 In a flameproof casserole or other large saucepan, cook the onion and garlic in 4 tbsp of the olive oil for 3-5 minutes, until softened, but not brown. Add tomatoes, wine, ½ cup of water, sugar, and a good grinding of black pepper, and simmer, covered, for 20 minutes.

2 Mash with a potato masher until the tomatoes are well crushed. Add the beans and another ½ cup of water and simmer very gently, covered, for 45 minutes to 1 hour, until the beans are tender and cooked through. Add a little more water if the beans are drying out.

3 Remove the pan from the heat and stir in the capers, basil, balsamic vinegar, and the remaining 2 tbsp olive oil. Season to taste and serve the dish warm or at room temperature.

Note If you do not grow cranberry beans, and cannot find fresh beans to buy, you can make this recipe using 1¼ cups of dried cranberry (borlotti) beans, soaked overnight and cooked according to package directions, before adding to the tomato and caper sauce.

Freeze vegetables

One of the best ways to preserve your home-grown vegetables is to freeze them. Most produce is best cooked before being frozen. Blanching vegetables, such as beans, before freezing them destroys the enzymes that cause their color, texture, and flavor to deteriorate in the freezer. Other vegetables can be griddled or puréed, then frozen on open trays, packed into freezer bags, labelled, and dated. Frozen cooked and raw vegetables (except corn on the cob) can be cooked when frozen, but cooked purées should be thawed before using.

1 **Blanch the beans** Bring a saucepan of lightly salted water to a boil. Add a handful of beans and bring back to a boil. Blanch each batch for 2–3 minutes.

2 **Cool the beans** Transfer each batch of beans immediately to a large bowl of iced water to halt the cooking process and set the color. The beans will cool very quickly.

Recipe Blanched beans

Makes approx. 1lb (450g) • **Prep** 8 mins
Keeps 6–12 months

INGREDIENTS

approx. 1lb (450g) Green beans, trimmed

Other vegetables to freeze

The best vegetables to freeze are those with a firm, less watery texture:

Runner beans Slice, blanch, and open freeze.
Peas Wait for pods to swell before shelling, then blanch briefly and open freeze.
Spinach Blanch briefly and squeeze out moisture.
Corn Blanch and freeze whole cobs or strip the kernels, blanch, cool, and freeze them.
Tomatoes Cook and freeze batches of sauce.
Carrots Peel, slice, blanch, and open freeze, or cook first and freeze as a purée.

3 **Drain and dry** Remove the beans, drain, and pat them dry on paper towels. Leave to one side until all the batches have been blanched, drained, and dried.

4 **Pack and freeze** Pack in convenient portions in freezer bags or containers. Alternatively, freeze on open baking trays, then store in larger freezer bags.

RUNNER BEANS

When to pick
Best eaten when young, before they become tough and stringy. Pick runner beans when no more than 6in (15cm) long. Pick often to encourage regrowth.

Eat and store fresh
Before cooking, trim strings from the sides and slice diagonally into strips. Cook as soon as possible after harvesting. Store in the fridge for up to 3 days.

How to preserve
Use runner beans in pickles, relishes, and chutneys.

Freezing options
Trim, slice, and blanch for 2 minutes, cool, and freeze for up to 12 months.

Left to grow too large, runner beans have a tendency to become tough and stringy. It is often difficult to eat them as fast as they grow. This chutney is an ideal way to use up larger beans.

Runner bean
and zucchini chutney

Makes approx. 2^1/$_4$ lb (1kg) or 3 medium jars • **Prep** 30 mins • **Cooking** 2 hours

INGREDIENTS

1^1/$_4$ lb (600g) runner beans, thinly sliced

4 zucchini , thinly sliced

12oz (350g) cooking apples, such as Granny Smith, peeled, cored, and chopped

2 onions, finely chopped

2^1/$_4$ cups light brown sugar

1 tsp mustard powder

1 tsp turmeric

1 tsp coriander seeds

2^1/$_2$ cups cider vinegar

METHOD

1 Put the beans, zucchini, apples, and onions in a preserving pan or a large, heavy, stainless steel saucepan. Then add the sugar, mustard powder, turmeric, and coriander seeds. Pour in the vinegar and stir.

2 Cook over gentle heat, stirring until all the sugar has dissolved, then bring to a boil and cook at a rolling boil, stirring occasionally, for about 10 minutes. Reduce to a simmer and cook for about 1^1/$_2$ hours, stirring from time to time, until the mixture thickens. Stir continuously near the end of cooking time so that the chutney doesn't stick to the bottom of the pan.

3 Ladle into warm, sterilized jars with non-metallic or vinegar-proof lids, making sure there are no air gaps. Cover each pot with a waxed paper disc, seal, and label.

Note Store in a cool, dark place. Allow the flavors to mature for 1 month and refrigerate after opening. The chutney will keep for 9 months unopened.

This light summer salad is a great way to use home-grown artichokes. You can either prepare raw artichokes, or take a short cut and use baby artichokes preserved in oil (see opposite).

Artichoke salad

Serves 4 • **Prep** 25 mins, plus cooling • **Cooking** 10 mins

ARTICHOKES

When to pick
The flower heads are best when harvested before the leaves open and flowers appear. Pick tight, firm heads from the center of the plant to encourage regrowth.

Eat and store fresh
Best eaten immediately. The whole plant can be steamed or boiled, or the heart can be eaten alone, after being steamed, boiled, or chargrilled.

How to preserve
Preserve cooked whole baby globe artichokes in oil, or char-grill just the hearts before preserving them in oil (see page 81).

Freezing options
Trimmed hearts can be blanched for 4 minutes, cooled, and then frozen for up to 12 months.

INGREDIENTS

4 globe artichokes

3 lemons

sea salt

2 large handsful of arugula

1oz (25g) chunk of Parmesan
    cheese

2 tbsp extra virgin olive oil

1 tbsp balsamic vinegar

freshly ground black pepper

METHOD

1 Trim the artichoke stems and snap off the hard outer leaves (about 5–6 layers), until you reach the paler, more tender ones. Cut about 1in (2.5cm) off the spiny tips and discard. Then slice in half and using a teaspoon, carefully remove the choke and discard. Place the artichokes in a bowl and pour the juice of 2 lemons over them.

2 Bring a saucepan of water to a boil. Add 1 tsp salt and the juice of the remaining lemon. Place the artichokes into the pan and cook for 10 minutes, or until tender. Drain well and set aside to cool.

3 When the artichokes are cool enough to handle, carefully cut them into quarters.

4 Divide the arugula and artichokes between the serving plates. Using a vegetable peeler, shave pieces of Parmesan cheese over each salad. Drizzle over with olive oil and balsamic vinegar, and season to taste with salt and freshly ground pepper.

Baby artichokes are a great delicacy. They taste delicious when stored in olive oil. Serve as antipasti, or add to fresh pasta with home-made arugula pesto (see page 55).

Baby artichokes in oil

Makes approx. 1lb (500g) or 1 small jar • **Prep** 35 mins• **Cooking** 10 mins

INGREDIENTS

10 baby globe artichokes

$1^1/_4$ cups white wine vinegar

1 tbsp sea salt

For the marinade

2 cups extra virgin olive oil

$^1/_4$ cup

white wine vinegar

handful of black peppercorns

METHOD

1 Trim the artichoke stems and snap off the hard outer leaves (about 5–6 layers), until you reach the paler, more tender ones. Cut about 1in (2.5cm) off the spiny tips and discard. Then slice in half and using a teaspoon, carefully remove the choke and discard.

2 Put the vinegar, salt, and $1^1/_4$ cups of water in a heavy, stainless steel saucepan, and bring to a boil. Add the prepared artichokes and blanch for 3–5 minutes in the simmering vinegar mix. They should still retain plenty of bite. Drain, cool, and then cut lengthwise into quarters.

3 To prepare the marinade, put the olive oil, vinegar, and peppercorns into a saucepan and bring to a boil. Add the artichokes and bring back to the boil. Turn the heat off, and leave to cool with the artichokes in the marinade.

4 Using a slotted spoon, remove the cooled artichokes and put them into a sterilized jar with a non-metallic or vinegar-proof lid. Pour the marinade over to cover the artichokes. Seal, label, and store in the fridge. Once open, keep refrigerated, top up with oil if necessary so the artichokes are always covered, and use within 2 months.

TOMATOES

When to pick
Harvest tomatoes with deep color and glossy skin. If signs of blight or disease show, pick any imperfect tomatoes immediately, to stop the disease spreading.

Eat and store fresh
Where possible, keep and eat tomatoes at room temperature for best flavor. Green tomatoes will keep for up to 2 weeks in a cool, dark place.

How to preserve
Tomatoes can be preserved in a number of ways, including in chutneys, sauces, or pickles. They can also be dried and preserved in oil (see pp. 38–9 and 92–3).

Freezing options
Tomatoes freeze well if they have been cooked first. Typically, they are skinned, chopped, and cooked down before being cooled and frozen for up to 6 months.

This is a luxury version of a classic tomato soup. Fresh, roasted, and sun-dried tomatoes are combined to give richness and depth of flavor to the finished dish.

Cream of tomato soup

Serves 4–6 • **Prep** 30 mins • **Cooking** 40 mins

INGREDIENTS

3 tbsp butter

1 tbsp extra virgin olive oil

2 onions, finely chopped

2 celery stalks, finely chopped

2 carrots, finely diced

2 garlic cloves, crushed

12 plum tomatoes, about $2^{1}/_{4}$lb (1kg), quartered, roasted, and coarsely chopped

8 plum tomatoes, about $1^{1}/_{4}$–$1^{1}/_{2}$lb (600–720g), peeled and finely chopped

6 sun-dried tomatoes, finely chopped

4 cups hot vegetable stock

2–3 tbsp heavy cream

sea salt and freshly ground black pepper

METHOD

1 Heat the butter and olive oil in a heavy saucepan over medium heat. Add the onions, and sauté for 8–10 minutes, stirring frequently, until very soft but not colored. Next, add the celery and carrots, and continue cooking gently without browning for another 10 minutes, stirring from time to time. Add the garlic and sauté for another 1-2 minutes, stirring.

2 Mix together the roasted plum tomatoes, fresh tomatoes, and sun-dried tomatoes. Add to the pan with juices, and cook, stirring, for 5 minutes to allow the flavors to combine. If the sauce looks too thick or starts sticking to the bottom of the pan, add a little of the hot vegetable stock. Pour in the remaining vegetable stock, and simmer the soup for 15–20 minutes.

3 Blend the soup to a smooth purée using a food processor or hand-held blender. Pass through a sieve or food mill into a clean pan, unless you prefer to make a coarse-textured soup. Add the cream a teaspoon at a time until you are happy with the taste and texture. Season with salt and pepper, reheat very gently if required, and serve.

A time-honored Spanish classic, this chilled tomato soup makes the best of high-summer produce. It is delicious served simply with platters of sweet Charentais melon and salty Parma ham.

Gazpacho

Serves 6–8 • **Prep** 30 mins

INGREDIENTS

1 red bell pepper,
   seeded and chopped

10 scallions, trimmed and
   chopped, or 1 red onion,
   finely chopped

5 garlic cloves, chopped

1 cucumber, finely chopped

$2^{1}/_{4}$lb (1kg) ripe tomatoes,
   finely chopped

1 tbsp chopped fresh thyme,
   marjoram, parsley, mint, or
   basil

3 slices of stale bread, torn into
   pieces

1 fresh chile, seeded and finely
   chopped, or $^{1}/_{2}$tsp cayenne
   pepper (optional)

2 tbsp red wine vinegar

3 tbsp extra virgin olive oil, plus
   extra to serve

sea salt and freshly ground
   black pepper

ice cubes

METHOD

1 Place a large serving bowl in the fridge. Put the chopped pepper, spring onions or red onion, garlic, cucumber, and tomatoes into a mixing bowl, and then add the herbs.

2 Process the bread in a blender to make bread crumbs, and then add to the mixing bowl along with the chile or cayenne pepper (if using), the vinegar, and oil. Gradually add chilled water; $^{1}/_{2}$ cup will give it a nice thick consistency, but you can use more if you prefer.

3 Transfer to the blender and process briefly, until you achieve your preferred texture. Season generously with salt and pepper. Transfer to the serving bowl, add a few ice cubes, and drizzle with olive oil.

This Indian-style fish dish is quick to prepare and cook, making it ideal for entertaining. It can also be made using fillets of sea bass, John Dory, or any other firm, meaty fish.

Grilled red bream
with tomato and cilantro salad

Serves 4 • **Prep** 15 mins • **Cooking** 6–8 mins

INGREDIENTS

4 red bream fillets,
    about 6oz (150g) each
lemon wedges, to serve

For the spice rub
3 tbsp walnut or
    extra virgin olive oil
4 tbsp chopped cilantro
2 garlic cloves, crushed
1 tsp coriander seeds, crushed
1 tsp fresh lemon juice
1 small hot green chile, very
    finely chopped

For the tomato salad
4 plum tomatoes, chopped
1 tbsp chopped cilantro
1$^{1}/_{2}$ tsp walnut or olive oil
1 tbsp coarsely
    chopped walnuts
sea salt and freshly ground
    black pepper

METHOD

1 Mix together all the ingredients for the spice rub and season with salt.

2 Line a baking sheet with foil and place the fish fillets on it, skin-side down. Brush the spice rub over the fish. Place under a preheated broiler for 4-6 minutes, until cooked through and lightly golden. Remove from the heat and keep warm.

3 Meanwhile, toast the walnuts in a dry frying pan, and then lightly crush them, and mix with the rest of the ingredients for the tomato salad. Serve the fish with the salad and some lemon wedges.

If you grow a variety of tomatoes, this salad is perfect for the best of the high summer crop, since any type and combination of tomatoes can be used. The freshness of the ingredients is key.

Tomato salad
with mozzarella

Serves 4 • **Prep** 10 mins

INGREDIENTS

8 ripe plum tomatoes, sliced
6 cherry tomatoes, halved
1 small red onion, sliced
handful of fresh basil
   leaves, torn
extra virgin olive oil,
   for drizzling
sea salt and freshly ground
   black pepper
2 handsful of arugula leaves
balsamic vinegar, for drizzling
2 balls of fresh mozzarella, torn
   into bite-sized pieces

METHOD

1 Put the tomatoes, red onion, and half the basil leaves in a bowl. Drizzle over plenty of olive oil, season well with salt and freshly ground black pepper, and toss through.

2 Arrange the arugula leaves on a serving platter, and drizzle over a little olive oil and some balsamic vinegar. Season with salt and black pepper, and spoon over the tomato and basil mixture.

3 Add the torn mozzarella. Scatter over the remaining basil leaves, and drizzle again with a little olive oil and balsamic vinegar. Serve immediately.

Heating this vinaigrette slightly brings out its strong, heady aromas. It works best served over freshly grilled tuna or salmon steaks, but is also good as a dressing for a pasta or rice salad.

Warm tomato
and garlic vinaigrette

Serves 4–6 • **Prep** 10 mins • **Cooking** 10 mins

INGREDIENTS

3 ripe, medium to large
    tomatoes

3 tbsp extra virgin olive oil

2 garlic cloves, crushed

1/4 tsp hot paprika

1 tbsp finely chopped
    fresh basil

1 tbsp finely chopped flat-
    leaf parsley

1 tbsp sherry vinegar

sea salt and freshly ground
    black pepper

METHOD

1 Place the tomatoes in a bowl, cover them with boiling water, and leave for 1 minute. Peel when they are cool enough to handle. Halve them, scoop out and discard the seeds. Remove the tomato core, chop the flesh finely, and set it aside.

2 Put the olive oil in a frying pan over very low heat, and add the garlic and paprika. Stir for 3–4 minutes. Add half the basil and parsley, and stir for 1 minute. Add the tomatoes and stir gently for 2–3 minutes until hot.

3 Take off the heat. Stir in the reserved basil and parsley, and then the sherry vinegar. Season with salt and pepper to taste and serve while still warm.

Using the ripest tomatoes and the best olive oil, this dish captures the flavors of the Mediterranean. Serve it with freshly baked bread and a green salad for an elegant and simple meal.

Baked ricotta
with roasted tomatoes

Serves 4 as a starter • **Prep** 15 mins • **Cooking** 25 mins

INGREDIENTS

2 tbsp extra virgin olive oil, plus
   extra for greasing
7 ripe cherry tomatoes,
   cut in half
sea salt and freshly ground
   black pepper
1 large red bell pepper
8oz (250g) piece of ricotta
   cheese, drained
2 tbsp freshly grated
   Parmesan cheese

METHOD

1 Preheat the oven to 425°F (220°C) and lightly grease a small roasting pan or dish. Reserve 2 tomato halves and place the rest in the pan, cut-sides up, drizzle with 2 tbsp olive oil, and sprinkle with salt and pepper. Bake 7–10 minutes, until soft. Remove from oven, set aside.

2 Place the pepper under a hot broiler and cook, turning frequently, for 4–5 minutes, or until blackened all over. Put the pepper in a plastic bag and set aside to cool completely, and then peel away the skin. Cut in half, discard the core and seeds, and cut into strips. Set aside.

3 Cut the ricotta in half horizontally. Remove tomatoes from the pan. Place the bottom half of the ricotta, cut-side up, in the pan and season lightly. Arrange the pepper strips on top, then the tomatoes. Drizzle with oil, and top with remaining ricotta, cut-side down.

4 Sprinkle with Parmesan and drizzle with olive oil. Return to oven and bake for 15 minutes, or until the cheese is hot and the crust is golden. Top with reserved tomato halves, and season with freshly ground pepper.

This wonderful jam is extremely versatile and delicious served with cold meats, sausages, and cheese. It is ideal for the end of the tomato season, when there tends to be a late glut.

Tomato and chile jam

Makes 12oz (350g) or 1 medium jar • **Prep** 10 mins • **Cooking** 35 mins

INGREDIENTS

1lb (500g) tomatoes

1 tsp crushed hot red
    pepper flakes

1 tsp mixed dried herbs

juice of 1 lemon

pinch of salt

1¼ cups granulated sugar

METHOD

1 Place the tomatoes in a bowl, cover with boiling water, and leave for 1 minute. Peel when they are cool enough to handle. Halve them, scoop out, and discard the seeds. Remove the cores, roughly chop the flesh, and set aside.

2 Put all ingredients except sugar into a preserving pan or large, heavy saucepan. Bring to a boil and simmer gently for 8 minutes, or until the tomatoes soften.

3 Add the sugar and heat gently, stirring until the sugar dissolves. Turn up the heat and bring to a boil. When the jam reaches a rolling boil, cook for 10–15 minutes or until it starts to thicken and becomes glossy, reaching the setting point. Stir occasionally to prevent the jam sticking or burning in the pan. Remove the pan from the heat while you test for a set (see page 187).

4 Ladle into a warm, sterilized jar, making sure there are no air gaps. Cover the surface with a disk of parchment or waxed paper, seal with a non-metallic or vinegar-proof lid, and label.

Note Store in a cool, dark place and refrigerate after opening. The jam will keep for 6 months unopened.

By the end of the summer you may be left with lots of slightly imperfect tomatoes from your garden. Chutneys and relishes are an ideal way to use up every last bit of your precious crop.

Tomato chutney
with roasted peppers

Makes approx. 3lb (1.35kg) or 3 medium jars • **Prep** 20 mins • **Cooking** 2 hours

INGREDIENTS

1 red pepper

1 orange pepper

1 yellow pepper

3lb (1.35kg) ripe tomatoes, plunged into boiling water for 1 minute, then peeled

2 onions, coarsley chopped

$2^1/_2$ cups granulated sugar

$2^1/_2$ cups white wine vinegar

METHOD

1 Preheat the oven to 400°F (200°C). Put the peppers into a roasting pan and bake for 25–30 minutes until they begin to char. Remove from the oven, seal in a plastic bag, and cool before removing stems, rubbing off the skin, seeding, and chopping coarsely.

2 Put the tomatoes, peppers, and onions in a food processor and pulse until chopped, but not mushy.

3 Tip the mixture into a preserving, or heavy, stainless steel saucepan, with the sugar and vinegar. Cook on low, stirring continuously, until the sugar has dissolved. Bring to a boil, reduce to a simmer for $1–1^1/_2$ hours, stirring occasionally, until it starts to thicken and turn jammy.

4 Ladle into warm, sterilized jars with non-metallic or vinegar-proof lids, ensuring there are no air gaps. Cover jars with parchment or wax paper discs, seal, and label.

Note Store in a cool, dark place. Leave to mature for 1 month, and refrigerate after opening. Keeps for 9 months unopened.

Dry vegetables

Many fruits and vegetables are suitable to dry. If you use top-quality produce, picked at its moment of perfection, and dry it correctly, it will taste superb. In warm countries, tomatoes are dried outdoors in the sun for up to 4 days. Similar results can be achieved by drying them in an oven set to very low heat. Other fruits and vegetables that dry well this way include mushrooms, cranberry beans, corn, figs, pears, peaches, apricots, apples, and citrus peel. Chiles and beans can be successfully air-dried (see right) for later use in recipes.

1 **Cut and score** Slice each tomato in half, round ones horizontally, plum ones vertically. Score the middle of each tomato with a cross shape and push the centers up from below.

2 **Sprinkle with salt** Arrange the tomato halves cut side up, on wire racks over baking trays. Sprinkle lightly with salt. Leave for a few minutes. Place cut side down.

Recipe Oven-dried tomatoes

Makes approx. 2lb (900g) • **Prep** 10 mins, plus
8–12 hrs drying, and cooling • **Keeps** 2 weeks
(12 months frozen)

INGREDIENTS

6½lb (3kg) ripe, but firm,
   medium-sized tomatoes

2–3 tsp sea salt

Air-drying beans and chiles

Beans that you can shell, such as cranberry and climbing green beans (kidney beans), and red chiles can be dried and stored at home.

Beans Dry the bean pods on newspaper, then shell the beans, arrange in trays, and place on a window sill until dry and plump, not wrinkled. Keep in storage jars, out of direct sunlight, for up to 1 year. Soak overnight before cooking.

Chiles Harvest red chiles and hang in garlands to air-dry in a warm, dry, airy place for 2 weeks. Use crumbled in recipes.

3 **Dry in the oven** Preheat the oven to 150–175°F (60–80°C) and dry for 8–12 hours, keeping the door slightly ajar. Remove and leave to cool on the racks.

4 **Store in jars** Pack into sterilized jars and store in the fridge. For long-term storage, freeze on open trays, pack into bags, and freeze. Thaw, cover with olive oil, and refrigerate.

When to pick

You can harvest peppers when they are still under-ripe (green), nearly ripe (yellow), or ripe (red). Generally the riper the pepper the sweeter the taste.

Eat and store fresh

Raw red peppers taste their best if eaten immediately, but all types of peppers will store well in the bottom of the fridge for up to 5 days.

How to preserve

Chutneys, pickles, and relishes are all good ways of preserving peppers. Char-grilling or roasting, or peeling and preserving in oil is another option.

Freezing options

Peppers can be frozen if they are first griddled, then cooled, and stored in batches for up to 6 months. They also make good freezer pickles.

The chickpeas in this soup add depth and texture, making it a meal in itself. You can roast bell peppers ahead of time and keep them loosely packed in olive oil in the fridge for up to a week.

Roasted red pepper
and chickpea soup

Serves 4 • Prep 25 mins • Cooking 35 mins

INGREDIENTS

3 red bell peppers

1 onion, chopped

2 carrots, chopped

1 large garlic clove, chopped

2 tbsp chopped fresh thyme

1 x 15.5oz can garbanzo beans
    (chickpeas), drained

3 tbsp extra virgin olive oil,
plus extra to garnish

1 tsp ground cumin

1 tsp ground cinnamon

2 tsp paprika

1/2 tsp finely grated ginger

3 cups chicken stock

1 tbsp tahini (sesame paste)

1 tsp honey

sea salt and freshly ground
black pepper

2 tbsp pitted, coarsely chopped
    black olives

METHOD

1 Preheat the oven to 400°F (200°C). Put the peppers in a roasting pan and cook for 25–30 minutes until they begin to char. Remove from the oven, seal in a plastic bag, and leave to cool before removing the stems, rubbing off the skin, seeding, and chopping coarsely.

2 Heat the oil in a large pan and cook the onion, carrots, and garlic over medium heat, stirring for 2 minutes until softened. Add the peppers, half the thyme, and all the remaining ingredients, except the olives. Bring to a boil, then reduce the heat, partially cover, and simmer gently for 30 minutes.

3 Purée using a hand-held blender or by transferring to a food processor, then reheat. Season to taste. Ladle into warm bowls, add a trickle of olive oil, a sprinkling of chopped olives and some of the remaining thyme to garnish each.

Note To save time, add raw, diced bell peppers in step 2. It is quicker, although the flavor is not as good.

In this Spanish dish, sweet red bell peppers are gently stewed, and then served cold. It is wonderful as tapas or as a side dish with a piece of grilled steak or meaty fish, such as tuna.

Red pepper salad

Serves 4 • **Prep** 10 mins • **Cooking** 25 mins

INGREDIENTS

3 tbsp extra virgin olive oil

6 red bell peppers, seeded and cut into large strips

2 garlic cloves, finely chopped

8oz (250g) ripe tomatoes, plunged into boiling water for 1 minute, then peeled, seeded, and chopped

2 tbsp chopped fresh parsley

sea salt and freshly ground black pepper

1 tbsp sherry vinegar

METHOD

1 Heat the oil in a large frying pan, add the peppers and garlic, and cook over low heat for 5 minutes, stirring, then add the tomatoes. Increase the heat, bring to a simmer, then reduce the heat to low, cover, and cook for 12–15 minutes.

2 Stir in the parsley, season well with salt and pepper, and cook for a further 2 minutes. Using a slotted spoon, remove the peppers, and arrange in a serving dish.

3 Add the vinegar to the pan, increase the heat, and simmer the sauce for 5–7 minutes, or until it has reduced and thickened. Pour the sauce over the peppers and allow to cool before serving.

Variation To make a red-pepper dressing, process the salad in a blender or food processor until smooth. With the machine running, gradually add in enough olive oil to make a dressing, and use to coat a mix of green leaves.

This savory scrambled-egg dish is a classic recipe from the Basque region of southwestern France, where the peppers have been sweetened by long hours of sunshine.

Pipérade

Serves 4 • **Prep** 5 mins • **Cooking** 20 mins

INGREDIENTS

2 tbsp extra virgin olive oil

1 large onion, thinly sliced
   or chopped

2 garlic cloves, crushed

1 red bell pepper, seeded
   and chopped

1 green bell pepper, seeded
   and chopped

3oz (85g) Serrano ham or
   Bayonne ham, chopped

4 tomatoes, chopped

8 eggs, lightly beaten

salt and freshly ground
   black pepper

2 tbsp chopped fresh parsley,
   to garnish

METHOD

1 Heat the oil in a large frying pan and cook the onion over medium-low heat until softened. Add the garlic and peppers, and cook for 5 minutes, stirring occasionally.

2 Add the ham and cook for 2 minutes, then add the tomatoes and simmer for 2–3 minutes, or until any liquid has evaporated.

3 Pour the eggs into the pan and cook, stirring frequently, until cooked well enough to suit. Season to taste with salt and freshly ground pepper, sprinkle with parsley, and serve.

A wonderfully spicy vegetarian dish, where the contrasting lime and chile work brilliantly well with the crunchy peanuts. Make it your own by adding the vegetables you have in season.

Fiery pepper noodles

Serves 4 • **Prep** 30 mins • **Cooking** 4–5 mins

INGREDIENTS

1 red bell pepper

1 green bell pepper

1 tbsp sunflower or
    vegetable oil

4 scallions, chopped

1 garlic clove, finely chopped

1 zucchini, finely chopped

1 or 2 green jalapeño or
    poblano chiles, seeded and
    chopped

1 tsp finely grated fresh ginger

1 tbsp chopped flat-leaf parsley

1 tbsp chopped fresh cilantro,
    plus a few torn leaves, to
    serve

finely grated zest and juice of
    1 lime

4 tbsp chunky peanut butter

3 tbsp soy sauce

1 tbsp dry sherry

1lb (500g) fresh egg noodles

1/4 cup chopped roasted
    peanuts, to serve

METHOD

1 Preheat the oven to 400°F (200°C). Put the peppers in a roasting pan and cook for 25–30 minutes until they begin to char. Remove from the oven, seal in a plastic bag, and leave to cool before removing the stems, rubbing off the skin, seeding, and chopping coarsely.

2 Heat the oil in a wok or large frying pan. Add the scallions, garlic, and zucchini, and cook, stirring and tossing, for 1 minute. Add the peppers, chiles , ginger, herbs, lime zest and juice, peanut butter, soy sauce, sherry, and 9 tbsp of water. Stir the ingredients until the peanut butter melts.

3 Add the noodles and toss for 2 minutes until piping hot. Pile into warm bowls and sprinkle with peanuts and a few torn cilantro leaves.

For a small plant, the chile can yield a surprising amount. A thin disc of chile butter adds a touch of spice to grilled meats or fish, and can be frozen for convenient slicing whenever you need it.

Chile butter

Makes 9oz (250g) • **Prep** 10 mins, plus chilling

INGREDIENTS

1 cup butter, at
    room temperature

2 tbsp crushed chili flakes, or
    less, to taste

2 tsp ground cumin

2 garlic cloves, crushed

4 tbsp finely chopped fresh
    cilantro or parsley

sea salt and freshly ground
    black pepper

METHOD

1 Place the butter, chili flakes, cumin, garlic, and cilantro in a mixing bowl and beat together until well combined. Season to taste with salt and pepper and stir again. Transfer to a sheet of parchment or wax paper and form it into a cylinder.

2 Roll the cylinder in the paper and twist the ends to seal. Chill in the refrigerator for 1 hour, or until firm enough to slice.

Note The chile butter can be made up to 3 days in advance and chilled until ready to use. Leftovers can be kept, wrapped in greaseproof paper, in the refrigerator, then sliced and melted for a quick butter sauce.

CHILE PEPPERS

When to pick
You can harvest chiles at any stage of their ripeness. Their color is an indicator of spiciness, so the darker and riper the chile, the hotter will be the taste.

Eat and store fresh
Store fresh chiles in the fridge for up to 5 days. If left in a bowl in the kitchen, chiles can be used at any stage, as they gradually start to dry.

How to preserve
Dry chiles by tying together with string, and hanging them in a sunny window. Use in chutneys, relishes, butters, and chile jelly (see page 102).

Freezing options
Chiles can be frozen if made into chile butter (see left).

This is a fantastically fresh, spicy salsa. Its Asian flavors and vibrant colors transform grilled or barbecued meat or fish. Replace Thai basil with another variety of basil, if preferred.

Lemongrass
and chile salsa

Serves 6 • **Prep** 20 mins, plus chilling

INGREDIENTS

2 stalks of lemongrass, tough
    outer leaves discarded
2 heaping tbsp chopped fresh
    Thai basil, plus 6 whole
    leaves to finish
1 tsp grated fresh ginger
1 whole hot red chile pepper,
    seeded and finely chopped
1 tbsp honey or 1 tbsp sugar
3 tbsp soy sauce
2 tsp Asian fish sauce
6 tbsp fresh lime juice

METHOD

1 Slice off the tops of the lemongrass stalks and discard them. Bash down on the bulb ends with the flat side of a large knife or pound using a kitchen mallet. Chop very finely and place in a bowl.

2 Add the basil, ginger, and chile. Pour in the honey, soy sauce, fish sauce, and lime juice, and stir well. Cover and chill for at least 1 hour to give the flavors time to develop.

3 Stir in the whole basil leaves just before serving.

Note Store in the fridge for up to 2 days.

Keep your chiles longer by hanging them up to air-dry in a warm, dry, airy place for two weeks until shrivelled. Crumble them to make your own chili flakes to use in recipes like this one.

Hot pepper jelly

Makes 1lb (450g) or 2 small jars • **Prep** 15 mins, plus straining • **Cooking** 1½ hours

INGREDIENTS

1½lb (675g) tart cooking
    apples, such as Granny
    Smith, skin on,
    coarsely chopped
3¾ cups
granulated sugar (see method)
juice of 1 lemon
1–2 tsp crushed chili flakes

METHOD

1 Put the chopped apples, with their cores and seeds, in a preserving pan or a large, heavy saucepan. Pour in 7 cups of cold water, bring to a boil, and simmer for 30–40 minutes, or until the apples are mushy and completely broken down. Mash them with a fork.

2 Spoon the pulpy mixture into a jelly bag or muslin-lined sieve, set over a large clean bowl. Leave the juice to drip through naturally overnight, and don't squeeze the pulp.

3 Measure the strained juice and calculate 2½ cups of sugar for every 2½ cups of juice. Pour the juice into a clean pan, bring to a boil, then add the sugar and lemon juice. Stir until the sugar has dissolved, then bring to a rolling boil and remove surface scum. Continue to boil, stirring occasionally, for 20–30 minutes or until the jelly reaches the setting point. Remove the pan from the heat while you test for a set (see page 187).

4 Leave to cool for 10 minutes, then stir in the pepper flakes. Ladle into warm sterilized jars, cover with discs of waxed paper, seal, and label.

Note Store in a cool, dark place, and refrigerate after opening. Keeps for 9 months unopened.

The eggplant in this dish are enlivened by the tangy flavor of pomegranate seeds. This is wonderful served as part of a mezze-style meal, or as a salad with red onion and feta cheese.

Grilled eggplant
and pomegranate vinaigrette

Serves 6 • **Prep** 10 mins • **Cooking** 10 mins

INGREDIENTS

6 tbsp extra virgin olive oil,
    plus extra for brushing
3 tbsp pomegranate syrup
    (pomegranate molasses)
3 tbsp chopped fresh cilantro
sea salt and freshly ground
    black pepper
3 large eggplants, cut into
    1/2in (1cm) thick slices
2 shallots, very thinly sliced
fresh pomegranate seeds, to
    garnish

METHOD

1 To make the vinaigrette, whisk together the extra virgin olive oil, pomegranate syrup, and cilantro, and season to taste with salt and freshly ground pepper. Set aside until ready to serve.

2 Preheat a grill pan over high heat. Brush both sides of the eggplant slices with olive oil, season to taste with salt and pepper, then grill on both sides until tender.

3 Layer the eggplant slices and shallots in a serving dish, and pour over the vinaigrette. Scatter with fresh pomegranate seeds and serve.

Variation Use thinly sliced red onion instead of the shallots and scatter with 1/2 cup crumbled feta cheese to make a salad.

EGGPLANT

When to pick
Pick all varieties of eggplant when they are a good size, with a dark, glossy color and smooth skin. Dull or wrinkled skin indicates an overripe fruit.

Eat and store fresh
Eggplant are best eaten as soon as possible after picking, but also store well in the bottom of the fridge for up to 5 days.

How to preserve
A really good candidate for char-grilling and preserving in oil, eggplant are also commonly used in chutneys, pickles, and relishes.

Freezing options
Eggplant can be frozen if they are first sliced and char-grilled, then cooled and frozen in batches for up to 6 months.

Home-grown eggplant taste far better than commercially produced ones. Small and sweet, they respond well to being steamed. This tastes delicious served alongside grilled lamb.

Eggplant salad

Serves 6 • **Prep** 15 mins • **Cooking** 10 mins

INGREDIENTS

2 medium eggplants, peeled
    and cut into ³/₄in (2cm) dice
¹/₂ cup crumbled soft
    goat cheese
2 ripe tomatoes, seeded
    and diced
1 small red onion, finely diced
1 handful of flat-leaf parsley,
    finely chopped
¹/₂ cup walnut halves and
    pieces, lightly toasted and
    coarsely chopped
1 tbsp sesame seeds,
    lightly toasted
sea salt and freshly ground
    black pepper

For the dressing
1 garlic clove, crushed
salt and freshly ground
    black pepper
¹/₄ cup walnut oil
juice of 1 lemon

METHOD

1 Cook the diced eggplant in a covered steamer basket placed over simmering water, for 10 minutes. Leave to cool slightly and then gently squeeze the dice to extract as much water as possible.

2 Combine all the remaining salad ingredients in a mixing bowl and toss gently. Whisk together the dressing ingredients, and then toss the dressing with the salad. Season to taste with salt and pepper.

Variation Replace the goat cheese and sesame seeds with feta cheese and pine nuts.

105

Combining eggplant, tomatoes, and basil, this confit is the essence of summer growing and eating. It makes a classy side dish for lamb or fish, finished with a drizzle of basil-infused oil.

Eggplant
and tomato confit

Serves 6 • Prep 5 mins, plus infusing • Cooking 5 mins

INGREDIENTS

2 tbsp extra virgin olive oil

5 tbsp vegetable oil

12oz (300g) eggplant, cut into
   sticks about 1/2 in (1cm)
   wide and 3in (7.5cm) long

1/4 cup garlic-infused olive oil

1/2 cup cherry tomatoes, halved

10 fresh basil leaves, torn into
   pieces, plus whole
   leaves to garnish

salt and freshly ground
   black pepper

METHOD

1 Heat the extra virgin olive oil and vegetable or sunflower oil in a large frying pan over medium-high heat, until they just begin to smoke. Add the eggplant and cook, stirring often, for 3 minutes, or until golden brown all over. Drain on paper towels.

2 Add the garlic oil to the pan, then add the cherry tomatoes. Cook, shaking the pan occasionally, for 1–2 minutes, or until softened.

3 Place the eggplant in a large bowl. Add the torn basil leaves and the tomatoes, and mix gently. Cover and leave to blend for up to 1 hour in a warm place in the kitchen.

4 Season to taste with salt and pepper and serve slightly warm with the whole basil leaves scattered on top.

The okra in this rich, classic dish from New Orleans provides a natural thickener and adds texture and color. The sausage adds extra spice and complements the seafood.

Seafood gumbo

Serves 6 • **Prep** 20 mins • **Cooking** 50 mins

INGREDIENTS

1 tbsp vegetable oil

1 onion, chopped

2 celery stalks, chopped

1 large garlic clove, chopped

4oz (115g) andouille sausage or chorizo, sliced

2 tbsp all-purpose flour

2½ cups fish or chicken stock

1 x 14.5oz (400g) can diced tomatoes

1 green bell pepper, diced

8oz (250g) okra, trimmed and cut into ½in (1cm) pieces

¼ tsp cayenne pepper

½ tsp dried oregano

½ tsp granulated sugar

sea salt and freshly ground black pepper

8oz (200g) mixed raw seafood, such as crabmeat and peeled and deveined shrimp

1¼ cups long-grain white rice

chopped parsley, to serve

METHOD

1 Heat the oil in a large pan. Add the onion and celery and cook gently, stirring, for about 5 minutes, or until softened but not browned. Stir in the garlic and andouille, and cook for 2 minutes. Add the flour and cook, stirring, until lightly golden, about 5 minutes. Remove from the heat and gradually blend in stock, then the tomatoes. Return to heat, bring to a boil, stirring.

2 Add the remaining ingredients, except the seafood and rice, bring back to a boil, reduce the heat, partially cover, and simmer gently for 30 minutes. Add the seafood and simmer for a further 5 minutes, stirring occasionally. Season again to taste.

3 Meanwhile, cook the rice in boiling, lightly salted water for 10 minutes, or until just tender. Drain in a fine sieve, rinse with boiling water, and drain again.

4 Spoon some rice into 6 large soup bowls. Ladle the gumbo over it, sprinkle with a little chopped, fresh parsley, and serve hot.

OKRA

When to pick
Pick okra often to encourage regrowth. It is ready to harvest when no more than 3in (7.5cm) long, and glossy green. It can become woody if left to grow larger.

Eat and store fresh
Eat okra as soon as possible after picking, or store for up to 2 days in the fridge. Tiny okra can be eaten raw, bigger ones should be cooked.

How to preserve
Use okra as an ingredient in chutneys, pickles, and relishes.

This sensational dish can be eaten hot or cold. Hot, serve simply with a green salad on the side, and cold it would make a great addition to a buffet.

Bulgur wheat
with shrimp and okra

Serves 8 • **Prep** 15 mins • **Cooking** 30 mins

INGREDIENTS

2$^1/_2$ cups bulgur wheat

$^1/_2$ cup extra virgin olive oil

2 large onions, finely chopped

1lb (450g) okra, trimmed, and
cut into chunks

6 garlic cloves, peeled and
grated, or finely chopped

1$^1/_2$lb (675g) shelled and
deveined large shrimp

$^1/_2$ cup dry white wine

large handful of fresh dill,
chopped

sea salt and freshly ground
black pepper

METHOD

1 Preheat the oven to 300°F (150°C). Put the bulgur in a heatproof bowl, and pour in enough boiling water to cover. Cover the bowl with a kitchen towel, leave for 5 minutes, then stir.

2 Meanwhile, heat the oil in a large flameproof casserole or other heavy saucepan, add the onions, and cook over medium heat for 5 minutes, or until they start to soften. Add the okra and cook for 2 minutes, then add the garlic and shrimp and continue to cook, stirring frequently, for 2–3 minutes or just until the shrimp start to turn pink.

3 Stir in the wine and dill, cook for 2 minutes, and then stir in the bulgur. Transfer to an ovenproof serving dish, if desired. Season with salt and pepper, and cover with foil. Bake, stirring occasionally, for 20 minutes or until heated through. Serve hot or cold.

CUCUMBERS

When to pick
Pick when small, to use whole or pickled, or grow longer for use in salads. Cucumbers should have a dark green, firm, glossy skin. Pick frequently to encourage regrowth.

Eat and store fresh
Eat small cucumbers soon after picking. Larger ones can be watery or bitter, so deseed and peel before use. Keep in the fridge for up to 5 days.

How to preserve
Cucumbers can be pickled, used in relishes, or salted for storage.

Freezing options
Cucumbers can be stored in the freezer as a freezer pickle (see pages 114–15).

This beautifully simple Scandinavian dish is an elegant accompaniment to a piece of grilled, or cold poached salmon. The cooling cucumber adds color as well as crunch.

Marinated cucumber
and dill salad

Serves 4–6 • **Prep** 10 mins, plus standing

INGREDIENTS

2 cucumbers, thinly sliced using a mandoline or food processor

2 tbsp coarse sea salt

2 tbsp granulated sugar

$1/4$ cup unseasoned rice wine vinegar, or white wine vinegar

freshly ground black pepper

handful of fresh dill, finely chopped

juice of $1/2$ lemon (optional)

METHOD

1 Put the sliced cucumber into a colander and toss in the sea salt. Place a slightly smaller bowl on top of the cucumber and weigh down with weights, or a few unopened cans of food. Leave over a sink for 1 hour to allow the cucumber to drain off excess water.

2 Remove the weighted bowl, wrap the cucumbers carefully in a clean towel, and squeeze out the excess water. Transfer to a bowl, cover, and refrigerate for at least 1 hour, until completely chilled.

3 Meanwhile, put 2 tablespoons of boiling water into a heatproof bowl and stir in the sugar to dissolve. Then add the vinegar, a generous grinding of pepper, and the dill, and place the bowl in the fridge to cool. Once the dressing and cucumber are thoroughly chilled , mix the two together. Adjust the seasoning to taste before serving. If using rice wine vinegar, add the lemon juice.

The classic Vietnamese flavors of lime, chile, and mint combine here to produce a wonderful summer salad. Be sure to obtain Asian fish sauce, since it is vital to the taste of the finished dish.

Vietnamese salad
with cucumber and prawns

Serves 4 • **Prep** 15 mins • **Cooking** 2–3 mins

INGREDIENTS

12 raw jumbo shrimp

2 tbsp vegetable oil

1 tsp unseasoned rice
   wine vinegar

1 tsp sugar

1 hot red chile pepper, seeded
   and very finely chopped

2 garlic cloves, crushed

2 tbsp Vietnamese fish sauce
   (nuac nam) or Thai fish
   sauce (nam pla)

1 tbsp fresh lime juice

1 tbsp chopped Vietnamese
   mint (rau ram) or other
   fresh mint leaves, plus a few
   sprigs to serve

1 green papaya, peeled, seeded,
   quartered lengthwise, and
   thinly sliced

$1/2$ cucumber, seeded and cut
   into thin strips

METHOD

1 Peel and devein the shrimp, removing and discarding the heads and tails. Spread them out on a foil-lined grill rack, brush with the oil, and grill under medium heat for 2–3 minutes, or until they turn pink.

2 Meanwhile, whisk the rice wine vinegar, sugar, chili, garlic, fish sauce, lime juice, and 75ml ($2^1/_2$fl oz) cold water together in a bowl until the sugar dissolves. Add the cooked shrimp to the bowl and stir well until they are coated in the dressing. Leave to cool completely.

3 Add the chopped mint, papaya, and cucumber, and toss together. Transfer the salad to a serving platter, with the shrimp on the top and garnish with mint sprigs.

Here the anise flavor of tarragon combines beautifully with cream to produce an unusual, delicate side dish. Serve as an accompaniment to a piece of grilled salmon or chicken.

Cucumber
with tarragon cream

Serves 4 as a starter • **Prep** 15 mins, plus standing and finishing

INGREDIENTS

1 large, firm, unblemished
  cucumber, peeled
  and thinly sliced
2 tbsp coarse sea salt
1/2 tsp granulated sugar
1 tbsp chopped fresh tarragon,
  plus 2 tsp to finish
1/4 cup half-and-half, or 3 tbsp
  sour cream
freshly ground black pepper

METHOD

1 Put the cucumber in a colander. Mix the salt, sugar, and tarragon, and sprinkle over the cucumber. Toss, then put a weighted plate on top. Leave for 30 minutes.

2 Rinse in plenty of cold water to get rid of any excess salt, drain well, and press down hard to extract all the moisture. Pat dry with kitchen paper.

3 Transfer to a serving bowl. Spoon over the cream, toss gently, and scatter over the reserved tarragon. Stir lightly, season with pepper, and serve.

Note This dish can be refrigerated overnight.

Make freezer pickles

Freezer pickles are a quick, modern way to achieve wonderfully fresh-flavored condiments with bite, and a great way to preserve the best of your garden vegetables. This cucumber pickle, which is so popular in sandwiches, can also be served with salads, cold meats, cheese, or barbecued fish. As with all frozen produce, only freeze fresh, top-quality vegetables and freeze as quickly as possible for the best results.

1 **Draw out moisture** Slice thinly and chop the vegetables. Put into a large bowl, sprinkle the salt over them, mix well, and leave for 2 hours to draw out the moisture.

2 **Drain water** Drop the vegetables into a colander, rinse in cold water, and drain, pressing down lightly to squeeze out moisture. Then put them into a clean, dry bowl.

Recipe Cucumber pickles

Makes 12oz–1lb (350–450g) • **Prep** 15 mins,
plus standing • **Keeps** 6 months

INGREDIENTS

2 large cucumbers

2 shallots

½ green pepper (optional)

1–2 tsp sea salt

½ cup cider or wine vinegar

⅛–¼ cup granulated sugar

pinch of ground turmeric

pinch of celery seeds or
dill seeds,

or ½–1 tsp
whole mustard
seeds

Other freezer pickles to try

Once you have learned the principles of making
freezer pickles, experiment with other vegetables,
using what is available from your garden.

Runner beans are ideal for a sweet and sour
treatment with brown sugar and soy sauce.
Leave the beans sprinkled in salt for 3 hours
to draw out the excess moisture.

Cauliflower works with cucumbers, red peppers,
and scallions to make crunchy pickles. Sprinkle
with salt and allow to stand for 3 hours.

3 **Soak in preserve** Mix the vinegar and
sugar to taste. Stir to dissolve the sugar,
then add the spices. Pour over the
vegetables, cover, and refrigerate overnight.

4 **Transfer to containers** Store in
freezer jars, leaving space at the top, seal,
label, and freeze. To use, thaw in the
fridge, keep refrigerated, and use in a week.

Make cold pickles

Cold pickling is a simple but worthwhile process that can be used to make a variety of delicious condiments to last you throughout the year. With cold pickling, vegetables are salted to draw out moisture then stored in cold vinegar. For crisp pickles avoid diluted vinegar. Keep the vegetables submerged in their liquor and make sure that the metal lids of storage jars are not in direct contact with the pickles when storing, since the vinegar in the pickles will react with metal. Lids with plastic-coated linings are suitable for this purpose.

1 **Cut into quarters** Snip the stalks and blossoms from the cucumbers. You can leave the cucumbers whole, cut them into quarters lengthways, or into ⅛in (3mm) slices.

2 **Salt the cucumbers** In a bowl, layer the salt and cucumbers, finishing with a layer of salt. Leave at room temperature for 24 hours. Rinse the cucumbers to remove the salt.

Recipe Tiny Pickles

Makes approx. 2¼lb (1kg) or 2 small preserving jars
Prep 20 mins, plus salting • **Keeps** 6 months

INGREDIENTS

1lb 2oz (500g) small
    pickling cucumbers,
    2–2½in (5–6cm) long,
    rinsed and rubbed dry
6 tbsp sea salt
3 or 4 shallots, peeled
1 or 2 garlic cloves, peeled

2–3 dried chiles (optional)
2–3 cloves (optional)
½ tsp dill seeds
2 sprigs of tarragon or dill
1 grape leaf (optional)
approx. 3 cups white
    wine vinegar

Other cold pickles to try

The basic recipe for pickling shown here can
be used with many other vegetables.

Cabbage Pick firm small or medium-sized
heads, for a colorful, crisp pickle.
Cucumbers Cook in hot vinegar for a soft pickle.
Mixed vegetables Combine cauliflower, onions,
carrots, tomatoes, and peppers for
a cold pickle.
Sweet shallots Lightly caramelize in balsamic
vinegar (see page 243).

3 **Store in sterilized jars** Pack into clean
sterilized jars, leaving ½in (1cm) of head
space. Add the rest of the ingredients and
enough vinegar to cover the cucumbers.

4 **Seal and store** Seal the jars with
non-metallic or vinegar-proof lids and
label. Store in a cool, dark place for 3–4
weeks to mature before eating.

ZUCCHINI

When to pick
Pick when no bigger than 6–8in (15–20cm) long, and before they become large, watery, and tasteless. Frequent picking encourages regrowth.

Eat and store fresh
Eat small zucchini raw in salads as soon as possible after picking. Keep larger ones in the fridge for 3–5 days.

How to preserve
Zucchini can be used in chutneys, pickles, and relishes, and can also be char-grilled and preserved in oil.

Freezing options
Slice smaller zucchinis and blanch for 1 minute, leave to cool, and freeze for up to 6 months.

Lovely when picked young, this member of the cucurbita family soon resembles the marrow if left to grow larger than your hand. To offset watery texture, salt larger zucchini before use.

Zucchini fritters
with dill tzatziki

Serves 4 (makes 12 small fritters) • **Prep** 20 mins, plus draining • **Cooking** 10 mins

INGREDIENTS

8oz (200g) zucchini, coarsely grated

sea salt and freshly ground black pepper

$1/2$ cup ricotta cheese

1 large egg

2 tbsp all-purpose flour

3 garlic cloves, crushed

small handful of fresh basil, chopped

small handful of flat leaf parsley, chopped

light olive oil, to fry

2 tbsp finely chopped fresh dill

1 cup Greek-style, plain yogurt

juice of $1/2$ lemon

METHOD

1 Sprinkle the zucchini with 1 tsp of salt and leave to drain in a sieve for 1 hour. Rinse and squeeze dry in a clean tea towel.

2 In a bowl, whisk together the ricotta cheese, egg, and flour. Add 2 of the crushed garlic cloves, the basil, and parsley, and season well. Mix in the zucchini.

3 Fill a frying pan with olive oil to a depth of $1/2$in (1cm) and place over medium heat. When hot, fry tablespoons of the batter, without crowding, for 2-3 minutes on each side, until golden brown. Drain the fritters on paper towels.

4 To make the tzatziki, mix the remaining clove of garlic with the dill, some salt and freshly ground pepper, and the yogurt. Add a squeeze of lemon juice, and then serve immediately with the hot fritters.

Garden owners know that zucchini are prolific and can double in size almost overnight. You can use larger zucchini here, as they are marinated and drained of excess water.

Zucchini
with chive marinade

Serves 4 as a starter • **Prep** 20 mins plus standing

INGREDIENTS

1lb (450g) zucchini

¼ cup extra virgin olive oil

finely grated zest and juice of 1 lemon

1 tsp finely chopped fresh chives, plus 2 tsp to finish

1 tsp finely chopped flat-leaf or curly parsley, plus 1 tsp to finish

1 tsp finely chopped fresh thyme

sea salt and freshly ground black pepper

METHOD

1 Rinse the zucchini, pat them dry, and then trim the ends. Using a vegetable peeler, shave each zucchini lengthwise into thin strips (it doesn't matter if some strips are only peel); if using larger zucchini discard the central seeds. Reserve on a plate lined with a double layer of paper towels .

2 In a bowl, mix 1 tbsp of the olive oil with the lemon juice and zest, chives, parsley, and thyme, and season lightly with salt and pepper. Add the zucchini strips and toss to coat. Allow the mixture to stand in a cool place for at least 40 minutes.

3 Tip into a colander. Drain well, pressing down gently, then pat dry with a paper towel.

4 Transfer to a serving bowl. Spoon over the reserved olive oil, chives, and parsley, and toss lightly. Taste and season with salt and pepper. Serve at room temperature.

Pea shoots, the first tendrils of the young plants, can be enjoyed raw in salads and other dishes. Combine them with fresh baby peas and raw zucchini in this vibrant, healthy dish.

Zucchini
and pea tortilla

Serves 10 as an appetizer • **Prep** 20 mins • **Cooking** 5 mins

INGREDIENTS

1lb 2oz (500g) zucchini, grated

1³/₄oz (50g) baby
  spinach leaves

grated zest and juice of 1 lemon

9oz (250g) baby peas

1³/₄oz (50g) toasted pine nuts

sea salt and freshly ground
  black pepper

10 wheat tortillas, halved

2 tbsp reduced-fat mayonnaise

large handful of mangetout
  (snow pea) sprouts and
  pea shoots

METHOD

1 In a large bowl, gently mix together the zucchini, spinach, lemon zest and juice, peas, and pine nuts. Season with salt and freshly ground pepper.

2 Heat a grill or a dry frying pan over high heat. Add the tortilla halves, 2 at a time, and cook for about 15 seconds on each side until soft. As you cook, set aside the softened tortilla halves under a clean kitchen towel to keep warm.

3 Lay one of the tortilla halves flat on a work surface , and brush lightly with mayonnaise. Take some of the zucchini filling, and place in the center. Arrange some of the sprouts and pea shoots on top, so that they stick out at one end, and then gently roll up the tortilla to enclose the filling. Repeat this process with the filling and remaining tortilla halves.

4 To serve, arrange the tortilla roll-ups seam-side down on individual serving plates, allowing 2 per person.

The vibrant green of grated zucchini combines with the creamy white of goat cheese to make this beautiful omelet. Strewn with fresh thyme, the finished dish looks almost too good to eat.

Grated zucchini
and goat cheese omelet

Serves 1 • **Prep** 10 mins • **Cooking** 5 mins

INGREDIENTS

3 eggs, lightly beaten

1 small zucchini,
   coarsely grated

sea salt and freshly ground
   black pepper

1 tbsp butter

$1/3$ cup crumbled soft
   goat cheese

small handful of fresh thyme,
   leaves picked, to garnish
   (optional)

METHOD

1 Put the eggs and zucchini in a pitcher. Season with salt and black pepper.

2 Melt the butter in a small, non-stick frying pan over medium-high heat until foaming, then pour in the egg mixture, swirling it around the pan to cover the bottom. Gently slide a spatula or knife under the edges of the omelet to allow the uncooked egg flow onto the bottom of the pan

3 When the omelet is beginning to cook around the edges, scatter over the goat cheese, so that it is evenly covered. Continue cooking until the center is almost cooked, but still just a little wet. Remove from the heat, and leave for 2 minutes to set; the retained heat will continue to cook the omelet.

4 Sprinkle over a little black pepper, and garnish with thyme leaves (if using). Carefully slide the omelet out of the pan and serve immediately.

CORN

When to pick
Pick corn when the silky tassels at the top of the plant are withering and brown. Ripe kernels should produce a milky white liquid when pressed.

Eat and store fresh
Eat corn as soon as possible after picking. If you must store it, keep the outer husk intact, and it will stay fresh for 2–3 days in the fridge.

How to preserve
Corn can be used in chutneys, pickles, and relishes (see pages 128–9).

Freezing options
Cut the corn off the cob with a sharp knife and blanch for 2 minutes, then cool and freeze for up to 12 months.

Home-grown corn is so tender that there is no need to cook it before making these fritters. The generous flavors used here will turn your corn into something the whole family will enjoy.

Corn fritters
with tomato salsa

Serves 4 (makes 14–16 fritters) • **Prep** 20 mins • **Cooking** 10 mins

INGREDIENTS

2 medium ears of corn

1 cup self-rising flour

1 tsp baking powder

2 large eggs

$1/4$ cup whole milk

1 tsp smoked paprika

2 scallions, finely chopped, green part separated

4 tbsp chopped fresh cilantro

1 hot red chile, seeded, finely chopped (optional)

sea salt and freshly ground black pepper

2 tbsp, or more sunflower or vegetable oil, as needed

2 ripe tomatoes, peeled and coarsely chopped

2 tbsp extra virgin olive oil

dash of hot pepper sauce

METHOD

1 Hold one ear of corn upright on a chopping board and, using a sharp knife, cut downward to shear the kernels from the cob. Repeat with the remaining ear of corn.

2 Sift the flour and baking powder into a bowl. Mix the eggs and milk together in a measuring cup, and gradually whisk them into the flour to make a thick batter. Add the corn, paprika, the white parts of the scallions, 2 tbsp of the cilantro, and the chile (if using). Mix well and season.

3 Heat the sunflower oil in a large frying pan. Working in batches, add tablespoons of batter without crowding. Use the spoon to spread the fritters slightly, and cook for 2–3 minutes per side until puffed and golden. Transfer to a plate lined with paper towels and keep warm. Continue until all the batter is used, adding a little oil as necessary.

4 Put the tomatoes, remaining cilantro, scallion greens, olive oil, and hot pepper sauce into a food processor or blender, and pulse the machine until well mixed but still chunky. Check for seasoning and serve hot fritters with salsa on the side.

The sweetness of freshly harvested corn cannot be beaten. We often cook corn on a stove right at the garden, but if any gets home, this is a wonderful soup to make.

Corn chowder

Serves 4–6 • **Prep** 10 mins • **Cooking** 30 mins

INGREDIENTS

4 ears corn
   (corn on the cob), husked
sea salt
2 bay leaves
2 tbsp extra virgin olive oil
1 large onion, chopped
4 fresh sage leaves, chopped,
   or $1/2$ tsp dried
   sage, crushed
1 tsp fresh thyme leaves, or $1/2$
   tsp dried thyme
1 medium carrot, chopped
2 celery stalks, chopped
1 large russet potato, peeled
   and chopped 7oz (200g)
   cream cheese, cut into
   pieces, at room temperature
$1/2$ cup whole milk
freshly ground black pepper
half-and-half, to serve
dusting of paprika, to serve

METHOD

1 Working one at a time, stand an ear of corn upright in a large bowl and strip off the kernels by cutting downward with a sharp knife. Set the kernels aside. Repeat with the remaining corn. Place the cobs in a large saucepan and add 2 cups water, 1 tsp salt, and the bay leaves. Bring to a boil and simmer, covered, for 15 minutes. Remove and discard cobs and bay leaves.

2 Heat the olive oil in a saucepan and cook the onions, stirring often, until translucent. Add the herbs and remaining vegetables, except the corn kernels. Cook for about 5 minutes, until softened. Add the corn cob stock and simmer until the potato pieces are breaking apart. Meanwhile, place the corn kernels in a saucepan and barely cover with cold water. Bring to a boil and cook for 2 minutes. Set aside.

3 Add the cream cheese and milk to the soup mixture, then puree until smooth using a hand-held blender or transferring to a food processor. Stir in the corn kernels with their cooking liquid. Process the chowder one more time, if desired, to break up the corn kernels slightly. Reheat and adjust the seasoning. Ladle into warm bowls. Drizzle with half-and-half and dust with paprika.

Make relish

Made from diced fruit or vegetables, relish is part pickle, part chutney, but cooked for a shorter time than a chutney. As its name implies, relish packs a tangy punch of flavor and is a classic accompaniment to barbecue and burgers. Be sure to prepare all the ingredients meticulously, since the final texture of your preserve is dependent on your care at this stage. Take the time to chop ingredients finely, unless you prefer a chunky relish. It is up to you what flavorings you add for spice. This recipe uses a chile pepper, but you can leave this out if you prefer. Relishes can be eaten immediately or stored.

1 **Strip and blanch** Strip the kernels from the cobs using a sharp knife. Blanch the kernels in a saucepan of boiling water for 2 minutes, then drain well.

2 **Simmer in the pan** Put the corn and the other ingredients into a saucepan, bring to a boil, and stir. Simmer gently, stirring frequently, for 15–20 minutes.

Recipe Corn relish

Makes approx. 2¼lb (1kg) or 2 small preserving jars
Prep 35–40 mins • **Keeps** 3 months

INGREDIENTS

4 ears of corn	1 onion, peeled and sliced
2 medium peppers, green or red, deseeded and diced	2 cups white wine vinegar
2 celery sticks, finely sliced	1 cup granulated sugar
1 red chile, deseeded and sliced	2 tsp sea salt
	2 tsp mustard powder
	½ tsp ground turmeric

Other relishes to try

There are many different relishes to make using your own fresh ingredients. Here are a few ideas to get your tastebuds tingling.

Tomatoes Combine with zucchini and peppers.
Carrots Delicious with coriander and ginger.
Beets Use for a sweet relish (see page 261).
Nectarines and cranberries A sweet-and-sour relish with coriander and cinnamon.
Zucchini Add mustard powder, turmeric, chile pepper for a sharp, spicy taste.

3 **Put into sterilized jars** Check the seasoning, then spoon into warm, sterilized jars. The relish should be a spoonable consistency and wetter than a chutney.

4 **Seal and store** Seal with non-metallic or vinegar-proof lids, leave to cool, and label. Store in a cool, dark place. Once opened, store in the fridge.

When to pick
Harvest fennel when the bulb is nicely rounded, but before it becomes elongated and starts to bolt. Eat young fennel raw, braise, or use older fennel in stews.

Eat and store fresh
Eat within 2 days of harvesting if using raw. Store older fennel for 1 week in the fridge. The leaves can be used like fennel herb, but have a stronger taste.

How to preserve
Use fennel in pickles or relishes, or cook and preserve in oil.

Freezing options
Slice and blanch for 2 minutes, then cool and freeze for up to 6 months.

This fresh salad makes a fantastic side dish for grilled fish. Alternatively, the addition of crumbled goat cheese and a few slices of apple or pear can turn it into a light lunch.

Shaved fennel salad

Serves 6 • **Prep** 10 mins, plus marinating

INGREDIENTS

1 fennel bulb, trimmed and thinly sliced

1½ tsp aged balsamic vinegar

3 tbsp extra virgin olive oil

1 garlic clove, crushed

sea salt and freshly ground black pepper

5 cups mixed salad leaves, such as watercress, baby spinach, arugula, or mâche (lamb's lettuce)

METHOD

1 In a bowl toss the fennel with a few drops of balsamic vinegar, 1 tbsp of oil, and the garlic, then season with salt and freshly ground pepper. Set aside to marinate for at least 1 hour before serving.

2 To serve, mix the salad leaves, fennel, remaining oil, and vinegar, then season to taste with salt and pepper, and divide the salad between individual plates.

Variation Scatter shavings of Parmesan cheese and pitted black olives over the salad.

If you want something easy, then one-pot recipes, such as this, are perfect. A bowl of creamy mashed potatoes is all that's needed to complement the sharp, tangy flavors of the fennel and lemon.

Chicken roasted
with fennel and lemon

Serves 4 • **Prep** 15 mins • **Cooking** 1 hour

INGREDIENTS

4 large chicken thighs, with
   skin on
sea salt and freshly ground
   black pepper
drizzle of extra virgin olive oil
juice of 1 lemon, and 2 small
   lemons, quartered
few sprigs of fresh thyme,
   leaves picked
1 large fennel bulb, trimmed
   and coarsely chopped
handful of green olives, pitted
$2/3$ cup dry white wine

METHOD

1 Season the chicken thighs generously with salt and black pepper. Drizzle over the olive oil and lemon juice, scatter over the thyme leaves, then transfer to a large bowl or plastic bag, and leave to marinate for 30 minutes. Preheat the oven to 400°F (200°C).

2 Using a slotted spoon, transfer the chicken to a small roasting pan and add the fennel and lemon wedges, which should fit snugly. Season well, then put in the oven for 20 minutes.

3 Take the roasting pan out of the oven and add the olives and wine, being careful that it does not spatter. Return the pan to the oven and cook for another 20 minutes, then turn the heat down to 350°F (180°C), cover the pan with foil, and cook for 20 minutes more, so that the alcohol evaporates but the chicken remains moist. Check to see if the chicken is ready by piercing the plumpest thigh with the tip of a sharp knife: if the juices run clear, it is cooked.

POTATOES

When to pick
Pick after the flowers have appeared and before the stems wilt. Potatoes keep growing if left in the ground but will be more vulnerable to pests and diseases.

Eat and store fresh
Freshly harvested potatoes taste delicious, but do not store well. To store, leave them in the sun for a few hours to dry. Rub the excess mud off and store in a cool, dark place in a burlap sack for up to 6 months, or in a pit (clamp) (see pages 140–1). Only store perfect potatoes.

This peppery dish was developed by the French settlers of Louisiana, and makes a delicious light lunch or side dish. Serve with a steak or on their own with a soured cream dip.

Cajun-spiced
potato wedges

Serves 6 • **Prep** 10 mins • **Cooking** 35–45 mins

INGREDIENTS

4 russet potatoes, unpeeled

3 small red onions, each cut into 8 wedges

1 lemon, cut into 6 wedges

12 garlic cloves

4 bay leaves

6 tbsp extra virgin olive oil

3 tbsp fresh lemon juice

1 tbsp canned tomato puree

1 tsp paprika

1 tsp dried oregano

1 tsp dried thyme

$\frac{1}{2}$ tsp ground cumin

$\frac{1}{2}$ tsp cayenne pepper

sea salt and freshly ground black pepper

METHOD

1 Cut the potatoes into thick wedges. Cook in a large pot of boiling, salted water for 3 minutes, drain well, and place in a large roasting pan with the onions, lemon, garlic, and bay leaves.

2 Whisk together the remaining ingredients with 6 tbsp water and pour evenly over the potatoes. Toss everything well to coat.

3 Roast for 30–40 minutes, or until the potatoes are tender and the liquid has been absorbed. Gently and frequently turn the potatoes during cooking, using a spatula. Serve hot.

Harvesting home-grown potatoes is so rewarding. If you have successfully grown your own potatoes, they deserve to be made into something as delicious as this spicy Spanish dish.

Patatas bravas

Serves 4 • **Prep** 15 mins • **Cooking** 1 hour

INGREDIENTS

6 tbsp extra virgin olive oil

1¹/₂ lbs (700g) white potatoes, peeled and cut into ³/₄in (2cm) dice

2 onions, finely chopped

2 tbsp dry sherry

finely grated zest of 1 lemon

4 garlic cloves, finely grated or finely chopped

1 tsp crushed hot red pepper flakes

1 cup canned, diced tomatoes, drained

handful of flat-leaf parsley, chopped

sea salt and freshly ground black pepper

METHOD

1 Preheat the oven to 400°F (200°C). Heat half the oil in 2 large non-stick frying pans, add the potatoes without crowding them in the pans, and cook, turning frequently, over medium-low heat for 20 minutes, or until starting to brown. Add the onions and cook for another 5 minutes.

2 Add the, sherry, lemon zest, garlic, and pepper flakes and allow to reduce for 2 minutes before adding the tomatoes and parsley. Season with salt and freshly ground black pepper, combine well, and cook over medium heat for 10 minutes, stirring occasionally.

3 Add the remaining oil, place all ingredients in a shallow baking dish, and cook in the oven for 30 minutes. Serve hot with a selection of tapas dishes.

Note You can cook the potatoes on the stovetop instead, although oven cooking intensifies the flavor.

A Spanish classic, this tortilla can be eaten warm or cold and makes perfect picnic food. Dice it into small squares and serve with olives and salted almonds before a meal, as do the Spanish.

Spanish tortilla

Serves 4 • **Prep** 10 • **Cooking** 45 mins

INGREDIENTS

$1^{1}/_{4}$ cups extra virgin olive oil, plus 1 tbsp for frying

5 medium russet potatoes, peeled and sliced, about $^{1}/_{4}$in (5mm) thick

3 medium onions, quartered and sliced

sea salt and freshly ground black pepper

5 eggs

METHOD

1 Put the olive oil in a large, deep-sided, ovenproof frying pan (preferably non-stick), add the potatoes, and cook at a gentle simmer for about 15 minutes, or until they are tender. Remove the potatoes with a slotted spoon and put them in a large bowl to cool.

2 Tip most of the oil out of the pan, add the onions and a pinch of salt. Cook over low heat until soft and beginning to brown. Add to the potatoes and leave to cool.

3 Whisk the eggs with a fork, then pour into the cooled potato and onion mixture, season with salt and pepper, and combine gently so all the potatoes get coated.

4 Preheat the oven to 400°F (200°C). Heat the 1 tbsp of olive oil in the frying pan until hot, then carefully slide in the egg mixture, spreading it evenly so it covers the bottom of the pan. Reduce the heat to medium-low and cook for 6–10 minutes, or until almost set.

5 Put in the oven, and cook for a further 10 minutes, or until set and golden. Alternatively, cook one side, then invert onto a plate and add back to the pan to cook the other side. Remove from the pan, leave to cool and set, then slice into wedges. Serve warm or cold.

Going by the delightful name of "wrinkly potatoes," this dish originates in the Canary Islands. Serve as tapas with other dishes, or as a light lunch with a crisp green salad.

Papas arrugadas

Serves 4–6 as tapas • **Prep** 15 mins • **Cooking** 45 mins

INGREDIENTS

2$\frac{1}{4}$lb (1kg) small, new
   potatoes, scrubbed
coarse sea salt and freshly
   ground black pepper
$\frac{1}{2}$ cup extra virgin olive oil
1 red bell pepper
juice of 1 lemon
2 heaping tbsp tomato purée
1 tsp smoked paprika
$\frac{1}{2}$ tsp ground cumin
pinch of chili powder,
   or to taste
1 garlic clove, crushed
2 tbsp chopped flat-leaf
   parsley or cilantro (optional)

METHOD

1 Preheat the oven to 400°F (200°C). Place the potatoes on a baking sheet, toss in salt and 1 tablespoon of the olive oil, and roast, turning occasionally, for about 45 minutes or until the potatoes are tender inside and golden brown on the outside.

2 Meanwhile, rub the pepper in olive oil and roast in the same oven for around 30 minutes, turning occasionally, until tender and soft. Remove the pepper from the oven, place it in a plastic bag for 2–3 minutes to loosen the skin, then cool, peel, and deseed. Roughly chop the cooked pepper.

3 Process the pepper, lemon, tomato purée, spices, and garlic, together with the remaining oil, in a food processor or using a hand-held blender to form a thick, unctuous dipping sauce. Add a little more oil if needed. Check the seasoning, add the parsley or cilantro (if using), and serve with the potatoes.

Note If you have leftover sauce, it can be stored in the freezer for 1 month.

A fantastically hearty supper dish, serve this twist on a classic Dauphinoise recipe with green beans or a salad. The emmental and pancetta lift the humble potato to a higher level.

Potato Dauphinoise with
emmental and pancetta

Serves 4–6 • **Prep** 20 mins • **Cooking** 45 mins

INGREDIENTS

8oz (200g) pancetta, diced

3lbs (1.5kg) white potatoes, peeled and evenly sliced about $1/8$in (.3cm) thick

$1^{1}/_{4}$ cups whole milk

$1^{1}/_{4}$ cups heavy cream

6oz (150g) emmental cheese, shredded or sliced

sea salt and freshly ground black pepper

METHOD

1 In a frying pan over medium heat, cook the pancetta until it is starting to crisp. Remove from the pan, and drain on paper towels.

2 Simmer the potatoes in the milk and cream for 10–15 minutes, then remove with a slotted spoon (reserve the milk and cream mixture).

3 Layer the potatoes in a shallow baking dish with the cheese and pancetta, and season. Pour over the milk and cream, cover with foil, and bake in the oven for 45 minutes until bubbly-hot. Remove the foil for the last 15 minutes of cooking time to brown the top.

These delicious little cakes can be eaten simply on their own or as a side dish. Try them with some smoked salmon, a poached egg, and a spoon or two of hollandaise sauce.

Potato cakes
with Parmesan

Serves 4 • **Prep** 20 mins • **Cooking** 20 mins

INGREDIENTS

1³/₄ lbs (750g) russet potatoes, peeled and cut into chunks

1 large egg yolk

¹/₂ cup freshly grated Parmesan cheese

sea salt and freshly ground black pepper

¹/₄ cup all-purpose flour

sunflower oil or vegetable oil for frying

1 tbsp capers, drained and patted dry

1 lemon, cut into wedges

METHOD

1 Place the potatoes in a large pot of cold, salted water, bring to a boil, and simmer for 15 minutes, or until tender. Drain well, then pass through a potato ricer or food mill, set over a bowl. Alternatively, mash well.

2 Add the egg yolk and Parmesan to the potatoes, season to taste with salt and freshly ground pepper, and mix. Divide into 8 equal balls and flatten into little cakes, each 2in (5cm) in diameter. Tip the flour onto a plate, season with salt and pepper, then coat the potato cakes in the flour, and refrigerate, loosely covered, up to 8 hours or until needed.

3 Pour enough oil into a frying pan to cover the bottom and set it over medium heat. Working in batches, cook the potato cakes, without crowding, for 2 minutes on each side, or until golden and hot. Remove from the pan and drain on kitchen paper.

4 Increase the heat and cook capers for 45 seconds, or until crisp. Drain on paper towels. Place cakes on warm plates, scatter on capers, and serve with lemon wedges.

Store under soil

Clamping is a traditional way of storing potatoes and other root vegetables, if you don't have a store room or a root cellar. Site a clamp in a sheltered spot, since it is not guaranteed frost-protection and is not suitable in areas where frosts are severe or common. You can use the technique to store fodder beets for livestock too. To prepare potatoes for clamping, carefully dig them up on a dry day, shake off the excess soil, and leave to dry outdoors for 1–2 hours to "set" the skins. Only use perfect specimens for clamping.

1 Dry potatoes Leave the potatoes to dry for 1–2 hours and dig a trench 4in (10cm) deep, 3ft (1m) in diameter, in a sheltered, well-drained site. Layer the trench with sand.

2 Form a pyramid Heap straw over the trench 8in (20cm) high, and arrange the potatoes in the center in a pyramid shape. Leave them to breathe for 1–2 hours.

Clamp Potatoes

Keeps 4–5 months

YOU WILL NEED

potatoes, to form a pyramid no bigger
    than 20in (50cm) high

clean straw

sand

spade

soil

an area of sheltered, well-drained soil

Store other crops under soil

Any crop with a tapering root can be stored in the ground until needed. Others may be stored inside in a cool, dark place over the winter.

Rutabagas, turnips, and winter radishes
Clamp and store for 3–4 months.
Celery roots, parsnips, Brussels sprouts, leeks
Leave in the ground and dig up as needed.
Carrots, beets, parsnips, and potatoes
Pick and store in boxes, under soil or other covering, through the winter (see pages 268–9).

3 **Add straw** Place a 4–8in (10–20cm) thick layer of straw over the top. Cover with a 6in (15cm) layer of soil. Leave a 2in (5cm) hole at the top and fill it loosely with straw.

4 **Pack down the soil** Pack the soil down around the sides of the clamp with the back of a spade. Dig a shallow drainage trench around the base of the clamp.

141

CILANTRO

When to pick
Pick cilantro when it is young and before the leaves start to yellow or become too large. If growing for seeds, leave the flower heads to dry on the plant before harvesting.

Eat and store fresh
Keep cilantro in a glass of water, in or out of the fridge, or wrapped in damp kitchen paper in the fridge for 2–3 days. Use fresh whenever possible.

How to preserve
Use cilantro in a pesto and store in the fridge for up to 2 weeks. Alternatively, dry the leaves flat or hang them to dry for 2 weeks, then store in sealed glass jars for up to 6 months (see pages 160–1).

Freezing options
Freeze in a herb butter or by adding oil and putting into freezer bags, or by freezing in ice cubes (see pages 148–9).

Try this tasty alternative to the more common basil and pine nut pesto. It can be used in the same way, with pasta or as a spread for crostini, topped with a piece of soft goat cheese.

Cilantro
and walnut pesto

Makes approx. 2/3 cup or 1 small jar • **Prep** 10 mins

INGREDIENTS

1 small bunch of cilantro, approx. 1oz (30g), stems removed

1 large garlic clove, lightly crushed

1/4 cup walnut pieces

sea salt and freshly ground black pepper

1/4 cup freshly grated Parmesan cheese

5 tbsp extra virgin olive oil

METHOD

1 Put the cilantro leaves in a blender or food processor with the garlic, walnuts, a generous grinding of black pepper, a pinch of salt, the cheese, and 1 tbsp of the oil. Blend the ingredients, stopping to scrape down the sides of the bowl as necessary.

2 With the machine still running, gradually add 3 tbsp of the remaining oil, a little at a time, until you have a thin paste. Alternatively, pound the cilantro and garlic using a mortar and pestle. Gradually add the nuts, crushing them to a paste with the herbs. Add the freshly ground pepper and salt, work in a little of the cheese, then a little of the oil, (reserving 1 tbsp of oil) and continue until both are used up and you have a glistening paste.

3 Spoon into a sterilized jar, top with the remaining 1 tbsp of oil to prevent air getting in, screw on the lid, and store in the fridge.

Note Keeps for 2 weeks, refrigerated. If you don't use all the pesto immediately, cover the remainder with another 1 tbsp of olive oil and screw the lid back on tightly.

BASIL

When to pick
Keep a pot of basil on your window sill and pick as required. If grown outdoors, pinch off the larger stems above a set of leaves, using larger leaves first.

Eat and store fresh
Store, wrapped in damp paper towels in the fridge for up to 2 days. Use fresh whenever possible. Older basil can be chopped and added at the end of cooking to many recipes.

How to preserve
Use basil in a pesto and store in the fridge for up to 2 weeks. Alternatively, dry the leaves flat or hang them to dry for 2 weeks, then store in sealed glass jars for up to 6 months (see pages 160–1).

Basil works particularly well in this very adaptable recipe, but you can try other green herbs, such as dill, sorrel, mint, or cilantro to match whatever you are serving it with.

Herbed mayonnaise

Makes about 2 cups • Prep 10 mins

INGREDIENTS

2 tbsp white wine vinegar

1 whole egg and 2 egg yolks

1 tbsp Dijon mustard

1 tbsp light brown sugar

1 garlic clove

sea salt and freshly ground
 black pepper

$1^1/_4$ cups sunflower or
 vegetable oil

1oz (30g) fresh basil, or other
 green herbs

METHOD

1 Put the vinegar, egg, egg yolks, mustard, sugar, and garlic in a food processor and add $^1/_2$ tsp each of salt and freshly ground pepper. With the motor running, slowly pour in the oil in a thin steady stream until the sauce is thick and creamy

2 Transfer to a bowl and stir in the finely chopped herbs until they are thoroughly incorporated.

Note A squeeze of lemon or lime juice, or a dash of chili sauce can also be added to the finished mayonnaise. This sauce may be made 2–3 days in advance, and refrigerated until ready to use.

The delicate flavors of this sophisticated, chilled custard work surprisingly well when paired with summer fruits, such as strawberries, raspberries, or black currants.

Basil and vanilla custard

Serves 4–6 • **Prep** 20 mins • **Cooking** 30 mins, plus cooling

INGREDIENTS

2 cups whole milk

3 tbsp fresh basil leaves, plus a few small leaves to decorate

2 vanilla beans, split lengthwise and seeded

3 large or 4 medium egg yolks

6 tbsp granulated sugar

1 tsp cornstarch

3 tbsp crème fraîche

Szechuan pepper (optional), to garnish

METHOD

1 Put the milk in a saucepan. Tear or crush the basil leaves and add to the milk. Add the vanilla bean pods and seeds and simmer over low heat, stirring occasionally. When the milk starts to bubble, reduce the heat to low, and cook gently, stirring frequently, for 10 minutes. Take off the heat and set aside.

2 In a large bowl, whisk together the egg yolks and sugar until smooth and pale. Whisk in the cornstarch.

3 Use a fine sieve to gradually strain the hot milk into the egg yolk and sugar, whisking well. Press the basil and vanilla against the sieve to release flavor, and discard.

4 Return the mixture to the pan over very low heat. Bring to a gentle simmer, stirring constantly, for 10 minutes or until the custard has thickened enough to coat the back of a spoon. Do not allow it to boil. If necessary, take it off the heat from time to time.

5 Leave to cool, stirring occasionally. Stir in the crème fraîche, and when completely cool, place it in the fridge. Serve cold, decorated with small basil leaves and with a little freshly ground Szechuan pepper (if using).

When to pick

Pick dill when the fronds are dark green and glossy. If you are growing it for the seeds, leave the flower heads to dry on the plant before harvesting.

Eat and store fresh

Keep dill in a glass of water, in or out of the fridge, or wrapped in damp paper towels in the fridge for 3 days. Use fresh where possible. Dill can be used in salads (see page 110), with fish, or new potatoes.

How to preserve

Hang sprigs tied with string to dry for at least 2 weeks in a dry, airy room out of direct sunlight. Store in sealed glass jars for up to 6 months (see pages 160–1).

Freezing options

Freeze in an herb butter, or by adding oil and putting into freezer bags, or by freezing in ice cubes (see pages 148–9).

Fresh and citrus, this salsa makes a perfect partner for all types of fish and seafood. Its robust flavors are also well suited to grilled or barbecued meats.

Dill and tomato salsa
with watercress and capers

Serves 4–6 • **Prep** 15 mins, plus chilling

INGREDIENTS

2 tbsp chopped fresh dill weed
leaves from 1 large bunch of
   watercress, coarsely
   chopped if large
9 small cherry tomatoes,
   halved
1 heaping tbsp capers, drained
juice and finely grated zest of
   $\frac{1}{2}$ lemon
sea salt and freshly ground
   black pepper
3 tbsp extra virgin olive oil

METHOD

1 Put the dill and watercress in a bowl. Gently squeeze the halved cherry tomatoes to discard some of the seeds, then slice into quarters, and add to the bowl. Stir in the capers (if they are large, chop them first), and lemon juice and zest. Chill for 30 minutes or until ready to use.

2 Stir, season with salt and pepper, and drizzle with olive oil. Stir again before serving.

This verdant summer soup is the ideal way to showcase the best of your herb garden. Herbs are too often an afterthought to a dish, but here their flavors are celebrated.

Cream of herb soup

Serves 4–6 • **Prep** 15 mins • **Cooking** 1 hour

INGREDIENTS

2 tbsp butter

2 tbsp each, chopped onion and carrots

3 tbsp each, diced celery and scallions

2 tbsp diced parsley root

2 tbsp all-purpose flour

sea salt and freshly ground black pepper

4 cups chicken stock

2 garlic cloves, finely chopped

1 bay leaf

5 whole black peppercorns

$^1/_2$ cup half-and-half

6 tbsp chopped mixed fresh herbs, such as dill, sage, basil, parsley, chervil, sorrel, lovage, oregano, thyme, or chives, in any combination

METHOD

1 Place a soup pot or medium saucepan over low heat and add 1 tbsp of the butter. Add the onion, cover, and cook over low heat for 5–10 minutes. Add the remaining vegetables and stir to coat with the butter. Cover and cook until soft, for 5–10 minutes.

2 Sprinkle the flour over the vegetables and give them a stir. Season lightly, then pour in the stock stirring. Raise the heat to high and bring the soup to a boil.

3 When it is boiling, turn down the heat and add the garlic, bay leaf, and peppercorns. Simmer uncovered for about 30 minutes. Skim off any foam that rises to the surface of the soup.

4 Stir in the half-and-half. Turn up the heat but do not boil. After 5 minutes, remove from the heat and strain the soup into a large bowl. Discard the vegetables and spices. Pour the soup back into the pot. . Whisk in the remaining butter and add the herbs, reserving some for garnish. Simmer for 5 minutes, stirring occasionally. Season to taste, spoon into bowls, garnish with herbs, and serve.

Freeze herbs

Freezing fresh herbs is a useful way to preserve them, and they retain a flavor for cooking that is almost as good as fresh. There are several easy ways of doing this. Make a mix of herbs and oil and spoon into freezer bags, or freeze with a little water in ice cube trays for use in pesto, sauces, and soups. Herb butters can add a fresh, aromatic touch to grilled or roasted meats. Simply slice into rounds as needed, straight from the fridge or freezer.

Herb oil mixes

1 **Chop the herbs and add oil** Coarsely chop the herbs in a food processor. Whizz briefly with the motor running and add enough olive oil to lightly coat the herbs.

2 **Store in freezer** Spoon the mixture into small freezer bags, seal them securely, label, and place in the freezer. Herbs in oil can be frozen for up to 4 months.

Quick herb butters

Many different herbs and combinations of herbs work as butters. Here are a few suggestions:

Watercress butter Combine watercress leaves with butter, seasoning, and lemon juice for a peppery butter to go with grilled meats and fish.

Parsley butter Combine butter with parsley, lemon juice, garlic, and seasoning for a butter that goes wonderfully well with chicken, fish, and snails.

Spinach and shallot butter Make a simple butter with chopped spinach leaves, shallots, some parsley, chervil, and tarragon. This is an ideal accompaniment to soups and bisques.

Oregano butter Add oregano, olive oil, and garlic to butter for a Mediterranean flavor.

Tarragon butter Mix tarragon, lemon juice, seasoning, and butter to enjoy with white fish.

Herb ice cubes

Freeze the cubes Fill an ice cube tray with herbs and pour water over to cover. Freeze until solid, for about 2 hours. Store in labelled freezer bags until needed. Use within 6 months.

Herb butters

Store the butter Combine chopped herbs and soft butter, shape into a cylinder, wrap in plastic wrap, and twist the ends to seal. Keep in the fridge for 1 week, or in the freezer 3 months.

PARSLEY

When to pick
Pick both flat-leaf and curly parsley when the leaves are dark green and glossy, and before they become too large. Pick frequently to encourage regrowth.

Eat and store fresh
Keep parsley in a glass of water, in or out of the fridge, or wrapped in a damp paper towel in the fridge for 3–4 days. Use fresh whenever possible. Often used in soups and stews.

How to preserve
Use parsley in a pesto and store in the fridge for up to 2 weeks. Alternatively, dry the leaves flat or hang them to dry for 2 weeks, then store in sealed glass jars for up to 6 months (see pages 160–1).

Freezing options
Freeze in an herb butter or by adding oil and putting into freezer bags, or by freezing in ice cubes (see pages 148–9).

This Mediterranean favorite is particularly good served with poached chicken or salmon, or grilled tuna. Change the amount and type of herbs you use, depending on what is available.

Sauce verte

Makes 1 cup • **Prep** 20 mins

INGREDIENTS

1 tbsp bread crumbs, made from day-old bread

1 tbsp white wine vinegar

1 tsp Dijon mustard

$^3/_4$ cup extra virgin olive oil

5 tbsp finely chopped flat-leaf or curly parsley leaves, plus their stems (optional)

3 tbsp finely chopped fresh basil

1 tbsp finely chopped fresh mint

2 garlic cloves, crushed

2 anchovy fillets, chopped

2 tbsp capers, drained, and finely chopped

finely grated zest and juice of 1 lemon

sea salt and freshly ground black pepper

METHOD

1 In a bowl, mix the bread crumbs and vinegar together with the mustard and 3 tbsp of the olive oil.

2 Add the herbs, reserving 1 heaping tbsp of the mixed herbs to finish, and beat well. If you like, chop a few parsley stems very finely and stir them in for extra flavor.

3 Add the garlic, anchovies, and half of the capers to the herb mixture, and beat again. The mixture will become a very thick, green paste.

4 Gradually beat in the rest of the olive oil, a little at a time, and then season to taste with salt and freshly ground pepper. Shortly before serving, stir in the lemon juice and zest, and add the reserved herbs and capers. Use soon or cover, chill, and use within 24 hours.

Tabbouleh, an herbed Middle Eastern salad, is always more about the herbs than it is about the bulgur wheat. In this recipe, the handsful of fresh herbs used produce a truly flavorful result.

Herbed tabbouleh

Serves 4 • **Prep** 25 mins

INGREDIENTS

For the dressing

1 garlic clove, crushed

sea salt

$^1/_2$ tsp Asian five-spice powder

finely grated zest and juice
    from $^1/_2$ lemon

1 tbsp pomegranate syrup
    (pomegranate molasses)
    or balsamic vinegar

$^1/_4$ cup extra virgin olive oil

freshly ground black pepper

For the salad

$^1/_2$ cup bulgur wheat

6 tbsp chopped
    flat-leaf parsley

1 tbsp finely chopped
    fresh mint

1 tbsp chopped fresh cilantro

4 scallions, finely chopped

4 small cherry
    tomatoes, chopped

METHOD

1 In a bowl, mix the garlic with a little salt, the five-spice powder, lemon juice and zest, and the pomegranate molasses or balsamic vinegar. Whisk in the olive oil and season with salt and pepper to taste. Leave it to stand while you prepare the ingredients for the salad.

2 Put the bulgur in a shallow, heatproof bowl, cover with boiling water, and leave to absorb for 2 minutes. Tip into a sieve, drain, and refresh with plenty of cold water, rubbing the bulgur grains between your fingers. Shake the bulgur, and then drain it well.

3 Tip the bulgur into the bowl with the dressing mixture. Add the parsley, mint, cilantro, scallions, and tomatoes. Toss just before serving and season with salt and pepper.

Variation You can add 2 or 3 tbsp pomegranate seeds for a crunchy, jewellike finish.

Also called Arabic salad, this dish is popular in Turkey and the Middle East. Laden with fresh herbs and spices, it's a perfect foil for grilled or barbecued lamb, or lemony chicken.

Shepherd's salad

Serves 4 • Prep 20 mins

INGREDIENTS

For the dressing

1/2 garlic clove, crushed

1/2 tsp sweet paprika

1/2 tsp ground sumac

1/2 tsp caster sugar

1/2 tsp ground cumin

2 tbsp lemon juice and
   1 tsp grated lemon zest

7 tbsp extra virgin olive oil

sea salt and freshly ground
   black pepper

For the salad

1 large cucumber, peeled

15 baby cherry tomatoes

1 head of romaine lettuce

12 black olives, pitted
   and chopped

3 scallions, chopped

2 tbsp each chopped, flat-leaf
   parsley, cilantro, and mint

2 tbsp chopped purslane
   or arugula

METHOD

1 In a bowl, mix all the ingredients for the dressing, and season with salt and freshly ground pepper to taste. Leave the mixture to rest while you prepare the salad ingredients.

2 Quarter the cucumber lengthwise; scoop out, and discard the seeds. Cut the flesh into small, neat chunks and reserve on a plate. Halve the tomatoes, scoop out and discard most of the seeds, and add the tomato halves to the cucumber. Tear or chop the lettuce into bite-sized pieces.

3 Stir the dressing. Put a layer of lettuce in the bowl (do not toss), scatter in some olives and scallions, and sprinkle in some parsley, purslane, cilantro, and mint. Add half the cucumber and tomatoes. Continue adding the ingredients until everything is in the bowl.

4 Toss the salad just before serving.

SAGE

When to pick
Harvest as needed, but use the leaves before they become too big and tough. Pick sage leaves individually, or pick whole stems for use in bouquet garnis or for drying.

Eat and store fresh
Store wrapped in damp paper towels in the fridge for 2 days. Leave stems to dry on a window sill. Store dried leaves in an airtight container for later use. Sage works well in pasta and risotto dishes.

How to preserve
Dry the leaves flat or hang them to dry for 2 weeks, then store in sealed glass jars for up to 6 months (see pages 160–1).

Freezing options
Freeze in an herb butter, or by adding oil and putting into freezer bags, or by freezing in ice cubes (see pages 148–9).

Sage is a perennial herb that is a valuable addition to any plot. Quickly fry the leaves for a tasty garnish or simply blend with wine and stock to make this simple sauce for grilled pork.

Fresh sage sauce

Makes 1 cup • **Prep** 10 mins • **Cooking** 10 mins

INGREDIENTS

2 bay leaves

$^1/_2$ cup chicken
   or vegetable stock

$^1/_2$ cup dry white wine

1 small sprig of fresh thyme

1 tbsp all-purpose flour

$1^1/_2$ tbsp slightly softened
   butter, plus 1 tbsp cold
   butter, diced, to finish

1 tbsp chopped fresh
   sage leaves, plus 3–5 small
   leaves to finish

sea salt and freshly ground
   black pepper

METHOD

1 Bruise the bay leaves with the back of a large knife or a kitchen mallet. Place in a saucepan over medium heat with the stock, wine, and thyme, and bring to a simmer.

2 Mash together the flour and softened butter, in a cup or on a saucer, using a fork until well mixed.

3 Whisk the butter-flour mixture into the simmering liquid. Continue whisking for 3 minutes over medium heat, until the liquid has thickened slightly.

4 Reduce the heat. Remove the bay leaves and thyme. Add the chopped sage and cook, stirring, for 2 minutes. Remove from the heat, cool for 2 minutes, and then season with salt and pepper.

5 Whisk in the diced, chilled butter, stir in the whole sage leaves, and serve.

This spicy, herbal sauce is a classic Argentinian accompaniment to grilled or barbecued steak. However, it also works well with grilled salmon or meaty fish, such as swordfish or tuna.

Chimichurri sauce

Makes 1 cup • **Prep** 5 mins

INGREDIENTS

6 garlic cloves

3 bunches fresh parsley, thick
  stems removed

6 tbsp extra virgin olive oil

2 tbsp white balsamic vinegar,
  or white wine vinegar

1 tbsp chopped fresh oregano

¼ tsp crushed hot
  red pepper flakes

salt and freshly ground
  black pepper

METHOD

1 Place all the ingredients and 2 tbsp cold water in a food processor or blender, and process until smooth.

2 Season to taste with salt and pepper, and keep covered until needed. Before serving, whisk in a little more olive oil or water for a thinner consistency.

OREGANO

When to pick
Use oregano leaves at any stage of their growth. However, they are best if picked just before the plant flowers. Harvest whole stems for drying or to be used in a bouquet garni.

Eat and store fresh
Pick and use fresh. Alternatively, store in a glass of water, in or out of the fridge, or wrapped in damp paper towels in the fridge for 2–3 days. Use raw in salads or as a stuffing for fish dishes.

How to preserve
Use oregano in a pesto and store in the fridge for up to 2 weeks. Alternatively, dry the leaves flat or hang them to dry for 2 weeks, then store in sealed glass jars for up to 6 months (see pages 160–1).

Freezing options
Freeze in an herb butter, or by adding oil and putting into freezer bags, or by freezing in ice cubes (see pages 148–9).

ROSEMARY

When to pick
Rosemary is a perennial plant, so harvest it as needed. Pick the bigger, outer stems first to encourage regrowth.

Eat and store fresh
Keep fresh rosemary wrapped in a damp paper towel in the fridge for up to 5 days. Serve with roast meats, such as lamb and pork.

How to preserve
Dry the leaves flat or hang them to dry for 2 weeks, then store in sealed glass jars for up to 6 months (see pages 160–1).

Freezing options
Freeze in an herb butter, or by adding oil and putting into freezer bags, or freeze in ice cubes (see pages 148–9).

Robustly flavored, this jelly is a classic accompaniment to roast lamb. It can be served alongside the meat, or added to the meat juices to form the basis of a sweet, herbal gravy.

Rosemary jelly

Makes 4$\frac{1}{2}$lb (2kg) or 6 medium jars • **Prep** 15 mins• **Cooking** 1$\frac{1}{2}$ hours, plus straining

INGREDIENTS

large handful of fresh rosemary
    sprigs, leaves stripped,
    stems reserved
2lb (900g) tart cooking apples,
    like Granny Smith, chopped
approx. 5 cups granulated
    sugar (see method)
juice of 1 lemon

METHOD

1 Preheat the oven to 300°F (150°C). Place the rosemary leaves in an even layer on a baking sheet and bake for 30–40 minutes, until very dry.

2 Put apples into a preserving pan. Pour in 5 cups of water and the rosemary stems . Bring to a boil, then reduce the heat to low and simmer for 30–40 minutes, or until the apples are mushy. Mash with a fork.

3 Put the pulp into a jelly bag or a muslin-lined sieve over a bowl and leave to strain overnight. Measure the strained juice and calculate the sugar. For every 2$\frac{1}{2}$ cups of juice, use 2$\frac{1}{2}$ cups of sugar.

4 Put the strained juice, sugar, lemon juice, and dried rosemary leaves into a saucepan over medium heat, stirring until sugar dissolves. Bring to a rolling boil and cook for 20 minutes or until jelly reaches the setting point. Remove from heat to test for a set (pages 186–7).

5 Leave to cool for 10 minutes. Ladle into warm sterilized jars, cover with waxed paper discs, seal, and label.

Note Store in a cool, dark place, and refrigerate after opening. Keeps for 9 months unopened.

Dry herbs

The flavor of herbs with woody stalks and tougher leaves, such as bay, thyme, and rosemary is well preserved by drying. Place individual leaves, fronds, and small sprigs on a piece of muslin stretched over a frame out of direct sunlight in a dry, airy room for at least 2 weeks until their color fades a little, and the herbs turn slightly brittle. Alternatively, hang in bundles to dry. Most home-dried herbs lose their flavor after 6 months, as their essential oils evaporate.

Drying flat

1 **Lay herbs flat** Place leaves of herbs, such as thyme, rosemary, marjoram, oregano, fennel, dill, bay, or sage, flat on a muslin cloth so they do not touch one another.

2 **Store in jars** Once dry (leave for at least 2 weeks) pack the herbs loosely in clean glass jars with tightly fitting lids. Seal the jars and store away from direct light.

Drying seeds and flowers

Fennel, dill, and coriander seeds, among others, can be home-dried for use in cooking. Both dried seeds and flowers should be used within 6 months.

Seeds Hang up bunches of stems, covering the seed heads with muslin and tying securely in place. After a week or so, collect the seeds and store in a paper bag.

Flowers Lavender, fennel, and chamomile flowers are easy to dry. Remove the stems, cut off the flowers, and dry on a muslin stretched over a frame for 3 weeks.

Hanging herbs

1 **Make herb posies** Tie together 3–4 stems of single herbs, such as bay, fennel fronds, rosemary, or thyme. Hang in an airy, dry room out of direct sunlight.

2 **Leave to dry** Hang strips of lemon peel alongside the herbs, if you like, and leave for 2 weeks until the color fades and the herbs are brittle. Untie and store in sealed jars.

MINT

When to pick
Pick the bigger leaves, to allow the smaller ones to develop. Pinch off sprigs just above a set of leaves, to encourage regrowth. Whole stems can also be picked.

Eat and store fresh
Keep mint in a glass of water or damp paper towel in the fridge for 2–3 days. Use with new potatoes, zucchini, peas, and to make mint tea.

How to preserve
Combine with vinegar and sugar for mint sauce. Dry leaves flat on muslin for 2 weeks, then store in sealed glass jars for up to 6 months (see pages 160–1).

Freezing options
Freeze in an herb butter, or coarsely chop in oil and spoon into individual freezer bags, or by freeze in ice cubes before transferring to bags (see pages 148–9).

This cordial has a delicate mint flavor. For a stronger taste, try doubling the quantity of mint leaves used. To serve, dilute with still or sparkling mineral water, or use as a base for cocktails.

Fresh mint cordial

Makes approx. $1^3/_4$ cup • **Prep** 20 mins, plus infusing • **Cooking** 5 mins

INGREDIENTS

2 cups fresh peppermint, Moroccan mint, or spearmint leaves

$1^1/_2$ cups granulated sugar

a few drops of natural green food coloring

a few drops of natural peppermint extract (only if using spearmint)

METHOD

1 Put the mint leaves in a large bowl, add the sugar, and pound with the end of a rolling pin, a cocktail muddler, or a pestle to bruise and crush them to a paste.

2 Pour over $1^1/_4$ cups of boiling water, stir, cover, and leave to infuse for at least 2 hours, or until the mixture is completely cold.

3 Strain through a sieve into a saucepan, pressing and squeezing the mint to extract the maximum flavor. Heat the pan over moderate heat, stirring until the sugar has dissolved. Then boil for 2 minutes. Stir in a few drops of natural green food coloring and peppermint extract (if using spearmint leaves).

4 Pour immediately into a warm, sterilized bottle using a sterilized funnel. Seal, label, and leave to cool. Then store in the fridge. Shake before use.

A lovely addition to fruity summer drinks and cocktails. Try diluting this fragrant syrup with mineral water or pouring it over vanilla ice cream for an instant dessert.

Mint and orange syrup

Makes approx. 1 cup • **Prep** 15 mins • **Cooking** 20 mins

INGREDIENTS

5 tbsp chopped, fresh mint, preferably Moroccan mint

finely grated zest of 1–2 large unwaxed oranges

1½ cups granulated sugar

½ cup freshly squeezed orange juice

2 tbsp Cointreau or any other orange liqueur

METHOD

1 Put the mint and grated orange zest in a double layer of muslin, bring up the edges, and tie with string. Put the sugar, orange juice, orange liqueur, and 1 cup water into a pan, and add the muslin bag.

2 Bring to a boil over moderate heat, stirring occasionally until the sugar has dissolved. Leave to simmer for 5–7 minutes, stirring from time to time until the syrup has thickened just a little.

3 Remove from the heat, cover, and leave to cool. Lift out the muslin bag and squeeze it over the pan to extract as much flavor as possible, then discard it. Strain the syrup through a fine sieve, lined with dampened muslin, into a warm sterilized bottle, and seal it.

Note Store in a cool place and use within 4–6 weeks.

This pretty, aromatic syrup is delicious poured over roasted peaches and served with Greek yogurt or crème fraîche. It is equally good when used to flavor meringues, cakes, and cookies.

Lavender syrup

Makes approx. 1 cup • **Prep** 15 mins • **Cooking** 15 mins, plus infusing

INGREDIENTS

2 tsp dried lavender flowers

1$\frac{1}{2}$ cups granulated sugar

peeled zest of 1 small
    unwaxed lemon, cut into
    narrow strips

METHOD

1 Put the dried lavender flowers, sugar, and lemon zest strips into a saucepan with 1$\frac{1}{4}$ cups water. Place over medium heat and stir.

2 Once the sugar has dissolved, after 3–4 minutes, stop stirring and remove from the heat. Leave to infuse for at least 30 minutes, stirring occasionally.

3 Return the pan to medium heat and bring to a boil without stirring. Turn the heat to high and let the syrup bubble for 5–7 minutes until thickened.

4 Remove from the heat. When the syrup is cool enough to handle, strain slowly and carefully through a fine sieve, lined with dampened muslin, into a warm sterilized bottle. Leave until completely cold before sealing.

Note Store in a cool place and use within 4–6 weeks.

LAVENDER

When to pick
Pick the flower heads or stems of lavender (if drying) when they first open. The leaves can be picked at any time and used sparingly for cooking.

Eat and store fresh
Lavender can be stored in a glass of water, in or out of the fridge, for up to 5 days. Use the leaves like rosemary to accompany roast lamb, or to add a wonderful aroma to baked goods.

How to preserve
Dry the picked flower heads on muslin for 3 weeks and store in sealed glass jars for up to 6 months (see pages 160–1), or tie whole bunches with string and hang up to dry.

Freezing options
Freeze chopped flowers with water in ice cube trays, and use in drinks and to flavor syrups, jellies, and baked goods.

GOOSEBERRIES

When to pick
Pick gooseberries when young and tart for cooking. Leave dessert varieties to grow plump for eating raw. Net plants to keep birds from feasting on them.

Eat and store fresh
Cook young gooseberries over gentle heat with a little sugar. Dessert gooseberries taste delicious in a fruit salad. Store in the fridge for up to 3 days.

How to preserve
Preserve gooseberries in jams, jellies, and chutneys. They can also be canned or used in cordials or for home brewing.

Freezing options
Open freeze whole on trays, as a cooked or uncooked purée, as a freezer jam (see pages 176–7), or blanched or poached in sugar syrup (see pages 194–5).

Like a dessert from the 1950s, this gooseberry tart has all the delicacy and demure simplicity of a bygone age. The gooseberries quiver in the just-set custard, all held together in a light pastry.

Gooseberry tart

Serves 6–8 • **Prep** 30 mins, plus chilling • **Cooking** 1 hour 10 mins

INGREDIENTS

1lb (400g) gooseberries

1 cup heavy cream

2 eggs

$^1/_4$ cup granulated sugar

For the pastry

1 cup all-purpose flour

2 tbsp granulated sugar

5 tbsp cold butter, cut into pieces

1 egg yolk

or prepared pastry for a 10in (24cm) tart pan

METHOD

1 To make the pastry: In a food processor, combine flour, sugar, and butter. Process, pulsing the machine on and off, until the mixture resembles fine breadcrumbs. Add the egg yolk and process until the mixture forms a ball, adding a little cold water, 1 tablespoon at a time, if necessary. Wrap pastry in plastic wrap and refrigerate 30 minutes.

2 Preheat the oven to 350°F (180°C). Meanwhile, remove the tops and stems from the gooseberries and set the berries aside. To make the custard, whisk together cream, eggs, and sugar in a bowl. Put the custard in the fridge.

3 On a floured work surface, roll out the pastry into a circle a little larger than a 10in (24cm) tart pan with a removable bottom. Line the pan with pastry, then line it with parchment and pie weights or beans; bake for 15 minutes. Remove beans and paper, and bake 10 more minutes until cooked through but still pale.

4 Remove from the oven and put a single layer of berries in the pastry shell. Pour the custard over and return to the oven for 35 minutes until the custard is set and golden at the edges. Leave to cool slightly before serving with whipped cream. Eat the same day as it does not store well.

An all-time favorite treatment for gooseberries, this chilled dessert is the epitome of summer eating. Try freezing the chilled purée so you can make this delicious fool whenever you like.

Gooseberry fool
with elderflower

Serves 4–6 • **Prep** 20 mins, plus chilling • **Cooking** 10 mins

INGREDIENTS

12oz (350g) gooseberries, tops
    and stems removed
$^1/_2$ cup granulated sugar
1 tbsp elderflower cordial
1 cup prepared custard
1 cup cream

METHOD

1 Put the gooseberries, sugar, and elderflower cordial into a pan and stir to dissolve the sugar. Cover and cook over low heat for 5 minutes until the gooseberries have released some water and started to swell. Remove the lid and cook for another 5 minutes.

2 Lightly mash the gooseberries with a potato masher to break up a few of the larger ones. Alternatively, if you prefer a smoother fool, purée the fruit in a blender or food processor. Leave the mixture to cool completely, and then chill in the fridge.

3 In a large bowl, whip the cream until it forms fairly stiff peaks.

4 Once the gooseberry mixture is completely cold, remove it from the fridge, fold it into the cream, and then fold in the cold custard to make a light, fluffy fool. Spoon the mixture into a serving dish or individual glasses and chill in the fridge for a few hours, or overnight, before serving.

Granitas are much simpler to make than ice cream and far more virtuous in the calorie count. Try this classic pairing of red summer berries for a refreshing iced dessert.

Red berry granita

Serves 6 • **Prep** 10 mins, plus freezing

INGREDIENTS

1 cup confectioners' sugar

1 tbsp fresh lemon juice

8oz (250g) strawberries, hulled

8oz (250g) raspberries

half-and-half,
    to serve (optional)

METHOD

1 Put the sugar and lemon juice in a blender or food processor with $^1/_2$ cup boiling water and process until the sugar has dissolved. Add the strawberries and raspberries, and process to a purée.

2 Transfer the mixture to a shallow freezerproof plastic container, cover, and place in the freezer for 3 hours. Remove from the freezer every hour and stir with a fork, breaking the mixture up into small pieces. When the mixture has completely broken up into frozen, gravelly pieces, serve straight from the freezer on its own, or with a drizzle of half-and-half.

Note The granita can be kept in the freezer for up to 1 month. Scrape with a fork before serving.

STRAWBERRIES

When to pick
Pick strawberries when dark red, firm, and glossy. Pick them with the hull and a little stalk intact as they will store longer. Harvest small fruits for jam or ice cream.

Eat and store fresh
Eat strawberries as soon as possible after picking. Keep them for up to 2 days in the fridge, and bring back to room temperature before eating.

How to preserve
A classic fruit for jam, strawberries can also be used to make cordials and syrups, and can be bottled.

Freezing options
Open freeze whole on trays, as a cooked or uncooked purée, as a freezer jam (see pages 176–7), or blanched or poached in sugar syrup (see pages 194–5).

If you're looking for new and interesting ways of using your crop of home-grown strawberries, this frozen dessert is a delicious alternative to eating them simply with cream and sugar.

Strawberry semifreddo

Serves 6–8 • **Prep** 20 mins, plus freezing

INGREDIENTS

8oz (225g) strawberries, hulled, plus extra whole strawberries and red currants to decorate

1 cup heavy cream

$\frac{1}{2}$ cup confectioners' sugar

4oz (115g) ready-made crisp meringues, coarsely crushed

3 tbsp raspberry-flavored liqueur

For the coulis

8oz (225g) strawberries, hulled

$\frac{1}{4}$ to $\frac{1}{2}$ cup confectioners' sugar

1–2 tsp lemon juice, brandy, grappa, or balsamic vinegar

METHOD

1 Brush an 8in (20cm) loose-bottomed, springform pan lightly with vegetable oil, then line the bottom with greaseproof or parchment paper and set aside.

2 Purée the strawberries in a blender. Whip the cream with the confectioners' sugar until it just forms soft peaks, and fold into the purée, then fold in crushed meringues and liqueur. Turn into the pan, smooth, cover with plastic wrap, and freeze 6 hours, or overnight.

3 Meanwhile, make the strawberry coulis. Purée the strawberries in a blender or food processor, then press them through a fine sieve to remove the seeds. Stir $\frac{1}{4}$ cup confectioners' sugar into the purée and taste for sweetness, adding more sugar if necessary. Flavor the coulis with the lemon juice.

4 Just before serving, release the sides of the springform pan, remove the semifreddo, peel away the lining paper, and using a warmed knife, cut into slices. Arrange the slices on individual plates, spoon the coulis around the base, and decorate with strawberries and red currants.

Note Store in the freezer for up to 3 months.

This delicate cake is a delicious twist on a baking classic. Adding fresh strawberries to the traditional filling gives it a summery elegance.

Victoria sandwich
with strawberries and cream

Serves 8 • **Prep** 20 mins • **Cooking** 25 mins

INGREDIENTS

1 cup butter, at room
    temperature
1 cup granulated sugar
4 large eggs, lightly beaten
1³/₄ cups self-rising flour

For the filling
¹/₂ cup heavy cream
6oz (175g) strawberries, hulled
    and sliced
confectioners' sugar, to dust

METHOD

1 Line the bottom of two 8in (20cm) round cake pans with baking parchment. In a bowl, mix the butter and sugar with an electric mixer until light and creamy.

2 Whisk in the eggs a little at a time, adding in a little of the flour if the mixture looks as if it is going to curdle.

3 Sift in the remaining flour and fold in gently with a spatula or large metal spoon. Divide the mixture between the pans and bake for 25 minutes, or until risen and firm to the touch. Leave to cool in the pans for 5 minutes, then transfer to a wire rack to cool completely.

4 To make the filling, place the cream in a bowl and beat with an electric mixer until soft peaks form. Spread over one of the cakes, then top with strawberries. Place the other cake on top, then dust with confectioners' sugar.

These delightful little cakes are perfect served with afternoon tea. For a party canapé, cut smaller versions, sandwich with a single slice of strawberry, and serve to your guests.

Chocolate strawberry
shortcakes

Serves 6 • **Prep** 15 mins • **Cooking** 10 mins

INGREDIENTS

1^1/$_2$ cups all-purpose flour

^{1}/$_4$ cup unsweetened cocoa
   powder

2 tsp baking powder

4 tbsp butter, at room
   temperature

^{1}/$_4$ cup granulated sugar, plus
   extra for sweetening

1 large egg

1 tsp vanilla extract

6 tbsp whole milk, or less, as
   needed

8oz (225g) strawberries

^{2}/$_3$ cup heavy cream, whipped

METHOD

1 Preheat the oven to 450°F (230°C). Sift the flour, cocoa, and baking powder into a bowl. Add the butter and rub in with fingertips. Stir in the sugar. Beat the egg with the vanilla and stir in. Add enough milk to form a soft, but not sticky, dough. Knead gently until smooth.

2 Pat out the dough to about ^{1}/$_2$in (1cm) thick. Cut into 6 rounds using a 3in (7.5cm) cookie cutter. Place on a lightly greased baking sheet. Bake in the oven for about 10 minutes until risen and the bases sound hollow when tapped. Transfer to a wire rack to cool for 5–10 minutes.

3 Halve 3 strawberries for decoration, leaving the green calyces intact, and reserve. Hull and slice the remaining strawberries in half, and sweeten with a little granulated sugar, if necessary.

4 Split the shortcakes, sandwich with the sliced strawberries and some of the cream. Top with the remaining cream and decorate with the reserved, halved strawberries.

This classic, soft-set conserve is for those times when you have so many strawberries that you just can't eat them all. Steeping the fruit in sugar stops it breaking up too much while cooking.

Strawberry conserve

Makes 3 medium jars • **Prep** 20 mins, plus standing • **Cooking** 25 mins

INGREDIENTS

2lbs (900g) juicy
    strawberries, hulled
5 cups granulated sugar
juice of 1 lemon
juice of 1 lime

METHOD

1 Layer the strawberries and sugar in a large bowl, cover, and leave for several hours or overnight.

2 Tip the fruit and sugar into a preserving pan or a large heavy saucepan. Cook over low heat, stirring constantly, until the sugar has dissolved. Then boil gently for about 5 minutes, just enough for the fruit to soften but not to break down too much. Remove the pan from the heat, cover it loosely with some muslin, and leave the cooked fruit in a cool spot overnight.

3 Remove the muslin, put the pan back on the heat, stir in the lemon and lime juice and bring to a boil. Boil gently for 5–10 minutes or until thickened and the setting point is reached, skimming off any foam that rises to the top, as needed. Remove the pan from the heat while you test for a set (see pages 186–7).

4 Ladle into warm sterilized jars, cover with discs of waxed paper, seal, and label.

Note Keeps for 6 months. Store in a cool, dark place, and refrigerate after opening.

Make freezer jam

Uncooked freezer jams are a great solution
for anyone who wants fresh-tasting, low-sugar
spreads. Very ripe, juicy fruits, especially those
low in pectin and acid, are difficult to set properly
as traditional jam (see pages 186–7), but are ideal
as thickened purées. This method uses agar, a healthy,
tasteless, Japanese gelling agent which gives these quick
jams a jelly-like set. They can be used thawed on toast, desserts, or yogurt.
Once thawed and opened, freezer jams should be used within 2 weeks.

1 **Crush berries** Wash the strawberries briefly, put them into a large bowl with the lemon juice, and crush with the back of a fork to a rough purée.

2 **Add the agar and simmer** Put 1 cup of water into a pan. Add the agar. Leave for 3 minutes, bring to a boil, and simmer for 5 minutes. Add the sugar and stir.

Recipe
Strawberry freezer jam

Makes approx. 1¼lb (600g) • **Prep** 15 mins, plus standing • **Keeps** 6 months

INGREDIENTS

1lb (500g) strawberries, no hulls; room temperature

1 tbsp fresh lemon juice

1 tbsp agar flakes or 1 tsp agar powder

(available in Asian markets)

¼ to ½ cup granulated sugar

Other fruits for freezer jams

Using the basic recipe shown here, make freezer jams using any of the fruits below.

Blackberries Add a little mixed spice for a delicious autumn jam.

Blueberries Use on their own or with other fruits such as raspberries (see page 183).

Cherries Halve and stone the fruit first.

Also suitable for freezer jams:
Figs, nectarines, melons, peaches, pears, raspberries, and tayberries.

3 **Add to the fruit** Pour the hot agar syrup onto the fruit, stirring constantly until it is well mixed (use a rubber spatula to scrape all the syrup out of the pan).

4 **Pot and store** Pour jam into clean freezer containers, leaving room for expansion. Leave to cool, then seal, leave in fridge overnight to thicken fully, and freeze.

RASPBERRIES

When to pick
Pick all varieties of raspberries when a deep color, but before they go too soft. They should be sweet to taste and should come away from the plant easily.

Eat and store fresh
Eat as soon as possible after picking. They will keep for 2 days in the fridge, but need to be brought back to room temperature before eating. If cooking, raspberries can be kept in the fridge for up to 3 days.

How to preserve
Delicious in jams and cordials, raspberries can also be bottled or made into fruit curds and cheese.

Freezing options
Open freeze whole on trays, as a cooked or uncooked purée, as a freezer jam (see pages 176–7), or blanched or poached in sugar syrup (see pages 194–5).

A delicate and impressive looking take on the traditional brûlée. Raspberries can lose some of their freshness when cooked, but the ground hazelnuts in this dessert act to enhance their flavor.

Raspberry and hazelnut
crème brûlée

Serves 4 • **Prep** 10 mins, plus chilling • **Cooking** 30 mins

INGREDIENTS

4oz (115g) raspberries

$^2/_3$ cup superfine sugar

1 tsp finely grated lemon zest

$1^3/_4$ cups heavy cream

2 eggs

$^1/_2$ cup ground hazelnuts

$^1/_2$ tsp vanilla extract

METHOD

1 Divide the raspberries between 4 ramekins. Sprinkle each with $^3/_4$ tsp of sugar and $^1/_4$ teaspoon lemon zest.

2 Whisk the cream with the eggs, hazelnuts, vanilla extract, and 1 tbsp of the sugar until well blended. Pour over the raspberries. Stand the dishes in a large frying pan with enough boiling water to come halfway up the sides of the dishes. Cover the pan with a lid or foil and cook very gently for about 30 minutes or until set. Don't let the water boil or the custard will curdle. Leave to cool, then chill in the fridge.

3 Remove from the fridge, sprinkle liberally with the remaining sugar and broil under high heat for 3–4 minutes until caramelized. Alternatively, move a cook's blowtorch over the top to caramelize the sugar. Allow to stand for 5 minutes, then serve.

This fragrant dessert is the perfect finale to a summer meal. Fresh raspberries are so delicious that I mostly eat them straight from the garden, yet an elegant recipe like this shows them at their best.

Cold raspberry soufflé

Serves 4 • **Prep** 30 mins

INGREDIENTS

1 tbsp sunflower or
    vegetable oil

4 tbsp rose water

1 x ¼oz (7g) envelope
    unflavored gelatin

12oz (350g) raspberries

1 tbsp fresh lemon juice

¾ cup confectioners' sugar,
    sieved

2 cups heavy cream

4 egg whites

mint leaves, to garnish

METHOD

1 Wrap double-thick strips of parchment or wax paper around the outsides of 4 ramekins so they sit 2in (5cm) above the rim, forming collars. Secure with adhesive tape. Brush the inside of the paper collars lightly with oil.

2 Place the rosewater in a small bowl, sprinkle with the gelatin, and leave to soften for 2 minutes, or until the mixture appears spongy. Set the bowl in a larger bowl, and carefully add enough boiling water to reach halfway up the sides of the smaller bowl. Stir to dissolve the gelatin. Remove from the heat and allow to cool slightly.

3 Place all but 8 of the raspberries in a food processor and purée. Strain through a sieve, discarding any seeds. Stir in the lemon juice and sugar, then stir in the gelatin mixture. Leave in a cool place until just beginning to set.

4 Whip the cream to soft peaks and fold into the raspberry mixture. In a separate bowl, using clean beaters, whisk egg whites until stiff and fold into the raspberry mixture. Pour into ramekins and chill until set.

5 Remove from the fridge, peel the paper from each and decorate with whole raspberries and mint leaves.

Soft fruit, such as berries do not keep for long after picking. One way to preserve their juicy freshness is by turning them into these tempting ice lollies to bring out later in the year.

Fruit lollies

Makes 4–6 small lollies • **Prep** 20 mins, plus freezing • **Cooking** 5 mins

INGREDIENTS

$^1/_2$ cup granulated sugar

1lb (500g) ripe berries, such as raspberries, strawberries, or blackberries, rinsed and patted dry

juice of 1 lemon

METHOD

1 Make a sugar syrup by placing the sugar and $^1/_2$ cup of water into a heavy saucepan. Place the pan over low heat and stir until the sugar dissolves.

2 Cook the syrup without stirring over medium to high heat to achieve a steady boil for 1-2 minutes. Then turn off the heat and allow the syrup to cool.

3 Purée the berries by pressing them through a sieve, discarding seeds. If the fruit is too firm to go through the sieve, process it with a hand-held blender, or in a food processor, to first make a purée, then sieve.

4 Add the lemon juice and sugar syrup to the bowl and mix them into the berry purée.

5 Pour the mixture into plastic pop molds or paper cups and freeze for 1 hour, until partially frozen. Insert the plastic sticks provided, or insert a frozen-dessert stick into the center of each cup. Freeze for 4 hours, or until very firm. Unmold or tear off the paper.

Note Freeze these for up to 6 months.

A lovely, light cake that is equally good eaten warm or cold. Although it suits tea in the garden on a summer's day, it would also work as a dessert, served warm with cream.

Raspberry bake
with lemon and almonds

Serves 8 • **Prep** 20 mins • **Cooking** 40 mins

INGREDIENTS

1 cup all-purpose flour

1 tsp baking powder

$^1/_2$ cup ground almonds

11 tbsp butter, cubed

1 cup granulated sugar

juice of 1 lemon

1 tsp vanilla extract

2 large eggs

7oz (200g) fresh raspberries

confectioners' sugar, to dust

METHOD

1 Preheat the oven to 350°F (180°C). Line the bottom and sides of an 8in (20cm) square cake pan with parchment paper.

2 Sift the flour into a bowl, add the baking powder and ground almonds, and mix well. In a saucepan, melt the butter, sugar, and lemon juice together, stirring this mixture until well combined.

3 Stir the syrupy mixture into the dry ingredients, then whisk in the vanilla extract and the eggs, one at a time, until the mixture is smooth and well combined. Pour into the prepared pan, then scatter the raspberries over the top. Bake for 35–40 minutes, or until golden and a skewer inserted into the cake comes out clean.

4 Cool in the pan for 10 minutes, then invert onto a wire rack, remove paper, and cool completely Dust with confectioners' sugar and cut into rectangles to serve.

This easy-to-make jam is wonderful served with thick, tangy yogurt as a low-fat dessert or at breakfast. To use, thaw overnight in the fridge, then keep refrigerated and use within two weeks.

Raspberry and blueberry
quick freezer jam

Makes approx. 1lb (500g) • **Prep** 10 mins • **Cooking** 12 mins

INGREDIENTS

8oz (225g) raspberries and 8oz (225g) blueberries, at room temperature

2 tsp fresh lemon juice

1 tbsp agar flakes
    or 1 tsp agar powder
    (available in Asian markets and health food stores)

$1/2$ cup granulated sugar

METHOD

1 Put the fruit in a heatproof bowl with the lemon juice and coarsely crush with a potato masher or fork; leave some texture, rather than reducing berries to a pulp.

2 Put 1 cup of water into a small saucepan, sprinkle the agar over it, and leave to soften for 2–3 minutes. Give the pan a gentle swirl, then bring the water slowly to a boil over low heat, without stirring. Simmer gently for 3–5 minutes, stirring occasionally to dissolve the agar.

3 Add the sugar and stir for 2–3 minutes over low heat until dissolved. Remove from the heat.

4 Pour the hot agar syrup over the fruit in the bowl, stirring the fruit until the ingredients are well mixed. Pour into clean freezerproof containers, leaving $1/2$in (1cm) space at the top. Leave to cool, then seal and label. Leave overnight in the fridge to thicken fully, then freeze.

Note Keeps for 6 months in the freezer.

Sometimes called jumbleberry jam, this can be made with any juicy summer fruits, although raspberries are essential. Try blackberries, black currants, or red currants in the mix.

Mixed berry jam

Makes approx. 1$^1/_2$ cups• **Prep** 10 mins • **Cooking** 15 mins

INGREDIENTS

1lb (450g) mix of raspberries, strawberries, and blueberries, hulled if needed
2$^1/_2$ cups granulated sugar
juice of 2 lemons

METHOD

1 Put the fruit into a preserving pan or a large heavy saucepan, and lightly crush the fruit with the back of a wooden spoon.

2 Add the sugar and heat gently, stirring until all the sugar has dissolved. Turn up the heat and bring to a boil. When the jam reaches a rolling boil, cook for 5–10 minutes, or until it reaches the setting point. Remove the pan from the heat while you test the mixture for a set (see pages 186–7).

3 Use a skimmer to skim off any foam that rises to the top . Leave the jam to cool slightly so that the berries are evenly distributed throughout the jam and a thin skin forms on top. Ladle into a warm, sterilized jar, cover with a waxed paper disc, seal, and label.

Note Keeps for 6–9 months. Store in a cool, dark place, and refrigerate after opening.

Make fruit jam

Jams are the simplest of preserves where fruit is cooked with sugar over high heat until set. This method, suitable for all soft-skinned berries, produces a soft-set jam. Once opened, refrigerate and use within 3 to 4 weeks. It is important to get the correct balance of sugar, acid, and naturally-occurring pectin as this helps the jam set. Some fruits, such as plums, have high pectin content. Others, including cherries and pears, which have low levels, need extra pectin added. Raspberries are a medium-pectin fruit and the lemon juice helps to achieve a set.

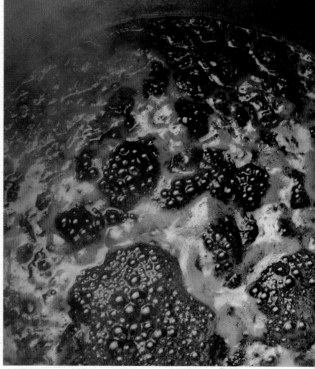

1 **Simmer fruit** Wash fruit and put into a preserving pan or large heavy saucepan. Add the lemon juice and water. Simmer gently for 3–5 minutes, add the sugar, and stir.

2 **Bring to a boil** Turn up the heat and bring the jam to a rolling boil for 5–10 minutes or until a setting point is reached. Take the pan off the heat to test for a set.

Recipe Raspberry jam

Makes approx. 1lb (450g) or 2 small jars
Prep 15 mins • **Keeps** 6 months

INGREDIENTS

1½lb (650g) raspberries
juice of ½ lemon
⅔ cup water
2¾ cups sugar

Tips on making fruit jams

When you think your jam has reached its setting point, you must test for a set.

Testing for a set Usually jams and conserves take 5–20 minutes, jellies 5–15 minutes, and marmalades 10–30 minutes to set. Remove the pan from the heat and follow step 3 below.

Sterilize bottles and jars To ensure successful preservation, sterilize all jars, bottles, and lids just before you need them. Wash in hot water, drain upside down, and put into a low oven, 275°F (140°C) for 15 minutes.

3 **Testing for a set** Put 1 tsp of jam on a chilled saucer, allow to cool, then push across it with your finger. If your finger leaves a trail and the jam wrinkles, it is set.

4 **Put into jars and store** Ladle the jam into warm sterilized jars using a clean jam funnel. Cover with waxed paper, seal, label, and store in a cool, dark place.

This is the ultimate in fast desserts, yet it looks impressive and is incredibly tasty. It is pleasing to think that an afternoon's blackberry picking can give such rewarding results.

Blackberry brioche
with mascarpone

Serves 4 • **Prep** 5 mins • **Cooking** 10 mins

BLACKBERRIES

When to pick
Pick blackberries when the fruits are dark purple, glossy, and sweet to taste. Slightly under-ripe berries are better for making jam.

Eat and store fresh
If eating raw, use blackberries within 2 days of picking and eat at room temperature. If cooking, they will keep for up to 3 days in the fridge before using.

How to preserve
Preserve blackberries in jams or jellies. Wild blackberries are often woody, and are better made into jelly. They can also be used in chutneys and fruit cheeses.

Freezing options
Open freeze whole on trays, as a cooked or uncooked purée, as a freezer jam (see pages 176–7), or blanched or poached in sugar syrup (see pages 194–5).

INGREDIENTS

4 tbsp butter

1/4 cup granulated sugar

16oz (400g) blackberries

4–8 slices of brioche

8oz (200g) mascarpone

METHOD

1 Melt the butter in a frying pan. Add the sugar and allow it to melt and start to turn golden brown; without stirring, shake the pan to dissolve the sugar.

2 Add the blackberries to the pan and allow them to cook over high heat for 2–3 minutes, until they are heated through and softened, but have not broken down. Leave the berries to cool slightly while you toast the slices of brioche.

3 Thickly spread the mascarpone over the slices of toasted brioche and top with the warm berries. Spoon over any juice that is left in the pan and serve.

Late summer blackberries often usher in autumn puddings, like this crumble. One of the best soft fruits for freezing, blackberries can deliver a welcome blast of vitamin C in the colder months.

Blackberry
and apple crumble

Serves 6–8 • Prep 15–20 mins • Cooking 45 mins

INGREDIENTS

2¼lb (1kg) apples, peeled, cored, and thickly sliced

12oz (350g) blackberries

1¼ cups dark muscovado or dark brown sugar

9 tbsp butter, diced

¾ cup all-purpose flour

¾ cup old fashioned oats

heavy cream or custard, to serve

METHOD

1 Preheat the oven to 350°F (180°C). Put the apples in a shallow, 2½ quart (2.25 liter) baking dish. Add the blackberries. Sprinkle about 3 tbsp of the sugar over the fruit. Cover with foil and bake for 15 minutes to soften the fruit.

2 Make the crumble by rubbing together the butter and flour until it resembles bread crumbs. Add the remaining sugar, and then the oats; you could do this in a food processor or blender, pulsing the machine on and off, and adding the oats last so they are not chopped too finely.

3 Remove the fruit from the oven, give it a quick stir, and spread the crumble all over. Bake for another 30 minutes or until the fruit is oozing out from beneath the golden crumble. Serve with cream or custard.

In this wonderful cheesecake recipe, the blueberries are reduced to a thick purée and swirled into the creamy topping. Its marbled appearance makes it look exceptionally pretty.

Blueberry-ripple
cheesecake

Serves 8 • **Prep** 20 mins • **Cooking** 40 mins

INGREDIENTS

3½ tbsp butter, plus extra
    for greasing

5oz (125g) British digestive
    biscuits or plain cookies,
    such as gingersnaps, vanilla
    wafers, or graham crackers

6oz (150g) blueberries

²/₃ cup granulated sugar, plus 3
    tbsp extra

14oz (400g) cream cheese

8oz (250g) mascarpone cheese

2 large eggs, plus 1 large egg
    yolk

½ tsp vanilla extract

2 tbsp all-purpose flour

METHOD

1 Preheat the oven to 350°F (180°C). Grease an 8in (20cm) springform pan. Put the cookies into a plastic bag and crush with a rolling pin. Melt the butter in a saucepan, then add the crumbs and stir until well-coated. Press the crumbs into the bottom of the prepared pan.

2 Put the blueberries and 3 tablespoons of sugar in a food processor and process until smooth, then push the mixture through a sieve into a small saucepan. Bring to a boil, then allow to simmer for 3–5 minutes, or until thickened and jammy. Set aside.

3 Put all the remaining ingredients into the cleaned food processor and whizz until well combined. Pour the mixture onto the crumb crust and smooth the top. With a teaspoon, carefully drizzle the blueberry mixture over the cream cheese mixture in a swirly pattern. Bake the cheesecake for 40 minutes, or until it has set but still has a slight wobble in the middle when you shake the pan . Leave to cool in the oven for 1 hour, then remove from the oven and cool completely before serving.

As long as you are able to protect them from the birds, blueberries are easy to grow and prolific. Here, a classic recipe is used to showcase one of the tastiest berries around.

Blueberry cobbler

Serves 4 • **Prep** 15 mins • **Cooking** 30 mins

INGREDIENTS

1lb (450g) blueberries

2 large peaches or 2 eating apples, such as Golden Delicious, sliced

finely grated zest of $\frac{1}{2}$ lemon

2 tbsp granulated sugar

For the cobbler

1$\frac{3}{4}$ cups self-rising flour

2 tsp baking powder

$\frac{1}{3}$ cup granulated sugar, plus 1 tbsp for sprinkling

pinch of salt

5 tbsp butter, chilled and diced

1 egg

$\frac{1}{2}$ cup buttermilk

handful of sliced almonds

METHOD

1 Spread the blueberries and peaches over the bottom of a shallow baking dish and sprinkle with the lemon zest and granulated sugar.

2 Sift the flour, baking powder, sugar, and salt into a bowl. Add the butter, and work with your fingers until the mixture resembles bread crumbs.

3 Break the egg into the buttermilk and beat well. Add to the dry ingredients and mix together to form a soft, sticky dough. Drop walnut-sized spoonsful of the mixture over the top of the fruit, leaving a little space between them. Press them down lightly with your fingers, then sprinkle over the almonds and 1 tbsp of sugar.

4 Bake for 30 minutes, or until golden and bubbling, covering loosely with foil if it is browning too quickly. The cobbler is done when a skewer pushed into the center comes out clean. Leave the cobbler to cool briefly before serving.

Making a simple jam like this is a great way of preserving your blueberries. It is undeniably sweet, and perfect on its own with natural yogurt or as an accompaniment to some warm scones.

Blueberry jam

Makes approx. 1lb (450g) or 2 small jars • **Prep** 5 mins • **Cooking** 35 mins

INGREDIENTS

2lb (900g) blueberries

juice of 2 lemons

3^1/$_2$ cups granulated sugar

METHOD

1 Put the blueberries, ^{1}/$_2$ cup of water, and the lemon juice into a preserving pan or a large heavy saucepan. Bring to a boil, then simmer for 10–15 minutes to extract the pectin and soften the fruit.

2 Add the sugar, stir until it dissolves, then increase the heat and bring the mixture to a boil. Boil rapidly for 10–12 minutes, or until it reaches the setting point. Take the pan off the heat while you test the jam for a set (see pages 186–7).

3 With the pan still off the heat, skim off any foam that rises to the top . Leave the jam to cool slightly, then ladle it into warm sterilized jars, cover with discs of waxed paper, seal, and label.

Note Keeps for 6–9 months. Store in a cool, dark place and refrigerate after opening.

Freeze fruit

A perfect way to preserve the flavor and nutritional content of fruit is to freeze it, but only freeze fresh, top-quality crops. Freezing breaks down the cell walls of the fruit, so whole fruit will be squashy when thawed, but its flavor will be just as delicious as fresh. All fruits are best frozen with sugar to help retain their texture when thawed. Remove any stones and cut larger fruits (apart from citrus fruits) in half or slices before freezing. The periods listed in the chart opposite are the maximum freezer storage times.

1 **Open freeze** Discard any overripe or blemished berries. Lay them in a single layer on baking trays. Sprinkle liberally with granulated sugar and put in the freezer.

2 **Put into bags** As soon as the fruit is frozen (after 1 hour or so), scrape it from the trays and put it into portion-sized freezer bags. Label, date, and return to freezer.

FREEZER TIMES FOR FRUITS

FRUITS	RAW			COOKED	
	Sprinkle with sugar and open freeze on trays (Months)	Pack in freezer jars, cover in syrup or sugar, and freeze (Months)	Purée, pack in freezer jars, and freeze (Months)	Blanch or poach in syrup, pack in freezer jars, cover in syrup, and freeze (Months)	Purée, pack in freezer jars, and freeze (Months)
Apples	9	9	—	9	9
Apricots (ripe)	9	9	6	9	9
Blackberries	12	12	6	9	9
Black currants	12	12	6	9	9
Blueberries	12	12	6	9	9
Cherries	6	6	6	9	9
Cranberries	12	12	6	9	9
Figs	9	9	6	9	9
Gooseberries	12	12	6	9	9
Melons	9	9	6	9	9
Nectarines	9	9	6	9	9
Peaches	9	9	6	9	9
Pears	—	—	—	9	9
Plums (all kinds)	9	9	6	9	9
Raspberries	12	12	6	9	9
Rhubarb	12	12	—	9	9
Strawberries	9	9	6	9	9

How to freeze purées and cooked fruit

Very juicy fruits such as peaches, raspberries, or strawberries can be puréed uncooked in a food processor with a little sugar and lemon juice. Fruit not perfect enough to freeze uncooked can be stewed lightly, baked, or poached in a sugar syrup. Freeze purées for up to 6 months and cooked fruit for up to 9 months, leaving ³⁄₄in (2cm) of space at the top of each container to allow for expansion.

195

When to pick
Black currants mature for a few days after turning black, so pick when almost bursting but before they start to shrivel. They should be sweet but still sharp.

Eat and store fresh
Eat black currants as soon as possible after picking if using them raw. If you are cooking them, they will keep for up to 3 days in the fridge.

How to preserve
A classic component of jams and jellies, they can also be bottled and used in both cordials and syrups.

Freezing options
Open freeze whole on trays, as a cooked or uncooked purée, as a freezer jam (see pages 176–7), or blanched or poached in sugar syrup (see pages 194–5).

Home-grown black currants are one of the treats of the allotment and are hard to find in shops. Here, the delicate fragrance of rosemary enhances this sweet, sharp, and creamy dessert.

Black currant
and rosemary cheesecake

Serves 8–10 • **Prep** 20 mins • **Cooking** 1–1hour 15 mins, plus chilling

INGREDIENTS

For the cheesecake

6 tbsp butter, plus extra
    for greasing
one 7oz (200g) package British
    digestive biscuits or plain
    cookies, such as gingersnaps
    or graham crackers
1 tbsp chopped fresh rosemary
1$\frac{1}{2}$lb (675g)) cream cheese, at
    room temperature
1 cup granulated sugar
2 eggs
1 tsp vanilla extract

For the topping

8oz (225g) black currants
sugar, to taste
1 tsp arrowroot

METHOD

1 Preheat the oven to 300°F (150°C). Grease an 8in (20cm) round springform pan with a removable bottom. Put the biscuits in a plastic bag and crush with a rolling pin. Melt the butter in a saucepan, then add the biscuit crumbs and rosemary, and stir until evenly moistened. Press the crumbs onto the bottom of the pan.

2 Beat the cheese with the sugar, eggs, and vanilla extract. Spoon the mixture over the prepared crumb crust. Smooth the surface with a spatula. Bake for up to 1$\frac{1}{4}$ hours, until set. Turn off the oven and leave until cool. Cover the pan with plastic wrap and refrigerate.

3 Cook the black currants in $\frac{1}{4}$ cup water until the juices are released , but the currants still hold their shape. Sweeten to taste. Blend the arrowroot with 1 tsp water and stir in. Cook, stirring, until thickened and clear. Cool.

4 Loosen the edges with a palette knife and release the springform. Place the cheesecake on a serving plate. Spoon the black currant topping over so that the fruits trickle down the sides a little.

Any fresh fruit combination can be used with this brûlée method. Here the black currants are lightly stewed, but summer fruits, such as strawberries and raspberries, could be used uncooked.

Black currant brûlée

Serves 4 • **Prep** 10 mins • **Cooking** 10 mins

INGREDIENTS

8oz (225g) black currants

3 tbsp apple juice

granulated sugar, to taste

2 tsp cornstarch

$1/4$ cup Greek-style or other
thick vanilla yogurt

2 tbsp light brown sugar

METHOD

1 Put the black currants in a saucepan with the apple juice and cook over medium heat for 3–5 minutes until tender. Sweeten to taste with a little sugar.

2 In a small bowl, blend the cornstarch with 2 tsp water, then stir into the black currants and cook over medium-low heat for 1 minute to thicken.

3 Spoon the mixture into 4 ramekins. Cover and leave to cool in the refrigerator. Just before serving, top each dish with 1 tbsp of vanilla yogurt, then cover with an even layer of brown sugar. Broil under high heat for 3–4 minutes until the sugar melts and caramelizes. Alternatively, move a cook's blowtorch over the top to caramelize the sugar. Let cool.

This classic English summer dessert is made with a variety of home-grown soft fruit picked when most juicy. Be sure to make it a day ahead, to allow the flavors to develop overnight.

Summer pudding

Serves 6 • **Prep** 20–25 mins, plus chilling • **Cooking** 5 mins

INGREDIENTS

12 slices white bread, crusts removed

5oz (125g) black currants

5oz (125g) red currants

$^2/_3$ cup granulated sugar

9oz (250g) mixed berries, such as strawberries, raspberries, mulberries, and blueberries

METHOD

1 Line a 4 cup pudding mold with bread slices, beginning with a circle cut to fit the bottom, then overlapping slices evenly around the sides.

2 Lightly cook the currants with the sugar until soft and the juices have run. Stir in the berries and cook for 1 minute, or until just softening.

3 Spoon some of the juices over the bread, then fill the mold with the fruit. Make sure the fruit is packed well into the basin. Cover the fruit with bread, ensuring that it is completely covered with an even layer.

4 If there is any juice remaining, spoon this over the top layer of bread. Stand the basin in a dish to catch any overspill of juice. Cover with plastic wrap plastic wrap and place a small plate on top. Put a weight on the plate and chill overnight.

5 Invert onto a serving plate. Serve with cream or ice cream.

Making a cordial is a wonderful way to prolong enjoyment of your home-grown produce. Dilute with sparkling or still mineral water, or pour over ice cream or thick Greek yogurt.

Black currant cordial

Makes about 4 cups or 1 large bottle • **Prep** 5 mins • **Cooking** 15 mins

INGREDIENTS

1lb (450g) black currants

1 cup plus 2 tbsp granulated
    sugar

zest and juice of 1
    unwaxed lemon

METHOD

1 Place the black currants, sugar, and 1 cup of water in a saucepan over low heat. Bring to a simmer, stirring occasionally. Gently mash the black currants to make sure that all the berries have broken open. Cook for 5–8 minutes, until the sugar has dissolved and the black currants have yielded their juice.

2 Stir in the lemon juice and zest, and remove the pan from the heat.

3 Slowly strain the contents of the pan through a funnel lined with dampened muslin, into a sterilized bottle. Allow the liquid to cool, then seal and refrigerate.

Note Use within 6–8 weeks. Once opened, it will keep for up to 3 days in the refrigerator.

Red currant jelly is a constant presence in my kitchen, as I find it indispensible for sweetening stews, sauces, and gravies. The high pectin content of the currants makes this an easy jelly to set.

Red currant jelly

Makes approx. 2$\frac{1}{4}$lb (1kg) or 3 medium jars • **Prep** 10 mins • **Cooking** 25–35 mins

INGREDIENTS

(2lb) 900g red currants,
    stalks included
approx. 5 cups
    granulated sugar
    (see method)

METHOD

1 Add the red currants, their stems , and 2$\frac{1}{2}$ cups of water to a preserving pan or a large heavy saucepan and bring to a boil over medium heat. Turn the heat down and cook for about 10 minutes or until the currants are soft. Mash to a pulp.

2 Tip the pulp into a fine sieve or a clean jelly bag set over a large bowl, and leave to strain for several hours or overnight until all the juice has dripped through.

3 Measure the strained juice; you should have about 4 to 5 cups. Calculate the quantity of sugar needed, allowing 2$\frac{1}{2}$ cups per 2$\frac{1}{2}$ cups of juice. Pour the juice into a clean preserving pan or a large heavy saucepan, add the sugar, and stir to dissolve.

4 Bring to a boil and cook on a rolling boil for 10–20 minutes or until the setting point is reached (start testing after 10 minutes). Remove the pan from the heat while you test for a set (see pages 186–7). Pot up in warm sterilized jars, cover with discs of waxed paper, seal, and label.

Note Store in a cool, dark place. Refrigerate after opening. Keeps for 6–9 months.

RED CURRANTS

When to pick
Red currants ripen on the bush after they turn red, so always taste before picking; they should taste sharp, almost sour, and look slightly translucent.

Eat and store fresh
Eat raw in a mixed summer fruit salad, as soon as possible after picking. They will keep for up to 3 days in the fridge before cooking.

How to preserve
Serve red currant jelly with lamb or game, and stir into gravies and stews for sweetness. Red currants can also be bottled and used in cordials and syrups.

Freezing options
Open freeze whole on trays, as a cooked or uncooked purée, as a freezer jam (see pages 176–7), or blanched or poached in sugar syrup (see pages 194–5).

This creamy, delicate dessert works marvellously well with the sweet sharpness of the hot berry sauce. Use whatever fresh berries you have available, but make sure they are well sweetened.

Chilled rice pudding
with warm berry sauce

Serves 4–6 • **Prep** 10 mins • **Cooking** 20 mins

INGREDIENTS

For the rice pudding

$3^1/_2$ cups whole milk

$3/_4$ cup long grain white or
    basmati rice

$1/_4$ cup granulated sugar

1 cup heavy cream

$1/_2$ cup blanched slivered
    almonds, toasted

1 tbsp sweet sherry

1 tsp vanilla extract

For the sauce

12oz (300g) mixed berries,
    such as black currants,
    raspberries, and
    blackberries

$1/_4$ cup granulated sugar

METHOD

1 Mix the milk, rice, and sugar in a large, heavy-bottomed saucepan and bring to a boil, stirring frequently to prevent the rice from sticking. Turn down the heat and simmer for about 15 minutes, stirring frequently, until the rice is tender. Turn the rice out into a large bowl and leave to cool.

2 While the rice cools, whip the cream until it forms soft peaks, then fold it into the cooled rice.

3 Cook the almonds in a dry frying pan over low heat, shaking the pan frequently, until golden. Leave to cool, and then chop. Fold the chopped almonds, sherry, and vanilla extract into the rice and leave in the fridge for 3–4 hours or overnight to chill before serving.

4 To make the sauce, heat the currants and berries gently with the sugar and 1 tbsp water, and simmer on low heat for 3–4 minutes until they are cooked through. Purée the sauce with a hand-held blender and pass through a sieve to remove the seeds. Pour the warm sauce over the chilled pudding to serve.

MELONS

When to pick
Pick melons when they start to smell fragrant. The area around the stalk starts to soften slightly and the stalk itself may start to crack. Ripe melons should also be heavy for their size, with unblemished skin.

Eat and store fresh
Eat all melons, except watermelon, at room temperature within a couple of days of picking. Store in a cool place for up to 5 days, depending on their ripeness. Watermelon is best served chilled.

How to preserve
Melons can be bottled or preserved in jams and pickles.

Freezing options
Open freeze in slices on trays, as an uncooked or cooked purée, or slices blanched in sugar syrup (see pages 194–5).

This salad, with its unlikely combination of ingredients, is becoming a modern classic. The sweetness of the ripe melon contrasts wonderfully with the salty feta and the heat of the chili.

Watermelon salad with
feta and pumpkin seeds

Serves 4 • **Prep** 10 mins • **Cooking** 5 mins

INGREDIENTS

1/4 cup shelled pumpkin seeds
sea salt
1/4 tsp chili powder
1/4 cup light olive oil
juice of 1 lemon
freshly ground black pepper
1lb (500g) watermelon, rind removed, seeded if necessary, and cut into 3/4in (2cm) squares
1/2 red onion, thinly sliced
4 large handsful of mixed salad leaves, such as watercress, arugula, or baby spinach
8oz (225g) feta cheese, cut into 1/2in (1cm) cubes

METHOD

1 Cook the pumpkin seeds in a dry wok or frying pan for 2 minutes, stirring and tossing, until they start to pop. Add a pinch of salt and the chili powder, and cook for 1 minute longer. Set aside to cool.

2 In a large bowl, whisk together the olive oil, lemon juice, and salt and freshly ground pepper to taste. Add the watermelon, red onion, and salad leaves, and toss gently to coat with the dressing.

3 Scatter the feta cheese and the seeds over the top of the salad and serve immediately.

This grown-up dessert is quick to prepare and visually appealing. Use ripe, fragrant melons. For best flavor, serve chilled, not cold.

Melon slices
with vodka and orange

Serves 6–8 • **Prep** 5 mins, plus 15 mins marinating

INGREDIENTS

1 honeydew melon, cut in
    quarters lengthwise, rind
    and seeds removed, and
    flesh sliced
1 watermelon, cut in half, rind
    and seeds removed, and
    flesh sliced
1–2 tbsp good-quality vodka
1–2 tbsp fresh, strained
    orange juice
handful of fresh mint leaves,
    coarsely torn

METHOD

1 Arrange the melon slices in a large flat serving bowl or platter, drizzle with the vodka and orange juice, then allow the fruit to sit for 15 minutes while it absorbs the vodka and juice.

2 Sprinkle with the mint and serve.

Note You can use any kind of melon, but always try to include watermelon, which will absorb the vodka.

A clafoutis is rather like a pastryless tart, where the cream, sugar, and eggs, are combined to make a rich batter. This French dessert is a fantastic way to use up a glut of cherries.

Cherry clafoutis

Serves 6 • **Prep** 12 mins, plus standing • **Cooking** 35–45 mins

INGREDIENTS

1¹/₂ lbs (750g) cherries, pitted

3 tbsp kirsch

¹/₃ cup granulated sugar

butter, for greasing

4 large eggs

1 vanilla bean, split

²/₃ cup all-purpose flour, sifted

1¹/₄ cups milk

pinch of salt

confectioners' sugar, to serve

METHOD

1 Toss the cherries with the kirsch and 2 tbsp of the sugar in a medium-sized bowl, and leave the fruit to stand for 30 minutes.

2 Meanwhile, preheat the oven to 400°F (200°C). Butter a 10in (25cm) flan tin or pie plate, and set aside.

3 Strain the liquid from the cherries and beat it with the eggs, the seeds from the vanilla bean, and the remaining sugar. Slowly beat in the flour, then add the milk and salt, and mix to make a smooth batter.

4 Arrange the cherries in the dish, then pour over the batter. Place in the oven and bake for 35–45 minutes, or until the top is lightly browned and the center is just firm to the touch.

5 Leave to cool slightly, then serve warm, dusted with confectioners' sugar. Clafoutis is also good served at room temperature.

Variation You can substitute damsons or other small plums for the cherries, adding more sugar if necessary, to compensate for the extra tartness.

CHERRIES

When to pick
Harvest cherries when they are a dark, glossy color, and as juicy as possible. Morello, or cooking, cherries are smaller and firmer than dessert cherries.

Eat and store fresh
Eat dessert varieties within 3 days of picking, if eating raw. Cooking cherries can be kept for 3–5 days in the fridge.

How to preserve
Cherries can be used to make all kinds of jams, jellies, cordials, and relishes, or can be bottled with alcohol (see pages 210–1). They can also be dried.

Freezing options
Remove pits and open freeze on trays, as a cooked or uncooked purée, as a freezer jam (see pages 176–7), or blanched or poached in sugar syrup (see pages 194–5).

This luscious jam has a hint of brandy in it to cut through the sweetness of the cherries. A cherry pitter is a useful device, but if you don't have one, halve the cherries and remove the stones.

Cherry jam

Makes approx. 2¼ lb (1kg) or 3 medium jars • **Prep** 20 mins • **Cooking** 30–35 mins

INGREDIENTS

1lb (500g) dark cherries, pitted, with the pits reserved

juice of 2 lemons

2½ cups granulated sugar, plus added pectin as per package instructions

2 tbsp brandy or cherry brandy

METHOD

1 Place the cherry pits in a small square of muslin, gather into a bag, and tie with kitchen string. Put the cherries in a preserving pan or a large heavy saucepan, with the bag of pits, and pour in 1¼ cups of water. Bring to a boil, then reduce to a simmer and cook for 10–15 minutes or until the cherries are tender and are beginning to soften. Discard the pits. If you want some of the cherries to remain chunky in the jam, don't cook them for too long.

2 Pour in the lemon juice and add the sugar and pectin mixture . Heat gently, stirring until all the sugar has dissolved. Bring to a boil and keep at a steady rolling boil, stirring occasionally, for about 10 minutes or until the jam reaches the setting point. Remove the pan from the heat while you test for a set (see pages 186–7).

3 Stir in the brandy, then ladle into warm sterilized jars, cover with discs of waxed paper, seal, and label.

Note Keeps for 9 months. Store in a cool, dark place, and refrigerate after opening.

Bottle fruit in alcohol

Many fruits bottle well in alcohol and make a luxurious treat that will taste better than anything available for sale. You will be spoiled for choice when deciding which seasonal fruits to treat this way. Fruits preserved in brandy, rum, whisky, vodka, gin, or eau de vie taste deliciously boozy. Serve with coffee, add to ice creams and other desserts along with the fragrant liquor, or use the fruits in cakes. This method particularly suits juicy, thin skinned berries, plums, and cherries. Once bottled, store in a cool, dark place for 2–3 months to mature before opening.

1 **Put cherries in jars** Carefully place the cherries in some wide-necked, sterilized preserving jars, packing them in tightly while taking care not to squash or bruise them.

2 **Fill with brandy** Add enough sugar to fill one-third of the jar and top with brandy. (As a general guide, use $1/4$–$1/3$ sugar and $3/4$–$2/3$ alcohol to fruit.)

Recipe Cherries in brandy

Makes approx. 3 cups, or 3 small preserving jars •
Prep 10 mins • **Keeps** 12 months or longer

INGREDIENTS

1lb (500g) firm but ripe
cherries (sweet or tart),
free of bruises, rinsed,
and stemmed (not pitted)

approx. ¾ cup
granulated sugar
approx. 1½ cups brandy

Other fruits to preserve in alcohol

Almost all fruits bottle well in alcohol, some exceptions being apples, melons, and rhubarb.

Blackberries Preserve in gin, vodka, or brandy.
Clementines Remove pith and preserve in vodka.
Nectarines and peaches Use sun-ripened, freshly-picked fruit, destone, and bottle in rum.
Pears Bottle in brandy or eau de vie.
Raspberries A classic fruit to add to a rumtopf, or to make liqueurs and cordials.
Plums Good in brandy with a cinnamon stick or star anise.

3 **Dissolve sugar** Tap the jar gently on a board and turn it to release air bubbles, and seal. Occasionally shake or turn the jar upside down to help the sugar dissolve.

4 **Leave to mature** Store in a cool, dark place for 2–3 months to allow the flavors to fully mature before opening. Refrigerate after opening.

When to pick
Pick peaches when they come away from the tree easily. They should give slightly if squeezed, and often have a pinkish blush and a sweet fragrance when ripe.

Eat and store fresh
Eat when slightly soft, at room temperature. Depending on when they are picked, they will keep for up to 5 days at room temperature.

How to preserve
Peaches can be sliced and dried, as well as used in all kinds of jams and jellies, savory chutneys, and preserves. They have a low pectin content, so crack the stones open and use the kernels to help setting, as with apricots.

Freezing options
Pit, slice, and open freeze on trays, as a cooked or uncooked purée, as a freezer jam (see pages 176–7), or blanched or poached in sugar syrup (see pages 194–5).

The classic peach melba is a delightful combination of vanilla ice cream, fresh peaches, and a raspberry sauce. The three flavors combine here to make a deliciously delicate and fragrant ice cream.

Peach melba ice cream

Serves 4–6 • **Prep** 30 mins, plus churning and freezing • **Cooking** 15 mins

INGREDIENTS

1$\frac{1}{4}$ cups heavy cream

1$\frac{1}{4}$ cups whole milk

3 large egg yolks

1 tsp vanilla extract

$\frac{3}{4}$ cup granulated sugar

4oz (100g) fresh raspberries

4 ripe peaches, peeled, pitted, and diced

METHOD

1 Heat the cream and milk gently in a saucepan until bubbles appear around the pan's edges, then remove the pan from the burner. In another bowl, whisk together egg yolks, vanilla extract, and $\frac{1}{2}$ cup of sugar until thick and pale yellow. Pour cream and milk over the egg mixture, whisking to blend. Return mixture to the cleaned pan. Bring to a boil, reduce heat to low, and cook 6–8 minutes, stirring until it coats the back of a spoon.

2 Transfer the mixture to a bowl and leave it to cool, stirring occasionally. Cover the surface with parchment or wax paper to prevent skinning.

3 Put raspberries and 2 tbsp of sugar in a bowl, mash, pass through a sieve and into a measuring cup. Mash peaches and 2 tbsp of sugar and pour into another bowl.

4 When cold, process the custard in an ice cream maker according to directions, or for 20–30 minutes, until nearly frozen. Add peach purée and process another 10–15 minutes to a frozen consistency. Transfer to a plastic container, drizzle raspberry purée over and draw it through to ripple. Freeze a few hours before eating.

This rich, chunky preserve is just as delicious spooned over ice cream as it is spread on freshly baked bread. Use only the ripest peaches for this sumptuous recipe.

Peach and walnut
preserve

Makes approx. 2¹/₄lbs (1kg) or 3 medium jars • **Prep** 25 mins • **Cooking** 20–25 mins

INGREDIENTS

2³/₄lb (1.25kg) ripe peaches

1 orange, peeled but with pith still attached, thinly sliced

5 cups granulated sugar

juice of 1 lemon

¹/₂ cup walnuts, coarsely chopped

1–2 tbsp brandy (optional)

METHOD

1 Cut a cross in the peach skins and plunge peaches into boiling water for 30 seconds. Plunge in cold water and peel away the skins. Cut them in half, remove the stones and reserve them, and then chop the flesh. Layer the peaches and orange slices in a large bowl with the sugar, cover, and leave for at least 4 hours or overnight.

2 Tip the fruit and sugar into a preserving pan or a large, heavy saucepan. Place the peach stones in a small square of muslin, gather into a bag, tie with string, and add it to the pan. Cook over gentle heat, stirring until the sugar dissolves. Bring to a boil and cook at a rolling boil for 15–20 minutes or until set. Remove the pan from the heat while you test for a set (see pages 186–7).

3 Remove the muslin bag of peach stones, then stir in the lemon juice, walnuts, and brandy (if using). Ladle into warm sterilized jars, cover with discs of waxed paper, seal, and label.

Note Store in a cool, dark place, and refrigerate after opening. Keeps for 6 months.

Here ripe peaches are surrounded with a delicate frangipane to produce a classic French fruit tart that would work equally well made with summer berries, apricots, plums, or nectarines.

Almond and peach
frangipane

Serves 8 • **Prep** 20 mins • **Cooking** 30 mins

INGREDIENTS

prepared dough for a 9in
     (23cm) pie or tart
7 tbsp butter, at room
     temperature
$1/2$ cup granulated sugar
2 large eggs
1 cup ground almonds
3 tbsp all-purpose flour,
plus extra to dust
4 peaches, halved and pitted
confectioners' sugar, to dust
     for serving

METHOD

1 Preheat the oven to 400°F (200°C). Put a heavy baking sheet in the oven to heat up. On a surface lightly dusted with flour, roll out the dough to a thickness of about $1/4$in (5mm), and line a rectangular tart pan measuring 5 x $14^1/_2$in (12 x 36cm). Trim off the excess dough with a knife and set the tart shell aside while you make the filling.

2 Place the butter and sugar in a bowl and beat with an electric hand mixer until creamy, then beat in the eggs, one at a time, until well blended. Mix in the ground almonds and flour just until well combined, then spread the mixture over the tart shell. Press the peach halves cut-side down into the almond mixture.

3 Place the pan on the hot baking sheet, and then bake for 30 minutes or until the crust is golden brown and the almond mixture is cooked through. Dust with confectioners' sugar before serving warm or at room temperature.

Pork works beautifully with soft fruits like apricots. The addition of cream and whiskey turns this speedy supper into something truly special. Wonderful served with mashed potato.

Caramelized pork
with pecans and apricots

Serves 4 • Prep 10 mins • Cooking 15 mins

INGREDIENTS

1–2 tsp light soft brown sugar

1½lb (675g) pork tenderloin
   (in one piece)

1 tbsp extra virgin olive oil

knob of butter

handful of pecans

handful of apricots, halved
   and pitted

splash of whiskey (optional)

1¼ cups (300ml) heavy cream

METHOD

1 Rub the brown sugar over the pork, then slice the pork crosswise into medallions about $^3/_4$ in (2cm) thick.

2 Heat the oil and butter in a frying pan over medium high heat. Brown the pork medallions for 3–4 minutes on each side until golden. Remove the pork from the pan and add the pecans, browning them in the hot oil for 2 minutes or until barely browned. Return the pork to the pan and add the apricot halves.

3 Increase the heat to high and add the whiskey (if using). Let it simmer for 2 minutes until the alcohol has evaporated. Reduce the heat to medium, pour over the cream and let it simmer for 2–3 minutes more, making sure that the apricots are tender but not collapsing.

APRICOTS

When to pick
Pick apricots when they have a deep color and a sweet fragrance. They should come away easily from the branch. Do not allow them to become too soft.

Eat and store fresh
Keep at room temperature and eat within 2–3 days of harvesting if eating raw. If cooking, they can be kept for 3–5 days in the fridge.

How to preserve
Apricots make delicious jams (see page 219) and jellies. Their low pectin content can be offset by adding some of the kernels, cracked and wrapped in muslin, to the pan to aid setting.

Freezing options
Pit, slice, and open freeze on trays, as a cooked or uncooked purée, as a freezer jam (see pages 176–7), or blanched or poached in sugar syrup (see pages 194–5).

This sticky, delicious concoction may not be the most elegant of desserts, but it certainly makes up for it flavor-wise. If you grow apricots, then this simple recipe is sure to become a favorite.

Apricot and toffee
brioche pudding

Serves 4 • **Prep** 10 mins • **Cooking** 8–10 mins

INGREDIENTS

4 tbsp butter

1¹/₃ cups light brown sugar

finely grated zest and juice
    of ¹/₂ lemon

4 thick slices of brioche, cut
    into large cubes

1lb (450g) apricots, pitted and
    quartered

Greek-style, or other thick
    yogurt, clotted cream,
    or ice cream, to serve

METHOD

1 Put the butter into a nonstick wok, or large frying pan. Place over medium heat until melted. Add the sugar, lemon zest, and juice. Continue to cook, stirring, until the sugar has melted. Turn down the heat. Add the brioche cubes and toss gently to coat, keeping the brioche as whole as possible.

2 Gently fold in the apricots. Cover and cook over low heat until the apricots are tender, for about 5 minutes. Leave the mixture to cool slightly and serve warm. Or, cool completely, and then chill before serving with Greek-style or other thick plain yogurt, clotted cream, or vanilla ice cream.

Note You can use any stone fruit for this recipe, but with tart fruit, add 1 tablespoon of water instead of lemon juice. You can also use challah or another bread if you prefer, but brioche gives a lovely richness and texture.

Apricots produce luscious, richly flavored jams. The dense, sugary sweetness of this preserve makes it perfect for an indulgent breakfast, served with fresh bread or a croissant.

Apricot jam

Makes approx. 1kg (2¼lb) or 3 medium jars • **Prep** 10 mins • **Cooking** 30–35 mins

INGREDIENTS

1½lb (675g) apricots, pitted
   and coarsely chopped
1 tbsp fresh lemon juice
3¾ cups granulated sugar, plus
   added
pectin as per package
   instructions

METHOD

1 Put the apricots, lemon juice, and ½ cup of water in a preserving pan or a large heavy saucepan. Gently bring to a boil and simmer, stirring occasionally, for 15 minutes or until the apricot skins are soft and the fruit is tender.

2 Add the sugar and pectin mixture to the pan and stir until completely dissolved. Increase the heat and bring the mixture to a boil. Boil without stirring for 10 minutes or until it reaches the setting point. Remove the pan from the heat while you test for a set (see pages 186-7).

3 With the pan still off the heat, use a skimmer to remove any foam that rises to the top. Ladle the jam into warm sterilized jars, cover with discs of waxed paper, seal, and label.

Note Keeps for 6–9 months. Store in a cool, dark place, and refrigerate after opening.

Make conserves

Conserves differ from jams in that they contain large pieces of fruit or whole fruits and can be made with less sugar. The fruits are steeped in sugar before cooking to firm them up, and they are boiled more gently than jam. They can be used in different ways, such as glazes for fruit tarts and flans, as cake fillings, or on yogurt. They can also be served like jam with bread. The best fruits for making conserves include apricots, blackberries, greengages, dessert plums, strawberries, cherries, and nectarines.

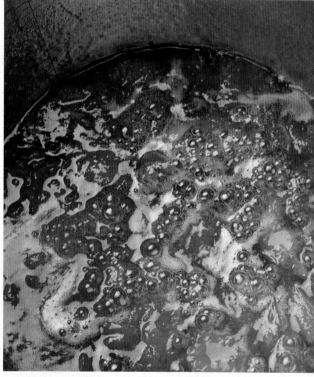

1 Layer the apricots and sugar Wash, halve, and destone the apricots. Layer them with the sugar in a bowl, cover, and leave for 2–3 hours or overnight at room temperature.

2 Bring to a boil Put fruit and sugar into a preserving pan with the lemon juice. Heat gently, stir. Do not break up the fruit. Bring to a steady boil for 7–10 minutes.

Recipe Apricot conserve

Makes 1½lb (700g) or 2 medium jars • **Prep** 25–30
mins, plus standing • **Keeps** 6 months

INGREDIENTS

1lb (500g) ripe apricots

1⅔ cups granulated sugar

juice of 1 lemon

Tips on making conserves

Adapt the basic conserve recipe shown here in
the following ways for slightly different results.

Use less sugar Use up to ¼ cup less sugar for
a fresher fruit flavor.

Make a luxurious conserve Add a small glass
of wine at the same time as the sugar, or a
splash of liqueur or spirit just before bottling.

Keep the fruit intact Try not to stir once
the sugar has dissolved. Set juicy fruit aside in
step 2. Boil the sugar and juices until reduced.
Add the fruit and complete the boiling process.

3 **Test for a set** Take the pan off the
heat, test for a set with a cold saucer
(see page 187), then leave to cool until
it has formed a wrinkle on the surface.

4 **Pot up and store** Ladle into clean, hot,
sterilized jars, ensuring an even amount of
juice and fruit per jar. Cover with waxed
paper, seal, label, and store in a cool, dark place.

AUTUMN

Pumpkins and squash	Sweet potatoes
Onions	Cranberries
Shallots	Grapes
Garlic	Apples
Kohlrabi	Pears
Celery	Quinces
Beets	Plums
Carrots	Figs

PUMPKINS AND SQUASH

When to pick
Pick summer squash often. Leave pumpkins and winter squash until the foliage is dying back, harvest with 4in of the stem, and leave them in the sun for 1 week to cure (see page 263).

Eat and store fresh
Store summer squash for up to 5 days in the fridge. Winter squash and pumpkins keep for up to 6 months in a cool, dark place.

How to preserve
Both varieties can be used in chutneys, pickles, and relishes.

Freezing options
Slice, blanch briefly, cool, and freeze summer squash for up to 6 months. Cut pumpkin and winter squash into chunks and freeze raw for up to 6 months.

In this delicious autumn soup, the natural sweetness of the pumpkin is offset by sharp apples. Garnishing the finished soup with toasted pumpkin seeds adds a welcome crunch.

Pumpkin
and apple soup

Serves 6 • **Prep** 20 mins • **Cooking** 40 mins

INGREDIENTS

4 tbsp unsalted butter

1 medium onion, finely chopped

8oz (200g) pumpkin, peeled, seeds removed, and diced

2 tart apples, such as Granny Smith, peeled and diced

5 cups cold vegetable stock or chicken stock

sea salt and freshly ground black pepper

$1/4$ cup hulled pumpkin seeds, to garnish

METHOD

1 Melt the butter in a soup pot or large saucepan, add the onion, and cook gently, stirring often, for 10 minutes, or until soft. Do not let it brown. Add the pumpkin and apples and stir to coat. Pour in $1/2$ cup hot water, cover with a lid, and leave on very low heat for 30 minutes, stirring from time to time. If the liquid evaporates, add a little more hot water into the pan. Vegetables and fruit should be very soft at the end of cooking.

2 Meanwhile, toast the pumpkin seeds in a dry frying pan over medium heat, just until browned. Set aside.

3 Stir the stock into the pumpkin-apple mixture, then puree with a hand-held blender, or in batches in a food processor. Pour the blended soup through a sieve, set over a clean saucepan. Press the contents through with the back of a ladle, a wooden spoon, or a pestle, and then discard the solids.

4 When the soup has been sieved, reheat it very gently, then season to taste with salt and freshly ground black pepper. Serve garnished with the toasted pumpkin seeds

Here a punchy combination of mint, lime, chili, and ginger enhances the sweetness of the squash. This is a fantastic side dish for roast beef or chicken.

Roasted squash
with ginger

Serves 3–4 • **Prep** 20 mins • **Cooking** 40 mins

INGREDIENTS

1 butternut squash, peeled, seeds removed and sliced into big, thick strips

5 tbsp extra virgin olive oil

1 tsp salt

2 hot red chiles, seeded and finely chopped

2oz (60g) fresh ginger, peeled and grated or thinly sliced

1 tbsp honey

freshly ground black pepper

handful of fresh mint leaves, torn

2 limes, cut into wedges

METHOD

1 Preheat the oven to 350°F (180°C). Place the slices of squash in a shallow roasting pan. Mix together 2 tbsp warm water, the olive oil, salt, chiles, ginger, honey, and pepper to taste. Drizzle the sauce over the squash, mixing to coat well.

2 Bake the squash for 40 minutes, or until tender, shaking occasionally during cooking to avoid sticking. If the squash dries out, add a little more olive oil.

3 Transfer the warm squash to a large serving dish, and scatter with the mint. Serve with lime wedges to squeeze over.

This spicy vivid orange dip can be served slightly chunky, or processed until smooth. Try it served on grilled sourdough bread with grilled pancetta on top.

Roasted pumpkin
and ginger dip

Serves 8 • **Prep** 20 mins • **Cooking** 30 mins

INGREDIENTS

$2^{1}/_{4}$lb (1kg) pumpkin, peeled, seeds removed, and cut into chunks

$^{1}/_{4}$ cup extra virgin olive oil, plus extra for drizzling over (optional)

4 whole garlic cloves, crushed with the flat side of a knife

1 tbsp grated or finely chopped fresh ginger

sea salt and freshly ground black pepper

1 medium-hot, long red chile, seeded and coarsely chopped

4 sprigs of flat-leaf parsley, leaves only

finely grated zest and juice of 1 lemon

$^{2}/_{3}$ cup Greek-style plain yogurt pinch of paprika

METHOD

1 Preheat the oven to 400°F (200°C). Put the pumpkin on a baking tray, and toss with the olive oil, garlic, and ginger. Season with salt and black pepper. Roast for about 30 minutes until tender and golden. Remove from the oven and leave to cool.

2 Transfer the cooled pumpkin to a blender or food processor, and add the chile, parsley leaves (reserving a few to garnish), and lemon zest and juice. Blend to a chunky or smooth puree, depending on preference.

3 Put the pumpkin puree and the yogurt in a bowl, and mix thoroughly. Season if needed, then spoon into a serving bowl. Top with a drizzle of extra virgin olive oil (if using). Garnish with the reserved parsley and paprika.

Variation The recipe works equally well with butternut squash.

Ripening pumpkins and squash herald the onset of autumn. This pasta dish is perfect for those slightly cooler days, since it has the comfort of cream and the warmth of red chiles.

Pasta with butternut
squash, chile, and Parmesan sauce

Serves 4 • **Prep** 20 mins • **Cooking** 30 mins

INGREDIENTS

8oz (200g) butternut squash, peeled, seeded, and diced

1–2 tbsp extra virgin olive oil

sea salt and freshly ground black pepper

1 garlic clove, crushed

1/2 hot red chile, seeded and finely chopped

8 fresh sage leaves, torn into pieces

1/2 cup half-and-half

1/4 cup freshly grated Parmesan cheese, plus extra to finish

12oz (350g) shell-shaped pasta (conchiglie)

METHOD

1 Preheat the oven to 400°F (200°C). On a baking sheet, toss the squash with enough olive oil to coat, season it well with salt and freshly ground pepper, and spread it in an even layer. Roast for 30 minutes or until soft. Remove it from the oven and leave to cool for a few minutes.

2 Meanwhile, cook the garlic, chile, and sage in a little olive oil over low heat for 1–2 minutes until fragrant.

3 Once the squash has cooled slightly, put it into a blender or food processor. Add the half-and-half, Parmesan, garlic mixture, plenty of black pepper, and a little salt. Process to a fine purée, adding 1–2 tablespoons of water if needed.

4 Cook the pasta in a pot of salted boiling water until al dente, and drain it in a colander. Quickly reheat the sauce in the pasta pot, adding more water if it seems too thick. Put the pasta back into the pot and mix it well, allowing the sauce to coat the pasta. Serve with plenty of freshly grated Parmesan to finish.

Most squash ripen once the summer is drawing to a close, and the cook's thoughts naturally turn toward autumnal fare. This spicy tagine fits the bill, using the best of the late-summer produce.

Butternut squash tagine

Serves 4 • **Prep** 20 mins • **Cooking** 1 hour

INGREDIENTS

¼ cup light olive oil

2 red onions, finely chopped

1 large red bell pepper, seeded, and diced

4 garlic cloves, chopped

1 thumb-sized piece of ginger, peeled and finely chopped

1 tbsp ground cumin

2 tsp smoked paprika

2 tsp ground coriander

1 tsp chili powder

1 tsp ground cinnamon

2 x 14.5oz cans diced tomatoes

3 cups vegetable stock

2 tbsp honey

sea salt and freshly ground black pepper

1lb (400g) butternut squash, peeled, seeded, and diced

1 cup cooked chickpeas

1 cup dried apricot halves, chopped

bunch of cilantro, chopped

METHOD

1 Pour the olive oil into a large saucepan over low heat. Add the onions, red pepper, garlic, and ginger, and cook, stirring often, for about 5 minutes until the vegetables are softened, but not brown.

2 Add the cumin, smoked paprika, ground coriander, chili powder, and cinnamon, and continue to cook for another 2 minutes over low heat, to release the flavors of the spices. Add the tomatoes, stock, and honey, and season well. Bring the sauce to a boil and turn down the heat. Simmer slowly, uncovered, for 30 minutes.

3 Add the butternut squash, chickpeas, and dried apricots and continue to cook for 10–15 minutes until the squash is soft, but not falling apart. Add more water if it is beginning to look a little dry. Season to taste and stir in the fresh cilantro before serving with some herbed couscous.

Note Canned chickpeas (garbanzo beans) can be used here, although dried ones that have been soaked overnight, then cooked until tender, give a better final texture.

Make this wonderful vegetarian tart in the early autumn when spinach and squash are readily available in the garden. If you grow chard, you can use it in place of the spinach.

Roasted squash
and Gorgonzola tart

Serves 6 • **Prep** 25 mins, plus chilling • **Cooking** 1 $\frac{1}{2}$ hours

INGREDIENTS

prepared dough for an 8in
(20cm) pie or tart
1lb (450g) butternut or other
winter squash, peeled, seeds
removed, thickly sliced
1–2 tbsp extra virgin olive oil
1lb (450g) spinach leaves
2 large eggs
1 egg yolk
1$\frac{1}{4}$ cups heavy cream
$\frac{1}{2}$ cup freshly grated Parmesan
cheese
pinch of freshly grated nutmeg
salt and freshly ground black
pepper
1 cup crumbled Gorgonzola
cheese

METHOD

1 Preheat the oven to 350°F (180°C). On a surface lightly dusted with flour, roll out the dough to about $\frac{1}{8}$in (3mm) thick in a circle a little larger than an 8in (20cm) tart pan with a removable bottom. Line the pan with the dough, trimming off any excess. Chill for 30 minutes.

2 Put the squash slices on a roasting tray and brush with olive oil. Bake for 30 minutes, or until tender. Meanwhile, place the spinach and a little olive oil in a large saucepan and cook over medium heat for 4 minutes until wilted. Drain and leave to cool. Whisk the eggs, egg yolk, cream, Parmesan, and nutmeg together, and season to taste.

3 Line the pastry shell with parchment paper, and fill with pie weights or beans. Bake for 15 minutes. Remove weights and paper, and bake another 10 minutes.

4 Squeeze the spinach dry and spread it in the tart shell, then add the squash and Gorgonzola. Pour the egg mixture over and bake for 30–40 minutes, or until the filling is set. Remove from the oven and cool 10 minutes. before serving.

A selection of vegetables is simmered in Indian spices and vinegar to give this colorful chutney its flavor. If you like a hotter chutney, add one or two finely chopped green chiles.

Indian-spiced
vegetable chutney

Makes approx. 3lb 3oz (1.5kg) or 3 large jars • **Prep** 30 mins • **Cooking** 2–2¼ hours

INGREDIENTS

2lbs (900g) butternut squash, seeds removed, peeled, and cut into bite-sized chunks

2 onions, finely chopped

8oz (225g) cooking apples, such as Granny Smith, peeled, cored, and chopped

3 zucchini, halved lengthwise and chopped

$^1/_2$ cup chopped pitted dates

2 cups cider vinegar

2 tbsp medium or hot curry powder

1 tsp ground cumin

1in (2.5cm) piece of fresh ginger, peeled and grated or finely chopped

$2^1/_2$ cups (450g) granulated or light brown sugar

METHOD

1 Put the squash, onions, apples, zucchini, and dates in a preserving pan or a large heavy, stainless steel saucepan. Pour over the vinegar, add the spices, and ginger, and mix well.

2 Bring the mixture to a boil, then reduce the heat and simmer for 40–45 minutes or until the vegetables are soft, stirring occasionally.

3 Add the sugar, stir until it has dissolved, then continue to cook on a gentle simmer for 1–1½ hours or until the chutney is thick and the liquid has been absorbed. Stir continuously near the end of the cooking time so that the chutney doesn't stick to the pan.

4 Ladle into warm sterilized jars with non-metallic or vinegar-proof lids, making sure there are no air gaps. Cover each jar with a waxed paper disc, seal, and label.

Note Keeps for 12 months. Store in a cool, dark place. Allow the flavors to mature for at least 1 month, and refrigerate after opening.

This subtly spiced jam is superb served with strong blue cheese, or as a sweet jam spread on toast or bread. Choose smaller pumpkins with smooth flesh and a good flavor.

Pumpkin and orange
spiced jam

Makes approx. 4½lb (2kg) or 4 large jars • **Prep** 15 mins • **Cooking** 35–45 mins

INGREDIENTS

3lb (1.35kg) pumpkin, peeled, seeded, and chopped

2 cooking apples, such as Granny Smith, peeled and chopped small

7½ cups granulated sugar

juice of 1 lemon

juice of 1 orange

pinch of ground cinnamon

pinch of freshly grated nutmeg

METHOD

1 Put the pumpkin and apple in a preserving pan or a large heavy saucepan. Pour in ¼ cup of water (just enough to keep the pumpkin from sticking and burning). Bring to a boil, then reduce to a simmer and cook for 10–20 minutes or until the pumpkin is soft. Mash roughly with a potato masher or fork, keeping a few chunks of pumpkin whole.

2 Add the sugar, lemon and orange juice, cinnamon, and nutmeg. Stir until all the sugar has dissolved. Then turn the heat up and bring to a boil. Cook at a rolling boil for 15–20 minutes or until the jam thickens and reaches the setting point. Remove the pan from the heat while you test for a set (see pages 186–7).

3 Ladle into warm sterilized jars, cover with waxed paper discs, seal, and label.

Note Store in a cool, dark place, and refrigerate after opening. Keeps for 6 months.

ONIONS

When to pick
Harvest onions when they reach a good size and the leaves begin to yellow. Leave to dry in the sun for 2 weeks to allow the skins to harden before storing.

Eat and store fresh
Milder red onions can be eaten raw in salads. All onions should be dried off and stored in a cool, dark place for 2–3 months (see pages 248–9).

How to preserve
A vital ingredient in pickles, relishes, and chutneys, onions can also star in recipes, such as red onion marmalade (see page 241).

This timeless, warming soup is one of the best ways to use onions through the winter months. The brandy is optional, but the crispy croûtes oozing with melting Gruyère are not!

French onion soup

Serves 4 • **Prep** 10 mins • **Cooking** 1 hour 20 mins

INGREDIENTS

2 tbsp butter

1 tbsp sunflower or vegetable oil

1¹/₂ lbs (675g) onions, thinly sliced

1 tsp granulated sugar

sea salt and freshly ground black pepper

¹/₂ cup dry red wine

2 tbsp all-purpose flour

6 cups hot beef stock

4 x ¹/₂in (1cm)-thick slices from a 1 day-old baguette

4 tbsp brandy

1 garlic clove, cut in half

1 cup shredded Gruyère or emmental cheese

METHOD

1 Melt the butter with the oil in a soup pot or large, heavy pan over low heat. Add the onions and sugar, and stir to coat. Season, then press a piece of damp parchment paper on the onions. Cook, uncovered, stirring occasionally for 40 minutes, or until the onions are a rich, dark brown. Take care not to let the onions burn.

2 Remove the paper and stir in the wine. Increase the heat to medium and stir for 5 minutes while the onions glaze. Sprinkle in the flour and cook for 2 minutes, stirring; then pour in the stock and bring to a boil. Reduce the heat to low, cover, and simmer for 30 minutes. Taste and season with salt and pepper.

3 To make the croûtes, toast the bread until golden. Alternatively, place on a baking sheet and bake in a preheated 350°F (180°C) oven for 15 minutes.

4 Preheat the broiler. Divide the soup among 4 flameproof bowls and stir 1 tbsp of the brandy into each. Rub the croûtes with cut garlic, place one croûte in each bowl. Sprinkle the croûtes with the cheese and broil for 2–3 minutes or until the cheese is bubbling and golden.

The saltiness of the anchovies gives a welcome piquancy to this mild onion tart, which can be prepared a day in advance and reheated. Serve with a green salad.

Onion and anchovy tart

Serves 4–6 • **Prep** 15 mins, plus chilling • **Cooking** 1¹/₄ hours

INGREDIENTS

prepared dough for an
    8in (20cm) pie or tart
2 tbsp extra virgin olive oil
2 tbsp butter
1lb (450g) onions, thinly sliced
1¹/₂lbs (750g) cottage cheese
¹/₂ cup whole milk
2 large eggs
1 tsp cumin seeds or caraway
    seeds, crushed (optional)
sea salt and freshly ground
    black pepper
1 x 2oz can of flat anchovy
    fillets packed in olive oil,
    drained and halved
    lengthwise

METHOD

1 On a surface lightly dusted with flour, roll out the dough to a thickness of about ¹/₈in (3mm) in a circle a little larger than an 8in (20cm) tart pan with a removable bottom. Line the tart pan with the pastry dough, trimming off excess. Chill for 30 minutes.

2 Heat the oil and butter in a pan, and add the onions. Cover and cook over low heat, stirring occasionally, for 20 minutes, or until the onions are soft, but not browned.

3 Preheat the oven to 400°F (200°C). Remove the pan from the fridge, line the tart shell with parchment paper, and fill with pie weights or baking beans. Bake for 15 minutes. Remove the weights and paper, and bake for another 10 minutes.

4 Reduce the oven temperature to 350°F (180°C). Spoon the onions into the pastry shell, spreading them in an even layer. Beat together the cottage cheese, milk, eggs, and spices, if using. Season to taste with salt and pepper, then pour over the onions. Lay the anchovy fillets in a lattice pattern on top, and bake for 25 minutes, or until the pastry is golden and the filling is set. Serve the tart while still warm.

This delicious marmalade made with sweet, sticky onions has become a modern classic. It is perfect served with cold meats and cheese.

Red onion marmalade

Makes approx. 1½lb (700g) or 2 medium jars • **Prep** 20 mins • **Cooking** 1 hour 10 mins

INGREDIENTS

2 tbsp extra virgin olive oil

2¼lb (1kg) red onions (approx. 6), peeled, halved, and sliced

sea salt and freshly ground black pepper

½ cup dry red wine

3 tbsp balsamic vinegar

3 tbsp white wine vinegar

6 tbsp light brown sugar

METHOD

1 Heat the oil in a preserving pan or a large, heavy, stainless steel saucepan. Add the onions, a pinch of salt, and some pepper. Cook over low to medium heat for about 30 minutes until the onions soften and turn translucent, stirring occasionally so they don't stick and burn. Slow cooking is essential at this point, since this is where the delicious caramel flavor is developed.

2 Raise the heat a little, add the wine and vinegars, and stir to combine. Bring to a boil, then reduce the heat, stir in the sugar, and cook on low heat, stirring occasionally, for another 30–40 minutes until most of the liquid has evaporated.

3 Remove the pan from the heat. Taste and adjust the seasoning as necessary, although the flavors will mature with time. Spoon into warm, sterilized jars with non-metallic or vinegar-proof lids, making sure there are no air gaps. Cover with waxed paper discs, seal, and label. Store in a cool, dark place for at least 1 month to allow the flavors to develop.

Note Keeps for 3 months. Refrigerate after opening.

These crispy fritters are made with besan flour, which is sold in Indian, Middle Eastern, or Asian markets. Serve with a simple raita made of Greek-style yogurt, crushed garlic, and mint.

Onion bhajis

Serves 4 • **Prep** 15 mins • **Cooking** 15 mins

INGREDIENTS

8oz (225g) onions, chopped

4oz (115g) besan (also called
    chickpea flour or gram flour)

2 tsp cumin seeds

$1/2$ tsp turmeric

1 tsp ground coriander

1 hot green or red chile, seeded,
    and very finely chopped

vegetable oil, for frying

METHOD

1 In a large bowl, mix together onions, besan, cumin seeds, turmeric, coriander, and chile . Add enough cold water (about $1/2$ cup) to bind the mixture into a batter.

2 Half fill a deep pan or deep-fat fryer with oil, and heat to 375°F (190°C). Carefully place spoonfuls of the mixture, the size of golf balls, into the hot oil without crowding. Turn occasionally, until all sides are golden.

3 Remove bhajis from the oil using a slotted spoon, and drain on paper towels. Repeat with the remaining batter.

4 Just before serving, return the bhajis to the hot oil and quickly fry for a second time, just until crisp and golden brown all over. Drain on paper towels and serve hot. The bhajis can be cooked up to the end of step 3 up to 4 hours in advance, and then given their second frying just before serving.

Variation To make vegetable bhajis, replace one-third of the onion with shredded spinach or grated carrot.

These smaller members of the allium family make a mild, sweet pickle using rich balsamic vinegar. Pour boiling water over the shallots for a few minutes, and then drain, for easier peeling.

Pickled sweet shallots

Makes approx. 1lb (500g) • **Prep** 10 mins • **Cooking** 30–35 mins

INGREDIENTS

1¼ lb (550g) shallots, peeled

a few sprigs of fresh thyme

1 tbsp extra virgin olive oil

¾ cup balsamic vinegar, plus extra if needed

METHOD

1 Preheat the oven to 400°F (200°C). Put the shallots and thyme sprigs into a shallow roasting pan, then add the olive oil, and mix with your hands to coat the shallots evenly. Roast for about 20–25 minutes or until the shallots are beginning to soften (they should no longer be crunchy).

2 Pour the balsamic vinegar into a stainless steel pan, bring it to a boil, and cook for a few minutes until it reduces. Don't let it cook away for too long, or it will become too sticky. Add the roasted shallots and thyme sprigs, and stir so that they all get evenly coated in the reduced vinegar.

3 Spoon the shallots, along with the vinegar and thyme, into a warm sterilized jar with a non-metallic or vinegar-proof lid. Pack the shallots in tightly and top up with extra balsamic vinegar so that the shallots are completely covered. Seal, label, and turn the jar upside down to combine the ingredients thoroughly.

Note Store in a cool, dark place for 2 weeks to mature. Refrigerate after opening. Keeps for 6 months.

SHALLOTS

When to pick
Harvest when the leaves turn yellow, and the shallots are a good size. Leave to dry in the sun for 2 weeks to allow the skins to harden before storing.

Eat and store fresh
Shallots are milder than onions, and can be used where the taste of onions would be too strong. After drying, store shallots in a cool, dark place (see pages 248–9).

How to preserve
Shallots can be used in the same way as onions in pickles, relishes, and chutneys. They can also be char-grilled and preserved whole in oil.

The allium family is indispensable to most cooks, yet we rarely find ways of allowing onions and shallots to take center stage. This simple lunch recipe gives shallots a starring role.

Caramelized shallot tart

Serves 4–6 • **Prep** 20 mins, plus chilling • **Cooking** 45 mins

INGREDIENTS

2 tbsp butter

2 tbsp extra virgin olive oil

1lb (400g) shallots, peeled and
    split in half lengthwise

2 tbsp balsamic vinegar

a few sprigs of fresh thyme

For the pastry

11 cups all-purpose flour

sea salt

5 tbsp cold butter,
    cut into pieces

or 1 sheet of prepared pie
    dough for a 9–10in
    (23–25cm) pie

METHOD

1 To make the pastry: In a food processor, combine flour, a pinch of salt, and the butter. Process, pulsing the machine, until the mixture resembles fine bread crumbs. With the motor running, add cold water, 1 tablespoon at a time, until the pastry sticks together to form a ball. Wrap pastry in plastic wrap and refrigerate 30 minutes.

2 Preheat the oven to 400°F (200°C) In a 9–10in (23–25cm) ovenproof frying pan, melt 2 tbsp butter with the olive oil. Add shallots, cut-side down, and cook gently over low heat for 10 minutes, until nicely browned. Turn them over and cook for another 5 minutes. Add the balsamic vinegar and 2 tbsp of water, then remove from the heat. Tuck the thyme sprigs between the shallots.

3 Roll out the pastry to a circle a little larger than the frying pan. Lay the pastry over the shallots, trim the edges, and tuck them inside the pan. Transfer to oven and bake 30 minutes until golden brown.

4 Remove the pan from the oven and tap it on the counter to loosen the shallots. Run a knife around the edges of the pastry, put a plate over the pan and invert quickly. Cut into wedges and serve warm with a salad.

Garlic is roasted before being added to this versatile, warm sauce. It works well with grilled meat or fish.

GARLIC

When to pick
Harvest garlic when the leaves droop and turn yellow. Leave it to dry in the sun for 2 weeks before storing. Harvest fresh "wet" garlic when the leaves are green.

Eat and store fresh
Wet garlic should be stored in the fridge and eaten within a week. Dried garlic can be stored for 4 months in a cool, dark place (see pages 248–9).

How to preserve
Garlic can be dried or smoked, and used in chutneys, pickles, and relishes.

Freezing options
Garlic can be crushed and mixed with a little water or oil, and frozen in ice cube trays. It can also be made into garlic butter (see page 149) and frozen.

Simple garlic sauce

Makes 1 cup (200–250ml) • **Prep** 15 mins • **Cooking** 1 hour 10 mins

INGREDIENTS

2 heads garlic, broken into
    unpeeled cloves

2 tbsp extra virgin olive oil

$^2/_3$ cup half-and-half

sea salt and freshly ground
    black pepper

METHOD

1 Preheat the oven to 250°F (130°C). Put the garlic cloves in a small bowl, drizzle with the olive oil, and mix with your hands to coat the garlic cloves. Line a shallow roasting pan with foil, add the garlic, and cover loosely with foil. Place in the oven and bake for about 1 hour, until the garlic becomes very soft.

2 Take out of the oven and tip the cloves onto a plate. Once cool, squeeze each clove to push the pulp into a bowl. Mash briefly with a fork.

3 Warm the half-and-half in a small saucepan placed over low heat. Take off the heat and thoroughly whisk in the mashed garlic pulp. Season with salt and pepper to taste, and reheat gently until hot but not simmering.

Variation Stir in 1 tsp ground cumin or coriander, and/or 2 tsp grated fresh ginger. Replace the half-and-half with the same quantity of drained, plain full-fat yogurt, or with stock, finishing the sauce by gradually whisking in 1$^1/_2$ tbsp diced cold butter until melted and smooth.

Note Sauce can be refrigerated for a day and reheated.

In southern France this rich sauce is used as an accompaniment to raw or lightly steamed baby vegetables and hard-boiled eggs. Try it with baby beans, peas, carrots, and zucchini.

Aïoli

Makes 1¹/₄ cups • **Prep** 20 mins, plus resting

INGREDIENTS

2 large garlic cloves, smashed
    with the flat side of a knife
    and peeled
sea salt
1 large egg yolk
freshly ground black pepper
³/₄ to 1 cup mild olive oil

METHOD

1 Using a mortar and pestle, pound the garlic with a small pinch of salt. Add the egg yolk and season with pepper. Beat for 1 minute and then leave to rest for 5 minutes.

2 Beat in some oil, a few drops at a time, to form an emulsion. Then gradually pour in the remaining oil in a thin trickle, beating always with the pestle moving in the same direction. The aïoli is ready once it has a thick texture. (A wooden pestle will almost stand up by itself in the bowl.)

3 Cover and refrigerate up to 24 hours until time to use.

Store onions, garlic, and shallots

Onions and garlic store well indoors and take up very little space. They can be strung up in nets or old stockings, or "cured" and plaited as shown here. Harvest mid- to late-summer, when the bulbs have swollen and leaves are yellowing. If plaiting, pick them before the outer leaves have suffered too much decay.

Plaiting garlic or onion bulbs

1 Clean the bulbs Brush the bulbs lightly to remove excess soil and dirty outer skins. Leave the stems still attached and cut off the roots at the base of each bulb.

2 Tie them together Take 3 onion or garlic bulbs, lay them on top of one another at angles so that the bulbs are nestled together.

Curing and storage conditions

Curing Ordinarily, onions, garlic, and shallots must be left to dry out, or "cured", before they can be stored and used for cooking. Once harvested, leave them to cure for 2 weeks in a warm, dry place, or outside in suitable weather on a dry path or on pallets or upturned boxes, turning them to expose all sides to the sun. They are ready to plait and store when the skins are papery and the stems have shrivelled. However, do not let the stems dry so much that they become brittle; there should still be a little moisture at the centre of them.

Storing plaits Hang in a well-ventilated, cold room, ideally 33–41°F (1–5°C), to prevent green shoots sprouting from the bulbs. Humidity and lack of ventilation will cause mould.

Storing shallots Harvest and cure shallots in the same way as onions and garlic. Store long-term in nets or boxes somewhere cool and airy, and when needed in the kitchen, move them to a basket or vegetable rack.

3 **Plait the garlic or onions** Set a bulb straight on top, and criss-cross 2 more over that. Divide the stems into 3 strands of 2 stems each and plait.

4 **Hang up to store** Continue to plait the stems, adding 3 new bulbs every time, until you have a plait long enough to hang up. Tie off in a knot at the end.

KOHLRABI

When to pick
Harvest kohlrabi when it is no bigger than a tennis ball, or it may turn woody.

Eat and store fresh
Small golf-ball-sized kohlrabi can be grated and eaten raw in salads or coleslaws, immediately after picking. Trim and store larger ones in the fridge for up to 5 days before cooking.

Freezing options
Freeze cooked purées and store in freezer pots. Thaw out before reheating to serve.

This is a variation of a classic potato dauphinoise, enlivened with the addition of finely sliced kohlrabi, a brassica that has the taste and crunch of a broccoli stem or cabbage heart.

Kohlrabi
and potato gratin

Serves 4–6 • Prep 15–20 mins • Cooking 1½ hours

INGREDIENTS

3 tbsp butter, at room temperature, plus extra for greasing

1lb (450g) evenly-sized waxy potatoes, peeled

1lb (450g) kohlrabi, peeled, trimmed, and quartered

sea salt and freshly ground black pepper

2½ cups heavy cream

1 garlic clove, cut in half

pinch of freshly grated nutmeg

2 tbsp butter, cut into bits

METHOD

1 Preheat the oven to 350°F (180°C). Butter a 1½ quart (1.4 liter) gratin dish.

2 Using a mandoline or a food processor, slice the potatoes and kohl rabi quarters into even rounds, about ⅛in (3mm) thick. Rinse the slices in cold water, drain, and pat dry with a paper towel or clean tea towel.

3 Arrange the potatoes and kohlrabi in layers in the prepared dish. Season with salt and pepper.

4 Bring the cream to a boil in a saucepan with the garlic and nutmeg. Discard the garlic, then pour the cream over the potatoes. Dot the top with the butter.

5 Cover with foil and place in the oven for about 1–1½ hours, or until the potatoes are tender. During the last 10 minutes of cooking, remove the foil and increase the oven temperature. Bake until a fine golden crust forms on the top. Serve hot, straight from the oven.

Kohlrabi takes its name from a combination of the German words for cabbage and turnip. Here, it is cut into wedges and roasted alongside partridge for a delicious early autumn meal.

Roasted partridge
with kohlrabi and pears

Serves 4 • **Prep** 15 mins • **Cooking** 50 mins

INGREDIENTS

4 sprigs of fresh thyme

4 partridges

6 tbsp butter

salt and freshly ground black
  pepper

8 bacon slices, cut crosswise
  into thirds

2 kohlrabi, cut into eighths

1 cup chicken stock

2 onions, cut into eighths

4 firm but ripe small pears,
  quartered and cored

$1/4$ cup walnut halves and
  pieces

$2/3$ cup pear or apple cider

METHOD

1 Preheat the oven to 400°F (200°C). Push a sprig of thyme inside each bird. Secure the legs to the bodies using toothpicks. Smear half the butter over the birds. Season lightly and lay 2 slices of bacon over each breast.

2 Boil the kohlrabi in stock for 2 minutes. Drain, reserving the stock. Melt the remaining butter in a roasting pan. Add the onions, kohlrabi, and pears, and toss to coat with butter. Push the vegetables and pears to one side. Put the walnuts in the the pan and place the partridges on top. Scatter vegetables and pears around the birds. Roast for 45 minutes until everything is golden and cooked through, stirring vegetables and pears once during cooking.

3 Lift the birds, pears, and vegetables out of the pan. Keep warm. Add the cider and reserved stock to the pan. Boil on high heat, stirring for about 3 minutes until well reduced and slightly thickened. Taste and season again.

4 Transfer the partridges, pears, and vegetables to warm serving plates. Remove toothpicks from the birds and spoon over the gravy. Serve immediately.

CELERY

When to pick
Pick celery when it is around 12in (30cm) high, after watering. Harvest young celery for eating raw; the more mature plants later, for soups and stews.

Eat and store fresh
Eat raw celery as soon as possible, but if necessary, store it in the fridge for up to 5 days. Crisp up the stems in cold water before eating.

How to preserve
Celery can be preserved in oil, having been char-grilled first (see pages 38–9). It is more commonly used as an ingredient in relishes, chutneys, and pickles.

In this salad, the strong tastes of celery and bitter leaves more than hold their own against the pungency of a blue cheese dressing, with walnuts adding crunch and texture.

Celery and apple salad
with blue cheese dressing

Serves 4 • **Prep** 10 mins • **Cooking** 2 mins

INGREDIENTS

$^1/_2$ cup chopped walnuts

10oz (300g) blue cheese, such as dolce latté or another Gorgonzola

$^1/_4$ cup cider vinegar

$^1/_4$ cup hazelnut or walnut oil

freshly ground black pepper

4 celery stalks, trimmed and sliced diagonally into $^1/_2$in (1cm) slices

2 green apples, cored and cut into thin wedges

4 large handsful of watercress or arugula

sea salt

METHOD

1 In a dry frying pan or wok, cook the walnuts for a couple of minutes, stirring and tossing, until they are golden and crispy. Set aside to cool.

2 In a food processor, combine 1 cup of crumbled blue cheese, the vinegar, oil, and a good grinding of black pepper. Process to a smooth, creamy dressing, with a thick pouring consistency. Add up to 1 tbsp of cold water to thin the dressing, if it is too thick.

3 In a large bowl, mix the celery, apples, and watercress. Add enough dressing to coat the salad and check it for seasoning. Top with the walnut pieces and the remaining blue cheese, crumbled or cut into bite-sized pieces.

This simple yet hearty soup can be prepared with any blue cheese, and the quantities can be easily scaled up or down as required. As with all soups, good quality stock is crucial.

Creamy celery
and Stilton soup

Serves 4 • **Prep** 10 mins • **Cooking** 25 mins

INGREDIENTS

4 celery sticks, chopped

2 medium russet potatoes, peeled and chopped

1 onion, chopped

approx. 2 cups hot vegetable or chicken stock

8oz (225g) Stilton cheese, crumbled

1 tbsp half-and-half or whole milk

sea salt and freshly ground black pepper

handful of fresh chives, chopped

METHOD

1 Put the celery, potatoes, and onion in a soup pot or large saucepan. Pour over the hot stock to cover the vegetables, and simmer gently for 30 minutes until tender.

2 Remove the pan from the heat and leave to cool slightly. Puree the vegetables and stock with the Stilton, using either a hand-held blender or transferring to a food processor or blender, working in batches if needed. Strain through a sieve to remove any celery strings, return to the pan, and cook gently over low heat. Stir in the half-and-half.

3 Season to taste and serve immediately, garnished with chives.

An unusual way to cook celery, here the heart is quartered and roasted with orange and walnuts. Delicious served with roast chicken, pork, or a piece of grilled halibut or monkfish.

Roasted celery
with orange and walnuts

Serves 4 • **Prep** 10 mins • **Cooking** 55 mins

INGREDIENTS

4 celery hearts, trimmed
    and quartered
zest and juice of 1 orange
extra virgin olive oil,
    for drizzling
1½ tbsp butter, melted
1 tsp granulated sugar
sprig of fresh thyme, leaves
    picked and chopped
handful of walnuts, chopped
sea salt and freshly ground
    black pepper

METHOD

1 Preheat the oven to 400°F (200°C). Put the celery hearts in a roasting pan and add the orange zest and juice. Drizzle with a little olive oil and the butter. Sprinkle over the sugar, thyme, and walnuts. Season with salt and pepper to taste.

2 Cover the roasting pan tightly with foil and cook in the oven for 40 minutes. Remove the foil and leave in the oven to brown for a further 15 minutes until tender and glazed. Serve hot or warm.

BEETS

When to pick
Pick beets when they reach between a golf ball and a tennis ball in size. Larger beets keep well in the ground. Some varieties can last until the first frosts, and be harvested as needed.

Eat and store fresh
Eat the tops as soon as possible, either raw in salads or stir-fried. Baby beets can be eaten raw, but larger beets need to be cooked. Boil, steam, or roast the roots, and stir-fry the leafy tops.

How to preserve
Use beets in pickles, relishes, and chutneys. Beets can be stored buried in sand in trays for several months (see page 262).

This deep pink soup is an ideal way to serve large beets. Smaller beets can simply be steamed or roasted, but the larger ones often need a little more attention to bring out their flavor.

Beet
and apple soup

Serves 6–8 • **Prep** 20 mins • **Cooking** 1 hour

INGREDIENTS

1 onion, halved

2 garlic cloves

3 tbsp extra virgin olive oil

salt and freshly ground black pepper

12oz (350g) beets, trimmed, peeled and halved

1 potato, halved

4 dessert apples, such as Golden Delicious, peeled and cored

6 cups hot vegetable stock or chicken stock

1–2 tbsp dark brown sugar

juice of 1 lemon

2 tbsp finely chopped parsley, chives, dill, cilantro, or a mixture

1 cup crème fraîche or Greek-style plain yogurt

METHOD

1 Grate the onion and garlic in a food processor. Heat the oil in a soup pot or large saucepan over low heat, add the onion, garlic, and a pinch of salt. Cook gently, stirring once or twice, for 5 minutes or until soft. Meanwhile, grate the beets, potato, and apples, in the food processor.

2 Add the beets, potato, and apples, to the pan and cook gently for 10 minutes, stirring occasionally. Pour in the stock, bring to a boil, then cover and simmer gently for 45 minutes or until the beets are cooked through.

3 Blend with a hand-held blender or, working in batches, transfer to a food processor and process until smooth. Season with the sugar, lemon juice, and some salt and pepper to taste.

4 Stir the chopped herbs into the crème fraîche, then ladle the soup into warm bowls and drop a big spoonful of the herbed cream into the middle of the soup.

This brightly colored risotto is amazing when cooked with freshly harvested beets. The deep, earthy flavor of beet and the sharp tang of goat cheese combine beautifully.

Beet risotto

Serves 4 • **Prep** 30 mins • **Cooking** 1 hour

INGREDIENTS

1lb (500g) beets, trimmed, peeled and diced

2 tbsp extra virgin olive oil, plus extra for brushing

sea salt and freshly ground black pepper

6 tbsp sunflower or vegetable oil

20 fresh sage leaves

2 medium onions, finely diced

2 garlic cloves, crushed

1¹/₂ cups arborio or other risotto rice

4 cups vegetable or chicken stock, heated

¹/₂ cup freshly grated Parmesan cheese

8oz (200g) firm goat cheese, cut into ¹/₂in (1cm) cubes

METHOD

1 Preheat the oven to 400°F (200°C). Toss the beets in a little olive oil, salt, and pepper. Wrap them in foil and bake in the oven for 30–40 minutes until soft.

2 In a small frying pan, heat the oil over high heat until smoking-hot. Working in batches if necessary, drop in most of the sage leaves and cook for 5 seconds, or until they stop sizzling, Remove and drain on paper towels.

3 Remove the beets from the oven and let cool slightly. Working in batches if necessary, purée in a blender or food processor with 4 tablespoons of water, 2 of the fried sage leaves, and some salt and pepper. Put aside.

4 Put the oil in a large, heavy frying pan over medium heat. Add the onions and cook 5–7 minutes until soft. Add garlic and cook 1 minute. Stir in the rice to coat.

5 Keeping the stock on a low simmer, add a ladle at a time to the rice, stirring continuously for about 15 minutes until the rice is almost cooked. Add the beet purée and cook, stirring, for another 5–10 minutes until the rice is tender.

6 Remove the rice from heat, season, and stir in two-thirds of the Parmesan and fold in the goat cheese. Serve garnished with the sage leaves and Parmesan.

The sweet, earthy flavors of the beets and sweet potatoes used here work beautifully with the peppery beef. Cook your beets in boiling water until tender then peel before roasting.

Peppered beef
with balsamic-roasted beets

Serves 4 • **Prep** 15 mins • **Cooking** 1 hour – 1 hour 50 mins

INGREDIENTS

4 medium beets

2½lb (1.1kg) beef tenderloin

1–2 tbsp freshly cracked black pepper

2–3 tbsp extra virgin olive oil

1 tbsp balsamic vinegar

4 sweet potatoes, peeled and quartered

salt

handful of fresh thyme sprigs

prepared cream-style horseradish, to taste

METHOD

1 Place the beets in a saucepan, cover with water, and bring to a boil. Simmer for 45 minutes to 1 hour or until tender. Drain, leave to cool, peel, and cut into quarters.

2 Preheat the oven to 375°F (190°C). Roll the beef in the pepper, covering it all over. Put 1 tablespoon of the oil in a flameproof roasting pan and set it over high heat. When very hot, add the beef, and cook for 5–6 minutes, turning, until lightly browned on all sides.

3 Toss the beets with the balsamic vinegar and add to the pan. Toss the sweet potatoes with the remaining oil and add to the pan. Season with a pinch of salt, sprinkle with the thyme, and put in the oven to cook to desired doneness; 20-30 minutes for rare beef, 35-40 minutes for medium, and 45-50 minutes for well done.

4 Remove the beef from the oven and keep it warm. Continue cooking the vegetables until they are golden and slightly charred. Slice the beef and serve with the beets, sweet potatoes, and horseradish.

This sweet relish with a hint of spice is perfect to serve with cheese or cold cuts. If you want to save time making the relish, you can cook the beets the night before.

Beet relish

Makes 2¼lb (1kg) or 3 medium jars • **Cooking** 2 hours 15 mins

INGREDIENTS

3lb (1.35kg) beets, trimmed

1 tsp plus 2½ cups granulated sugar

1lb (450g) shallots, finely chopped

2½ cups cider vinegar, or white wine vinegar

1 tbsp pickling spice blend, placed in a small muslin bag and tied with cotton string

METHOD

1 Put the beets in a preserving pan or a large heavy, stainless steel saucepan. Pour over enough water to cover them, and add the 1 teaspoon of sugar. Bring to a boil and simmer for 1 hour or until the beets are tender. Drain and leave to cool. When cool enough to handle, peel and dice into small, neat pieces.

2 Put the shallots and vinegar in the rinsed preserving pan or saucepan and cook for 10 minutes on low heat. Add the chopped beets and the muslin bag of pickling spices. Give the mixture a stir, add the 2½ cups of sugar, and cook gently until the sugar has dissolved. Bring to a boil and cook at a rolling boil for 5 minutes, then reduce the heat to a simmer and cook for about 40 minutes or until the mixture thickens.

3 Remove and discard the spice bag, then ladle the relish into warm, sterilized jars with non-metallic or vinegar-proof lids, making sure there are no air gaps. Seal, label, and store in a cool, dark place. Allow the flavors to mature for 1 month, and refrigerate after opening.

Note Keeps for 9 months unopened.

Store crops naturally

Storing crops in their natural state in a cool, protected environment, is the next best thing to picking produce fresh from the garden. It allows you to extend an autumn harvest from the garden. Low-tech methods, such as storing in trays or boxes, hanging produce, and storing on shelves in cool rooms, mean that treasured home-grown fruit and vegetables can be savored and enjoyed for months to come.

Storing beets in trays

1 **Cleaning and trimming** Cut off leaves and remove soil with a brush. Don't brush too hard, however, or trim the roots, since cuts could cause rot.

2 **Burying in sand** Fill the bottom of a tray with sand, layer the roots on top so they are not touching, and cover with more sand. Store in a cool room or root cellar.

Other options for natural storage

Some crops can be stored in clamps or in the ground (see pages 140–1); other options include hanging indoors or storing in boxes.

In boxes Crops including carrots, parsnips, potatoes, rutabagas, turnips, celery roots, and kohlrabi buried in compost or sand, in boxes, in a cool, ambient store room (see pages 268–9).

Hanging indoors Dried or "cured" pumpkins, squashes, garlic, onions, and shallots can be hung in nets, allowing the air to circulate around them.

Tips on storing crops

To keep your produce in tip-top condition it is vital to select suitable crops, store them properly, and dispose of deteriorated ones.

Select best produce Only store the best quality crops. Damaged crops spread disease.
Handle carefully Bruising of crops leads to rot.
Storage conditions Avoid damp spaces and extremes of temperatures.
Check regularly Remove any crops showing signs of disease immediately.

Storing pumpkins

1 **"Curing" the fruit** Cut off the squash leaving 4–6in (10–15cm) of stem. Leave in the sun to cure for 7-10 days, turning daily, so the skin hardens.

2 **Store in a cool room** Put on a raised shelf or hang in a net bag where air can circulate. They will keep for months but check regularly for signs of deterioration.

CARROTS

When to pick
Harvest from 10 weeks after planting to eat raw. Carrots for cooking can be left in the ground for longer and harvested as needed until winter sets in.

Eat and store fresh
Eat young carrots washed but unpeeled, in salads. Store larger carrots in the fridge, or in boxes for 2 months or more (see pages 268–9).

How to preserve
Use carrots as an ingredient in chutneys, pickles, and relishes.

Freezing options
Wash, peel, chop, and blanch for 2–3 minutes, then cool and freeze for up to 6 months.

This richly-colored salad is more than just pretty; it's packed with beneficial antioxidants too. Choose young, fresh vegetables as they are best eaten raw straight from the garden.

Carrot and beet salad
with balsamic vinaigrette

Serves 4–6 • Prep 30 mins • Cooking 3–4 mins

INGREDIENTS

For the salad

1¼ lb (600g) carrots, trimmed

1 bunch beets, about 1¼ lb (600g), trimmed, peeled and halved

small bunch of parsley, chopped, or watercress, snipped

For the vinaigrette

6 tbsp extra virgin olive oil, plus 1 tsp for toasting the seeds

3 tbsp balsamic vinegar

1 garlic clove, crushed through a press (optional)

¼ cup unsalted sunflower or pumpkin seeds

1 tsp soy sauce (optional)

salt and freshly ground black pepper

METHOD

1 Coarsely grate the carrots and beets and combine.

2 For the vinaigrette, put the oil, vinegar, and garlic (if using), in a screw-top jar, put the lid on tightly and shake to blend.

3 Gently heat the remaining 1 teaspoon of olive oil in a small frying pan and toast the seeds for 3–4 minutes over medium heat, stirring frequently to prevent burning. Add the soy sauce at the end of cooking (if using). Most of the sauce will evaporate, leaving a salty taste and extra browning for the seeds.

4 Add the parsley to the carrots and beets. Shake the vinaigrette again, pour over the vegetables, then season to taste. Toss the salad gently, scatter the toasted seeds over the top, and serve.

Note The vegetables, vinaigrette, and seeds can be prepared and stored separately in the fridge for up to 24 hours. Return to room temperature and combine before serving.

A light, refreshing soup with a hint of spice, this is the perfect start to a summer meal. Use fresh, young carrots and try adding a swirl of cream or plain yogurt before serving.

Spicy carrot
and orange soup

Serves 4 • **Prep** 10 mins • **Cooking** 45 mins

INGREDIENTS

2 tsp light olive oil
   or sunflower oil
1 leek, trimmed and sliced
1lb (450g) carrots, trimmed,
   and sliced
1 small russet potato, peeled
   and chopped
$1/2$ tsp ground coriander
pinch of ground cumin
$1^1/_4$ cups orange juice
2 cups vegetable or chicken
   stock
1 bay leaf
sea salt and freshly ground
   black pepper
2 tbsp chopped fresh cilantro,
   to garnish

METHOD

1 Place the oil, leek, and carrots in a large saucepan and cook over low heat for 5 minutes, stirring frequently, or until the leek has softened. Add the potato, cilantro, and cumin, then pour in the orange juice and stock and stir. Add the bay leaf and season with salt and pepper.

2 Increase the heat, bring the soup to a boil, then lower the heat, cover, and simmer for 40 minutes, or until the vegetables are very tender.

3 Allow the soup to cool slightly, then purée to a smooth consistency using a hand-held blender or by transferring to a food processor, working in batches if necessary.

4 Return to the saucepan and add a little extra stock or water if the soup is too thick. Bring back to a simmer, then transfer to heated serving bowls and sprinkle with chopped cilantro.

Note The soup can be stored in the freezer for up to 3 months.

This is a wonderfully moist cake that works just as well without the frosting. For an alternative, try grated zucchini instead of carrots and ground hazelnuts rather than almonds.

Carrot cake
with cream cheese frosting

Serves 8-10 • **Prep** 30 mins • **Cooking** 35–40 mins

INGREDIENTS

For the cake

1 large orange

1 cup butter, softened

2 cups light brown sugar

4 large eggs

$^3/_4$ cup whole wheat flour

$^2/_3$ cup self-rising flour

$^1/_2$ cup ground almonds

2 tsp baking powder

1 tsp pumpkin pie spice blend

2 large carrots, trimmed, and grated

For the frosting

8oz (225g) cream cheese

finely grated zest and juice of $^1/_2$ orange

$^1/_2$ cup confectioners' sugar, sifted

METHOD

1 Preheat oven to 350°F (180°C). Grease two 8in (20cm) round cake pans; line with parchment. Thinly pare zest of half the orange, cut into strips, boil 2 minutes, drain; cool. Grate remaining zest; squeeze juice.

2 Cream butter and sugar together until light and fluffy, 2-3 minutes. Beat in eggs one at a time; then beat in grated zest and orange juice, until blended. In a medium bowl, whisk together whole wheat flour, self-rising flour, ground almonds, baking powder, and allspice. Gradually add flour mixture to batter, until blended. Stir in carrots.

3 Spoon mixture into prepared pans. Bake 35–40 minutes until risen, golden, and firm to touch. Cool in pans 10 minutes, turn onto a rack, remove paper, cool.

4 For the frosting, beat cream cheese with zest and confectioners' sugar. Beat in juice until soft peaks form. Sandwich cake with half the frosting and spread the remainder over the top. Decorate with strips of zest.

Store root crops in boxes

Many root vegetables can be left in the garden through the winter months, but it may be more convenient to lift and store them indoors. They will also be less prone to damage caused by frost, disease, and pests. Carrots, parsnips, beets, and potatoes, among others, can be stored in boxes. Only store the best produce to avoid disease spreading. Keep in a cool, dark place, such as a garage or spare room for two months or more. Use as required, and keep remaining vegetables covered.

1 **Preparing the carrots** Harvest on a dry day, shake off excess soil, and twist off the tops. Don't scrub or wash the carrots, since this may damage the skins.

2 **Line the box** Line a shallow box with newspaper or burlap. Cover with a thin layer of spent compost, moist sand, coir, untreated sawdust, vermiculite, or leaf mold.

Store Carrots

YOU WILL NEED

carrots

shallow box or tray

newspaper or burlap

spent compost, sand, coir,
   untreated sawdust,
   vermiculite or leaf mold

Storing potatoes in boxes

If you don't have a large garden, or don't have enough outdoor space to accommodate potato clamps (see pages 140–1), store crops of potatoes in cardboard boxes with covers on top to block the light. These covers are essential, or the potatoes will turn green (the green parts are toxic, and must be cut away). Alternatively, store them in strong paper bags, folded or tied loosely at the top. Store the potatoes in a cool, dark place: 41–50°F (5–10°C). Cut away any sprouts before eating.

3 Position the first layer Arrange the carrots side by side on the compost so that they are not touching. Position the carrots so that they lie head to toe.

4 Cover and repeat Add another layer of compost over the carrots and repeat until the container is full. Finish with a layer of compost to block light and close the box

SWEET POTATOES

When to pick
Sweet potatoes grow well in warm climates and take around 4–5 months to mature. Harvest them when the foliage starts to wilt and turn yellow.

Eat and store fresh
They can be stored in the fridge for up to 1 week or stored like ordinary potatoes (see pages 140–1). Delicious baked, roasted, or thinly sliced and chargrilled to accompany chicken or fish dishes.

Freezing options
Griddle slices and open freeze on trays, or freeze as a cooked purée, for up to 9 months.

The inspiration for this dish comes from a classic Japanese dish known as *daigakuimo*. It is a wonderfully simple recipe that turns the humble sweet potato into something special.

Soy and sesame glazed
sweet potatoes

Serves 4 • **Prep** 10 mins • **Cooking** 40 mins

INGREDIENTS

2 tbsp soy sauce

2 tbsp light brown sugar

2 tbsp rice wine, such as mirin

1 tbsp Asian sesame oil

2 garlic cloves, crushed

1lb (500g) red-skinned sweet potatoes, peeled and cut into wedges

1 tbsp toasted sesame seeds

METHOD

1 Preheat the oven to 400°F (200°C). Put all the ingredients except the sweet potatoes and sesame seeds into a small saucepan. Bring to a boil, reduce the heat to low and cook for 2 minutes.

2 Put the potato wedges on a lightly oiled baking sheet and pour the sauce mixture over them, tossing well to coat. Spread into an even layer and scatter the sesame seeds over the top; cover the baking sheet with foil.

3 Bake for 20 minutes then turn up the oven to 425°F (220°C). Remove the foil and bake for another 20 minutes. Turn the potatoes several times while cooking until they have absorbed all the sauce and are tender, glazed, and sticky. These are superb eaten alongside a piece of grilled mackerel with some wilted greens.

The vegetables for this soup are cooked in the oven, which brings out their naturally sweet flavors. The harissa adds depth and a spicy edge. Delicious served with warm pita bread.

Moroccan roasted
sweet potato soup

Serves 4 • **Prep** 20 mins • **Cooking** 50 mins

INGREDIENTS

1½lb (675g) red-skinned sweet potatoes, peeled and cut into large chunks

6 large shallots, quartered

3 large garlic cloves, unpeeled

1 carrot, cut into large chunks

1 tbsp harissa*, plus extra to serve

2 tbsp extra virgin olive oil

salt and freshly ground black pepper

3¾ cups (900ml) hot vegetable stock

1 tsp honey

generous squeeze of lemon juice

plain yogurt, to serve

pita bread, to serve

METHOD

1 Preheat the oven to 400°F (200°C). Put the sweet potatoes, shallots, garlic, and carrot in a roasting pan. Mix the harissa with the oil, then pour over the vegetables and toss together so they are coated well. Season with freshly ground black pepper, then roast, turning occasionally, for 40 minutes or until tender and turning golden. Remove from the oven.

2 Squeeze garlic cloves out of their skins and back into the roasting pan. Stir in the stock and honey, then scrape up all the browned bits from the pan's bottom. Working in batches, carefully transfer the roasted vegetable mixture to a blender and process until smooth. Pour the pureed mixture into a large saucepan and reheat gently.

3 Add the lemon juice and season to taste with salt and freshly ground black pepper. Swirl the yogurt with a little harissa and top each bowl with a spoonful. Serve with warm pita bread.

* Look for small cans of this Tunisian hot sauce at Middle Eastern markets and well-stocked supermarkets.

A simple one-pot dish, the sweet-spicy sauce works wonderfully well with the earthiness of the sweet potatoes. Sweet potatoes can break up easily, so be sure that they don't cook for too long.

Garlic and chile chicken
with honeyed sweet potatoes

Serves 4 • **Prep** 15 mins • **Cooking** 1¼ hours

INGREDIENTS

8 chicken pieces (a mixture of thighs and drumsticks), skin on

salt and freshly ground black pepper

4 red-skinned sweet potatoes, peeled and cut into large chunks

1–2 tbsp honey

2 tbsp extra virgin olive oil

2 medium-hot red chiles, seeded and sliced

a few sprigs of fresh thyme

½ head of garlic, cloves separated, peeled, smashed flat with knife blade

½ cup dry white wine

1¼ cups chicken stock, or more, as needed

METHOD

1 Preheat the oven to 400°F (200°C). Season the chicken liberally with salt and freshly ground black pepper, and coat the sweet potatoes with the honey.

2 In a heavy flameproof casserole, preferably cast-iron, heat 1 tablespoon of the oil over medium heat. Working in batches if necessary, add the sweet potatoes and cook, stirring, for about 5 minutes until beginning to color; the honey should caramelize but not burn. Remove from the casserole and set aside.

3 Increase the heat to medium-high and heat the remaining oil in the same pan. Brown the chicken for about 5 minutes on each side until nicely golden all over. Add the chiles, thyme, and garlic. Return the sweet potatoes to the pan, and season well.

4 Pour in the wine and stock, cover the pan, and transfer to the oven to cook for 1 hour. Check the casserole a few times during cooking; give it a stir if needed, or add a small amount of stock if it is too dry. Serve hot with chunks of fresh crusty bread.

CRANBERRIES

When to pick
Pick cranberries at the end of summer, when the fruits are dark red, glossy, and bursting with juice. Leave on the bush and harvest as needed.

Eat and store fresh
Cranberries can be eaten raw, but they are extremely tart. They can be stored in the fridge for 3–5 days and cooked in pies or compôtes.

How to preserve
Cranberries are traditionally preserved in cranberry sauce (see page 276). They can also be used in jams and jellies, savory chutneys, and relishes.

Freezing options
Open freeze whole on trays, as a cooked or uncooked purée, or blanched or poached in sugar syrup (see pages 194–5).

This delicious autumnal dish makes a great accompaniment to a traditional roast, but is equally good scattered over some bitter leaves and eaten as a warm winter salad.

Squash with cranberries
and chestnuts

Serves 4 • Prep 10 mins • Cooking 30 mins

INGREDIENTS

1–2 tbsp extra virgin olive oil

1¹/₂ tbsp butter

pinch of allspice

pinch of cinnamon

1 butternut squash, peeled, halved, seeded, and cut into bite-sized chunks

salt and freshly ground black pepper

one 8oz (200g) vacuum-sealed jar or package of ready-cooked, unsweetened, peeled whole chestnuts, halved if large

¹/₂ cup fresh or frozen cranberries

sugar, to taste (optional)

METHOD

1 Preheat the oven to 400°F (200°C). Heat the oil and butter in a large frying pan, add the allspice, cinnamon, and squash. Season well with salt and pepper, and cook over medium-low heat, stirring occasionally, for 15 minutes, or until the squash begins to soften. Add a little more oil, if needed.

2 Add the chestnuts and stir so they are coated with the oil. Cook over low heat for 5–10 minutes, then add the cranberries and cook for 5-10 minutes longer, until the cranberries begin to burst.

3 Taste and season again, if needed, adding a little sugar if the cranberries are too tart (then cook a few minutes longer, until the sugar has dissolved).

A classic accompaniment to roast turkey at Christmas time, making your own cranberry sauce is a simple affair and tastes far superior to anything you would buy.

Cranberry sauce

Makes 1¼ cups • **Prep** 5 mins • **Cooking** 15 mins

INGREDIENTS

2 cups fresh or frozen
   cranberries
1 small shallot, finely chopped
½ cup light brown sugar
finely grated zest and juice of
   1 orange
¼ cup fruity red wine or
   port wine

METHOD

1 Put the cranberries in a saucepan with the shallot, sugar, orange zest, juice, and wine. Bring to a boil, stirring, until the sugar dissolves.

2 Simmer gently for 5–10 minutes, or until the cranberries are beginning to burst.

3 Leave to cool, then transfer to a serving dish or storage jar.

Note Cranberry sauce is good served with turkey, or other poultry. Keep refrigerated for up to 1 week and frozen for up to 2 months.

The fresh grapes and sweet white wine used here complement the rich flavor of the partridge breasts. Keep the partridge legs and use them in a slow-cooked stew for another day.

Roast partridge breasts
with grapes in Sauternes

Serves 6 • **Prep** 30 mins, plus soaking • **Cooking** 35 mins

INGREDIENTS

6 whole partridges,
   thawed if frozen

4 tbsp butter

12 fresh sage leaves

12 strips of bacon, thin slices of
   Parma ham, or prosciutto

extra virgin olive oil, for
   browning

For the sauce

2 shallots, finely chopped

1^1/$_2$ cups French Sauternes, or
   other sweet white wine

1^1/$_2$ cups chicken stock

^{3}/$_4$ cup white seedless grapes,
   each sliced in half

salt and freshly ground
   black pepper

2 tbsp butter, chilled and diced

METHOD

1 Preheat the oven to 375°F (190°C)). Pour Sauternes over grape halves and leave to soak for at least 1 hour.

2 Cut breasts off the partridges, or ask a butcher to do it. Place 1 teaspoon of butter and 1 sage leaf on the underside of each, then wrap with 1 slice of bacon.

3 Heat a little olive oil in a frying pan over medium-high heat and brown the wrapped partridge breasts on both sides, place in a flameproof roasting pan and set aside.

4 To make the sauce, fry the shallots in the same frying pan until softened, adding more oil if needed. Strain the Sauternes into the pan, reserving the grapes. Bring to a boil, simmer for 10 minutes, or until the wine is reduced, then add the stock, and bring back to a boil. When the sauce has reduced again, add the grapes, and simmer gently until ready to serve.

5 Roast the partridge breasts for 12 minutes, turning once. Bring the sauce back to a gentle simmer, and whisk in the butter. Serve the partridge with the sauce.

GRAPES

When to pick
Leave grapes on the vine as long as possible, until they are sweet and juicy, but before the skin shrivels. The longer they are left to mature, the sweeter they will be.

Eat and store fresh
Keep grapes at room temperature and eat raw within 3–5 days of picking.

How to preserve
Apart from being the main ingredient in wine, grapes can also be used in jams, jellies (see pages 280–1), and pickles, as well as being made into cordials and syrups.

This delightful cake can either be served warm as a dessert with cream or custard, or eaten cold with a cup of coffee. The grapes turn into a layer of sticky fruit on top of the cake and keep it moist.

Red grape
and cinnamon cake

Serves 6–8 • **Prep** 30 mins • **Cooking** 50 mins

INGREDIENTS

12oz (300g) seedless red
    grapes, halved lengthwise
2 tbsp light brown sugar
$^3/_4$ cup granulated sugar
11 tbsp butter, softened
3 eggs
$^1/_2$ tsp vanilla extract
1 cup self-rising flour
1 tsp ground cinnamon
1 heaping tsp baking powder

METHOD

1 Position the oven rack in the center of the oven, and preheat to 350°F (180°C). Grease the bottom and sides of an 8in (20cm) cake pan and line the bottom with parchment or wax paper. Spread the grapes, skin-side down, evenly over the bottom of the prepared pan, and scatter the brown sugar over the top.

2 In a food processor, mix together the granulated sugar and butter until well blended. When the mixture is smooth, mix in the eggs, one at a time. Mix in the vanilla. Add the flour, cinnamon, and baking powder, and process, pulsing the machine on and off, just until blended.

3 Carefully spread the batter over the grapes, taking care not to disturb them. Place the pan on a baking sheet and bake for approximately 50 minutes, or until risen and golden brown, and a skewer inserted into the center comes out clean. Use a blunt knife to loosen the cake from the sides of the pan. Invert the cake onto a serving plate, and carefully peel away the paper to reveal the grape topping. Serve warm.

Make jelly

The queen of preserves, jelly is made from the strained juice of fruit which produces clear, jewel-like results. Use perfect fruit, slightly under-ripe, and boil for the minimum time to achieve a set. Prolonged boiling is detrimental and may mean the jelly will not set. The quantity of strained juice always varies so calculate the sugar after measuring the juice. Allow $2\frac{1}{2}$ cups of sugar for every $2\frac{1}{2}$ cups of juice. Adding the lemon ensures there is enough pectin to achieve a set. Store in a cool, dark place and keep refrigerated once opened.

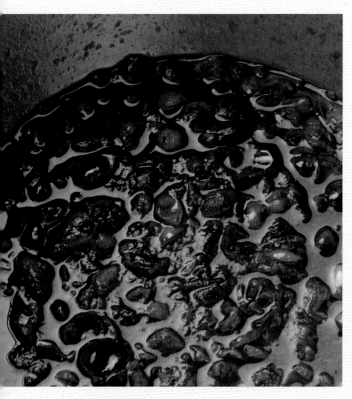

1 **Cook the grapes** Put the fruit and lemon into a preserving pan or large, heavy saucepan with the water. Bring to a boil, cover, and cook gently for 35–40 minutes.

2 **Remove the pulp** Strain the fruit through a jelly bag or clean nylon sieve over a clean bowl. Measure the juice and calculate the quantity of sugar (see above).

Recipe Grape jelly

Makes approx. 2¼lb (1kg) or 3 medium jars
Prep 50 mins–1 hour, plus straining • **Keeps** 12 months

INGREDIENTS

3lb (1.5kg) under-ripe red
   grapes (with seeds),
   stemmed, rinsed, and
   coarsely chopped
1 lemon, rinsed and
   coarsely chopped
1¼ cups (300ml) water

4 cups granulated sugar
½ tsp whole cloves

Other good fruits for jellies

Jellies require fruits that are juicy or high in pectin, and preferably both.

Apples Choose sour apples or windfalls (high in pectin), and include the core.
Quinces Wait until the skins have turned yellow before using.
Cranberries Good partners for apples, oranges, and cinnamon, or simply on their own.
Blackberries Combine with apples and flavor with cinnamon, cloves, or allspice.

3 **Add the sugar** Put the juice, sugar, and cloves back into the pan, bring gently to a boil. Stir to dissolve the sugar. Boil rapidly for 5–10 minutes to reach the setting point.

4 **Bottle and store** Remove the pan from the heat and test for a set (see page 187). Remove cloves and skim. Pour into warm sterilized jars, cover, seal, and label.

When to pick
Pick both cooking and eating apples when they come away easily from the branch with a little twist.

Eat and store fresh
Eat early varieties within a week or two of picking. Store later apples wrapped in paper or in a single layer (without touching) in a cool, dark place. Store only perfect fruits.

How to preserve
With their high pectin content, apples are used with soft fruits when making jams and jellies. They are also often the main ingredient in savory chutneys and apple butter.

Freezing options
Peel, slice, and dip in lemon, then freeze loose, or poach in syrup, then freeze, or freeze as cooked purée (see pages 194–5).

Apple trees are so prolific it is easy to run out of ideas at harvest time, and a savory side dish makes a change from the usual desserts. Caramelized apple slices are a perfect partner to pork.

Roast pork with apples

Serves 6 • **Prep** 30 mins, plus standing • **Cooking** 1 hour 20 mins–1³/₄ hours

INGREDIENTS

¹/₂ organic, free range pork
    belly, about 2lb (900g)
3 onions, cut in half
salt
dry sherry, white wine, or
    unsweetened apple cider

For the marinade
6 garlic cloves, peeled
¹/₂ tsp fine sea salt
¹/₂ tsp fennel or dill seeds
5 juniper berries
8 white or black peppercorns
1 tsp coarse-grain mustard

For the caramelized apples
4 apples, peeled, quartered,
    sliced and tossed in lemon
    juice to prevent browning
5 tbsp butter
3 tbsp light brown or
    granulated sugar

METHOD

1 To make the marinade, crush garlic, sea salt, fennel seeds, juniper berries, and peppercorns in a mortar and pestle to make a paste, then add the mustard. Score the skin and underside of the pork, and trim away excess fat. Rub the paste over. Rub the skin side with salt. Leave to stand for 30 minutes, then wipe off the liquid and excess salt. Put the onions in a shallow flameproof roasting pan, cut-side down, with the pork on top, skin-side up.

2 Preheat the oven to 475°F (240°C). Pour water ¹/₂in (1cm) deep into the roasting pan and cook the pork for 40–45 minutes. Turn the oven down to 300°F (150°C), and cook for another 30–45 minutes; add water, if necessary. Remove from the oven and leave to rest.

3 Add the apples to a frying pan with butter. Sprinkle over sugar. Cook apples until colored on both sides. Remove from the pan and keep warm.

4 Slice the pork. Pour fat from roasting pan. Place pan over high heat and add sherry, wine, or cider. Cook, stirring to loosen browned bits, until slightly thickened. Strain into a pitcher and serve with pork and apples.

Looking rather like freshly cooked doughnuts, biting into these warm fritters reveals instead, sweet soft apple and the delicate flavors of aniseed and cinnamon.

Portuguese
apple fritters

Makes 20–25 • **Prep** 20 mins, plus resting • **Cooking** 15–20 mins

INGREDIENTS

3 sweet apples, such as Golden Delicious, cored and sliced into $^1/_8$–$^1/_6$in (3–4mm) thick rings

2 tbsp fresh lemon juice

$^1/_4$ cup anise liquor, such as Anis del Mono, Ouzo, Sambuca, or anisette

$^2/_3$ cup granulated sugar

2 eggs

9 tbsp whole milk

5 tbsp extra virgin olive oil

2 cups all-purpose flour

$1^1/_2$ tsp baking powder

$^1/_4$ tsp ground cinnamon

vegetable oil, for deep frying

confectioners' sugar, for dusting

METHOD

1 Place the apples in a bowl, sprinkle with the lemon juice, liquor, and 4 tbsp of the sugar. Toss gently to mix and set aside for 30 minutes.

2 Meanwhile, to make the batter, mix the eggs, milk, and olive oil with the remaining sugar. Sift in the flour, baking powder, and cinnamon, and stir well to make a thick, smooth batter. Set aside for 30 minutes, to rest.

3 Heat the vegetable oil in a large frying pan. Dip the apple rings in the batter and fry in batches, turning once, until golden and crisp all over. Drain on paper towels and serve warm, dusted with confectioners' sugar.

This dish is like a sweet version of the British classic toad-in-the-hole. It makes a large tray, and can be served warm as a dessert with custard or cream, or left to cool and served with coffee.

Cinnamon apple cake

Serves 8–12 • **Prep** 30 mins • **Cooking** 25–30 mins

INGREDIENTS

$^{1}/_{2}$ cup butter, diced, plus extra
    for greasing

$1^{1}/_{2}$ cups all-purpose flour, plus
    extra for dusting

3 large or 4 medium cooking
    apples, such as
    Granny Smith

1 tbsp fresh lemon juice

3 eggs

$1^{1}/_{4}$ cups granulated sugar

6 tbsp whole milk

$^{1}/_{4}$ cup half-and-half

1 tbsp baking powder

2 tsp ground cinnamon

METHOD

1 Preheat the oven to 400°F (200°C). Grease a 9in (23 cm) square baking pan with butter, dust with flour, and shake out the excess.

2 Peel, core, quarter, and slice the apples, and put in a bowl of water with lemon juice to prevent browning.

3 Whisk the eggs and 1 cup of the sugar until thick and pale, and the whisk leaves a trail when lifted out.

4 Put the butter, milk, and half-and-half in a sauce pan and heat gently until the butter melts, then bring to a boil. Take off the heat and allow to cool briefly, then gradually whisk into the egg mixture. Sift the flour and baking powder over the surface and fold in with a metal spoon or rubber spatula. Pour into the prepared pan.

5 Drain the apples well and arrange attractively on top of the batter. Mix the remaining $^{1}/_{4}$ cup sugar with the cinnamon and sprinkle over. Bake for 25–30 minutes until golden and cooked through. Leave to cool in the pan, then cut into squares.

If you have an apple tree you probably have everything else you need for this simple yet delicious dessert in your storage cupboard, making it an ideal standby recipe.

Apple brown betty

Serves 4 • **Prep** 30 mins • **Cooking** 35–45 mins

INGREDIENTS

6 tbsp butter

1¹/₂ cups fresh bread crumbs

2lb (900g) apples, such as
    Bramley, Granny Smith, or
    Golden Delicious

¹/₂ cup light or dark
    brown sugar

1 tsp ground cinnamon

¹/₂ tsp pumpkin pie spice blend

finely grated zest of 1 lemon

2 tbsp fresh lemon juice

1 tsp vanilla extract

METHOD

1 Preheat the oven to 350°F (180°C). Melt the butter in a saucepan, add the bread crumbs, and mix well to moisten evenly.

2 Peel, quarter, and core the apples. Cut into slices and place in a bowl. Add the sugar, cinnamon, pumpkin pie spice, lemon zest and juice, and vanilla extract, and toss gently to mix well.

3 Put half the apple mixture into a 4 to 5 cup (1.2 liter) baking dish. Cover with half the bread crumbs, then put in the rest of the apples and top with the remaining bread crumbs.

4 Bake for 35–45 minutes, checking after 35 minutes. If it is getting too brown, reduce the oven temperature to 325°F (160°C), and cover with parchment paper. It is done when the crumbs are golden brown and the apples are tender. Serve warm.

This substantial, adaptable chutney gets better with age and should be left for at least a month before opening. For a darker result, use light or dark brown sugar instead of white sugar.

Apple chutney
with dates and raisins

Makes 4lb (1.8kg) or 5 medium jars • **Prep** 45 mins • **Cooking** 1$\frac{1}{2}$ hours

INGREDIENTS

4$\frac{1}{2}$lb (2kg) cooking apples,
   such as Granny Smith,
   (approx. 8–10 large apples),
   peeled, cored, and chopped
3 onions, peeled and
   chopped finely
1in (2.5cm) piece of fresh
   ginger, peeled, and
   chopped finely
1 cup golden raisins
1 cup pitted dates, chopped
1 tsp mustard seeds
4 cups cider vinegar
2$\frac{3}{4}$ cups sugar

METHOD

1 Put the apples, onions, ginger, raisins, dates, and mustard seeds in a preserving pan or a large, heavy, stainless steel saucepan. Stir everything together, then pour in the cider vinegar and add the sugar.

2 Cook over low heat, stirring until the sugar dissolves, then bring to a boil, reduce the heat, and cook gently for about 1$\frac{1}{2}$ hours. Stir continuously near the end of the cooking time so that the chutney does not stick to the base of the pan. The mixture is ready when it is thick and sticky.

3 Ladle into warm, sterilized jars, making sure there are no air gaps. Cover the surface with a disk of waxed paper, seal with a non-metallic or vinegar-proof lid, and label.

Note Store in a cool, dark place. Allow the flavors to mature for 1 month, and refrigerate after opening. Keeps for 9 months unopened.

Oven-dry fruits

Dried fruits make healthy snacks and are an excellent addition to granola, baked goods, sauces, pies, and many savory and sweet dishes. Choose ripe fruits, since they dry quickly and have a better flavor. The same recipe works for many kinds of fruit including tropical fruits, cherries, cranberries, grapes, nectarines, and plums. Keep the oven on its lowest setting and dry for 8–24 hours, depending on the temperature and preferred texture. Leave longer for a crunchier version.

1 **Core the apples** Briefly rinse the apples in cold water, then core and slice them into ⅛–¼in (3–5mm) rings. Discard the top and bottom rings with the most skin on.

2 **Prevent browning** In a bowl, add lemon juice or citric acid to 2½ cups water. Drop in apples, drain on kitchen towel, and lay on wire racks over baking sheets.

Recipe Dried apples

Makes approx. 4–8oz (115–225g) • **Prep** 15–20 mins, plus drying and cooling • **Keeps** 6 months if dried properly (12 months frozen)

INGREDIENTS

2¼lb (1kg) ripe apples,
   with bruised or damaged
   areas removed

2 tbsp fresh lemon juice, or
   ½ tsp citric acid

Drying different fruits

Keep the door of an electric oven ajar with a skewer to create airflow so that the fruit is dried rather than cooked.

Stone fruits Remove the stones first.
Fruits with rind Remove thick rind and peel.
Fruits with whole skins Dip fruits with skins left on, such as grapes and cherries, into boiling water for 30 seconds to split the skins first.
Larger fruits Cut fruits like peaches and large figs in half, and dry them cut-side up.

3 **Dry in the oven** Dry for 8–24 hours in the oven at 120–140°F (50–60°C), turning occasionally, until they look and feel like soft chamois leather.

4 **Store in jars** Remove from the oven, cover with paper towels, leave for 24 hours, turning occasionally. Pack into sterilized, airtight jars and store in a cool, dark place.

When to pick

Harvest pears when they come away from the tree easily. Cooking pears should be picked when slightly under-ripe, dessert pears can be left a little longer.

Eat and store fresh

Eat dessert pears when slightly soft. Store cooking pears wrapped in paper or in a single layer (without touching) in a cool, dark place for 2–3 months. Check them regularly.

How to preserve

Pears can be used in jams and jellies, chutneys, and pickles.

Freezing options

Freeze for up to 9 months as a cooked purée, or poached and covered with syrup in freezer containers (see pages 194–5).

Pears are delicious in sweet desserts, but they also work well with strong, savory flavors. Salty Parma ham and bitter crunchy chicory make a perfect foil for the sweet, ripe fruit.

Parma ham
with pears and nectarines

Serves 4 • **Prep** 15 mins

INGREDIENTS

2–3 heads chicory or curly endive, leaves separated and rinsed

3 firm but ripe pears, cored and sliced

3 ripe nectarines, halved, pitted, and sliced

12 slices Parma ham or prosciutto

handful of whole, natural almonds (skins on)

For the dressing

1/3 cup extra virgin olive oil

2 tbsp unsweetened apple juice

1 tbsp balsamic vinegar

salt and freshly ground black pepper

METHOD

1 First, make the dressing. Put the oil, apple juice, and balsamic vinegar in a jug or small bowl, and whisk together. Season well with salt and black pepper.

2 Arrange the chicory leaves in a single layer on a large serving platter and drizzle over a little of the dressing.

3 Arrange the fruit slices over the chicory leaves with the Parma ham, and toss together gently. Scatter over the almonds, then drizzle with a little more dressing. Season again, to taste. Serve immediately with some fresh crusty bread.

You can easily produce this dessert from some ripe pears and a few storage cupboard ingredients. The fruit keeps the cake moist for several days.

Pear and ginger
upside down cake

Serves 6 • **Prep** 5 mins • **Cooking** 20 mins

INGREDIENTS

1/2 cup butter at room
    temperature, plus extra
    for greasing
2/3 cup light brown sugar, plus
    extra for sprinkling
2 pears, peeled, cored, and
    halved
2 eggs, lightly beaten
3/4 cup whole wheat flour
2 tsp ground ginger
2 1/2 tsp baking powder

METHOD

1 Preheat oven to 375°F (190°F). Generously grease an 8in (20cm) round cake pan with butter and sprinkle evenly and liberally with brown sugar.

2 Lay the pear halves attractively in the pan on top of the butter and sugar.

3 In a bowl mix the butter and the 2/3 cup brown sugar with an electric hand mixer until light and creamy, 2–3 minutes. Gradually whisk in the eggs, then fold in the flour, ginger, and baking powder with a large metal spoon or rubber spatula. Spread the batter over the top of the pears and bake for 20 minutes or until the cake is just firm to the touch. Leave to cool in the pan for 5–10 minutes, then carefully invert onto a serving plate and transfer to a wire rack to cool. Serve slightly warm with cream or custard.

This impressive dinner party dessert is made with a few simple ingredients. Prepare a day in advance to allow the colors and flavors of the sauce to soak into the fruit.

Pears poached
in red wine and thyme

Serves 4 • **Prep** 20–30 mins • **Cooking** 50 mins, plus cooling

INGREDIENTS

1 bottle (750ml) dry red wine

1 cup granulated sugar

2 sprigs of fresh thyme

1 cinnamon stick

1 orange, preferably seedless

4 firm but ripe pears,
    such as Bosc

METHOD

1 Mix the wine, sugar, thyme, and cinnamon in a medium saucepan. Bring to a boil and then reduce the heat to low.

2 Using a vegetable peeler, remove the orange zest in large strips and add to the pan. Cut the orange in half and squeeze the juice into the pan.

3 Peel the pears, leaving the stems intact but slicing off the base of each pear so they will stand flat. Add the pears to the pan, so they are covered with the liquid, topping up with water if necessary. Cover and simmer over low heat for about 20 minutes, until the pears are tender when pierced with a sharp knife.. Leave to cool in the liquid and refrigerate overnight.

4 Before serving, remove the pears with a slotted spoon and return the poaching liquid to the heat. Bring to a boil; then reduce the heat to medium and cook until the liquid has reduced to a depth of about $1/2$in (1cm), or until thickened and slightly sticky. Taste the sauce, to make sure the flavors are strong, but not burned tasting. Strain and serve the cold pears with the hot sauce poured over.

When to pick
Pick quinces when golden yellow in color, and when they come away easily from the branch. They are a very hard fruit, so do not wait for them to soften.

Eat and store fresh
Quinces can be kept for several weeks in a cool, dark place before cooking.

How to preserve
The traditional Spanish preserve, membrillo (see right), is a well-known way of preserving quinces, but they can also be used in jams, jellies, and pickles.

❄ **Freezing options**
Best frozen as a cooked purée, or blanched or poached in sugar syrup (see pages 194–5).

This Spanish preserve is a fruit cheese made with quinces. Quince trees are often old and productive, but the fruits cannot be eaten raw. This is one of the best ways to unlock their subtle flavor.

Membrillo

Makes approx. 1lb 10oz–2^{1}/$_{4}$lb (750g–1kg) • **Prep** 10 mins • **Cooking** 1^{1}/$_{2}$ hours

INGREDIENTS

2^{1}/$_{4}$lb (1kg) quinces, scrubbed and coarsely chopped
juice of ^{1}/$_{2}$ lemon
approx. 2^{1}/$_{2}$ cups granulated sugar (see method)

METHOD

1 Place the chopped quinces (along with cores and seeds) in a preserving pan or a large heavy saucepan with 2^{1}/$_{2}$ cups of water. Add the lemon juice, bring to a boil, and simmer for 30 minutes. When soft, crush the fruit into a pulp with a potato masher. Leave to one side to cool.

2 Sieve the pulp in batches over a large, clean bowl, pressing hard against the sieve with a wooden spoon. Measure the purée: for every 2 cups , add 2^{1}/$_{2}$ cups of sugar. Put the puree and sugar back in the pan and stir over low heat to dissolve the sugar.

3 Bring the mixture to a boil. Simmer gently for 45–60 minutes, stirring occasionally. The purée will reduce down to a dark, thick, glossy paste. It is ready when it makes a "plopping" noise and sticks to the spoon.

4 Grease 6 warm sterilized ramekin dishes or molds with a little oil. Spoon in the paste and level the top. Seal with waxed paper discs and cellophane or plastic wrap if leaving in the ramekins. Otherwise, leave to cool completely; then loosen with a palette knife, turn out, and wrap airtight in waxed paper and plastic wrap and store in the refrigerator. When firm, cut into thin slices to serve.

The quince is a relative of the pear and apple, with a similar shape, but a bitter taste until cooked. Try these preserved quinces as a dessert with cream, or as a side dish to game.

Quinces in spiced syrup

Makes 2 small preserving jars • **Prep** 10 mins • **Cooking** 1¼ hours

INGREDIENTS

2lb (900g) quinces, scrubbed

1 tbsp fresh lemon juice

1¼ cups granulated sugar

2 star anise, 1 cinnamon stick, or 2 cloves

METHOD

1 Place the quinces in a saucepan, add 2½ cups of water, bring to a boil, and simmer for 2 minutes. Remove the quinces from the pan and plunge them into cold water. Reserve the pan of water. Peel, core, and quarter the quinces and put into cold water with the lemon juice.

2 Stir the sugar into the reserved pan of water. Heat the pan gently until the sugar dissolves, then stir well. Drain the quince quarters and add them to the syrup along with the spices. Bring to a boil, reduce the heat, cover and poach gently for 12–15 minutes, or until just tender.

3 Preheat the oven to 300°F (150°C). Pack the quinces into the warm sterilized preserving jars, leaving ½in (1cm) space at the top. Bring the syrup back to a boil and pour over the fruit to cover it completely. Tap the jar gently on a wooden board to remove air bubbles. Fit the rubber band or metal lid seal, and clamp on the lid. If using screw-band jars, loosen by a quarter turn.

4 Place the jars on a baking sheet lined with parchment in the oven for 40–50 minutes. Remove, and tighten the clips or screw bands (fit plastic screw bands at this point).

Note Keeps for 12 months if heat-processed.

PLUMS

When to pick
Pick dessert plums when as ripe as possible, but still firm. They should come away from the branch easily. Cooking plums can be picked earlier if needed.

Eat and store fresh
Eat plums within a few days of picking, before they become too soft. If cooking, store for up to 5 days in the fridge before use.

How to preserve
Use plums in jams or savory chutneys. You can also crystallize them or use them to make plum wine.

Freezing options
Pit, cut in half, and freeze .If using in jams and chutneys, freeze whole. They can also be poached in syrup and frozen (see pages 194–5).

This stunning dessert recipe is equally delicious when made with damsons or cherries, but instead of putting the marzipan in the fruit cavities, dot little pieces in between each fruit.

Plum and marzipan
clafoutis

Serves 6 • **Prep** 30 mins • **Cooking** 50 mins

INGREDIENTS

For the marzipan

1 cup ground almonds

$1/4$ cup granulated sugar

$1/2$ cup confectioners' sugar

a few drops of almond extract

$1/2$ tsp fresh lemon juice

1 egg white, lightly beaten

For the clafoutis

5 tbsp butter

4 eggs plus 1 egg yolk

$1/2$ cup granulated sugar, plus extra for dusting

$3/4$ cup all-purpose flour, sifted

2 cups whole milk

$1/2$ cup half-and-half

METHOD

1 Mix the marzipan ingredients together with enough of the egg white to form a stiff paste. Push a tiny piece of the paste into the cavity in each plum half.

2 Grease a shallow, ovenproof dish, large enough to hold the plums in a single layer, with 1 tbsp of the butter. Arrange the plums cut-side down in the dish, with the marzipan underneath. Melt the remaining butter and leave to cool.

3 Preheat the oven to 375°F (190°C). Add any leftover egg white from the marzipan to the 4 eggs and egg yolk. Add the sugar, and whisk until thick and pale. Whisk in the melted butter, the flour, milk, and half-and-half to form a batter. Pour over the plums. Bake in the oven for about 50 minutes until golden and just set. Serve warm, dusted with confectioners' sugar.

Note You can use store-bought white marzipan for speed.

Use up the contents of your autumn fruit bowl in this delicious, easy-to-make dessert. Even more mouthwatering when served with crème fraîche or ice cream.

Caramelized autumn
fruit sauté

Serves 6 • **Prep** 10 mins • **Cooking** 20 mins

INGREDIENTS

3 Granny Smith apples, peeled, cored, and quartered

3 firm but ripe Bosc or Conference pears, peeled, cored, and quartered

4 firm but ripe red plums, quartered and pitted

4 tbsp butter

¼ cup granulated sugar

2 tbsp orange juice or water

METHOD

1 To make the caramel, heat the butter in a large frying pan over medium heat. Add the sugar and orange juice and cook, stirring, until the sugar dissolves. Increase the heat and boil without stirring until the mixture turns golden brown.

2 Add the apples and cook gently, stirring, until they start to soften, then add the pears and cook until tender.

3 Add the plums and continue to cook, stirring occasionally, until all the fruit is softened, but not falling apart, and is coated in caramel. Serve warm.

Variation You could also make this with summer fruits, such as apricots, peaches, and blackberries.

The addition of port and cinnamon turns this simple plum jam into something special, with more than a hint of festive flavors. In a pretty glass jar, this would make an ideal Christmas gift.

Spiced port
and plum jam

Makes approx. 4¹/₂lb (2kg) or 6 medium jars • **Prep** 15 mins • **Cooking** 20–28 mins

INGREDIENTS

4lb (1.8kg) dark plums, halved
   and pitted
1 cinnamon stick, broken in half
juice of 1 lime
7¹/₂ cups granulated sugar
2–3 tbsp port wine (to taste)

METHOD

1 Put the plums, cinnamon stick halves, and lime juice into a preserving pan or a large, heavy saucepan, and then pour over 2¹/₂ cups of water.

2 Simmer gently on low heat for 15–20 minutes or until the plums begin to break down and soften.

3 Add the sugar, and stir until it has all dissolved, then bring to a boil and keep at a rolling boil for 5–8 minutes or until the jam begins to thicken and reaches the setting point. Skim off any foam that rises to the top. Remove the pan from the heat while you test the jam for a set (see pages 186–7).

4 Discard the cinnamon sticks and stir in the port. Ladle into a warm, sterilized jar, making sure there are no air gaps. Cover the surface with a disk of waxed paper, seal with a non-metallic or vinegar-proof lid, and label.

Note Store in a cool, dark place, and refrigerate after opening. Keeps for 9 months unopened.

Make chutney

Chutneys are versatile sweet-sour mixtures of vegetables, fruits, spices, and dried fruits cooked until soft. They are usually eaten with cold meats and cheeses. This recipe shows the basic method, which can be made with all kinds of seasonal produce. For the best chutney, always prepare ingredients carefully to achieve the desired texture. Ideally, grind your own spices for the freshest flavor, and cook the chutney slowly and gently, stirring often to prevent the mixture from burning in the bottom of the pan.

1 Prepare the fruit Put all the ingredients into a preserving pan or large heavy saucepan and bring to a boil slowly, stirring to dissolve the sugar.

2 Simmer and stir Simmer gently for 1½–2 hours until a wooden spoon drawn across the base of the pan leaves a trail. Stir frequently towards the end.

Recipe Plum chutney

Makes approx. 3lb (1.35kg) or 3 large jars
Prep 1 hour 50 mins–2 hours • **Keeps** 12 months

INGREDIENTS

2$\frac{1}{4}$lb (1kg) plums, halved,
    destoned, quartered

2 small cooking apples,
    cored, peeled, diced

1 large onion, sliced

1$\frac{1}{2}$ cups light
    brown sugar

$\frac{3}{4}$ cup dark raisins

1 tsp sea salt

1 tsp each, ground allspice,
    cinnamon, and coriander

$\frac{1}{2}$ tsp crushed hot pepper

2$\frac{1}{2}$ cups white wine
    or cider vinegar

Best fruits and vegetables for chutney

There are endless combinations of ingredients
that can be used in chutneys.

Apples A key fruit for chutneys, since its flavor
blends well with other ingredients.
Onions Essential for all chutneys. Try red or
white onions, and shallots for a milder flavor.
Pears Combine with fresh ginger or spices,
such as cardamom, cinnamon, and allspice.
Peppers These add sweetness and color.
Plums Add for rich chutneys with lots of body.
Rhubarb Use tender, less fibrous stems.

3 Put into jars The chutney should now
look thick and glossy. Check the seasoning,
add more salt if necessary, and pot into
warm sterilized jars, leaving no air gaps.

4 Cover and store Cover with waxed
paper, seal, label, and store in a cool, dark
place. Leave to mature and mellow for at
least 1–2 months before using.

FIGS

When to pick
Pick figs when they are fully colored and slightly soft. Sticky nectar oozing out of one end is an indicator of ripeness. Figs for cooking may be picked earlier.

Eat and store fresh
Eat figs raw within a couple of days of picking. Less ripe figs can be stored in the fridge and used in cooking up to 5 days after harvesting.

How to preserve
Figs can be used in jams, chutneys, and pickles as well as being bottled or dried.

Grilling figs seems to enhance their rich flavor. The addition of a creamy blue cheese, such as Gorgonzola, gives a welcome contrast to the natural sweetness of the figs and honey.

Grilled figs
with Gorgonzola and honey

Serves 4 • **Prep** 10 mins • **Cooking** 10 mins

INGREDIENTS

12 ripe figs, halved

6oz (175g) Gorgonzola cheese, crumbled

honey, to serve

METHOD

1 Heat a ridged grill pan over medium-high heat. Add the figs, placing them cut-side down without turning, and grill for 5 minutes, or until browned.

2 When the figs have nice grill marks, gently turn them over and cook on the other side for another couple of minutes.

3 Remove the figs from the pan and place them in a shallow serving dish. Sprinkle with the Gorgonzola, drizzle with honey, and serve immediately.

Note These are good with predinner drinks, or served at the end of a meal.

A richly dense, fruity jam like this can be served with sweet or savory food. For a spicier alternative, add a couple of teaspoons of chopped, crystallized ginger to the figs as they cook.

Ripe fig
and vanilla jam

Makes approx. 2¹/₂lb (1.1kg) 3 medium jars • **Prep** 10 mins • **Cooking** 40–45 mins

INGREDIENTS

1¹/₂lb (675g) ripe figs with soft skins, trimmed and cut into quarters

finely grated zest and juice of 1 lemon

1 small cooking apple, such as Granny Smith, peeled, cored, and coarsely chopped

1 vanilla bean, sliced lengthwise

7¹/₂ cups granulated sugar

METHOD

1 Put the figs in a preserving pan or a large heavy saucepan with the lemon zest and juice, chopped apple, and vanilla bean. Cook over low heat for about 20 minutes or so, stirring occasionally, until the figs have softened and broken down.

2 Add the sugar and cook over low heat, stirring continuously, until all the sugar has dissolved. Then bring to a boil and cook at a rolling boil, stirring occasionally, for about 15–20 minutes or until it reaches the setting point. Skim off any foam that rises to the top. Remove the pan from the heat while you test for a set (see pages 186–7).

3 Carefully remove the vanilla bean, ladle the jam into warm, sterilized jars, making sure there are no air gaps. Cover the surfaces with disks of waxed paper, seal with a non-metallic or vinegar-proof lid, and label.

Note Store in a cool, dark place, and refrigerate after opening. Keeps for 6 months unopened.

WINTER

Broccoli

Brussels sprouts

Asian greens

Kale

Cabbages

Leeks

Belgian endive

Celery root

Jerusalem artichokes

Rutabagas

Turnips

Parsnips

BROCCOLI

When to pick
Harvest the central flower head when it is no bigger than your hand, and the buds are tight. Do not leave until the flowers open. Side shoots can be cooked as individual spears.

Eat and store fresh
Broccoli can be stored in a cool place or in the fridge for up to 5 days. Eat before yellowing appears.

Freezing options
Wash, divide into florets, blanch for 2 minutes, cool, and freeze for up to 12 months.

In Italy, this warm, garlicky dip is traditionally served with raw vegetables, such as baby carrots and radishes, but I've found it's perfect with simply steamed, sprouting broccoli.

Steamed broccoli
with bagna càuda

Serves 4, makes about 150ml (5fl oz) dipping sauce • **Prep** 10 mins • **Cooking** 10 mins

INGREDIENTS

1lb 2oz (500g) purple or young green broccoli spears, trimmed

4 oil-packed anchovies, drained and chopped

2 garlic cloves, crushed

$1/2$ cup extra virgin olive oil

2 tbsp cold butter, cut into small pieces

1 tsp fresh lemon juice

sea salt and freshly ground black pepper

METHOD

1 Steam the broccoli for no more than 5 minutes, until it is *al dente*.

2 Put the anchovies into a mortar and pestle, and grind them to a paste. Put them in a small saucepan along with the garlic and oil, and heat gently for 2 minutes until the garlic is lightly colored, but not brown.

3 Remove the pan from the heat and use a wire whisk to add the cold butter in small pieces, beating well between each addition.

4 Add the lemon juice and continue to whisk until the mixture emulsifies slightly. Check the seasoning and add freshly ground black pepper, and a little salt, if necessary. Serve the dipping sauce warm with the broccoli.

Here is a quick and simple way to make the most of your delicious young sprouting broccoli. The spicy chile and zesty lemon flavors are perfect for the winter months.

Spicy spaghetti
with broccoli

Serves 4 • **Prep** 5 mins • **Cooking** 20 mins

INGREDIENTS

7oz (200g) white, purple, or
green sprouting broccoli
1lb (450g) dried spaghetti
extra virgin olive oil,
for cooking
1 bunch of scallions, chopped
$1/2$ tsp crushed hot red pepper
flakes
juice of $1/2$ lemon
sea salt and freshly ground
black pepper
$1/4$ cup Parmesan cheese, or
hard sheep's cheese, freshly
grated

METHOD

1 Trim the broccoli and separate any multiple florets into single heads so that all are similar sized for even cooking. Peel the stems and cut in half lengthwise if large. Slice the stems diagonally.

2 Cook the spaghetti in a large pot of boiling salted water until tender yet still firm to the bite. Drain and return to the pot.

3 Meanwhile, heat the olive oil in a nonstick wok or large frying pan, then add the broccoli and cook over medium heat for 5–7 minutes or until just tender. Stir in the scallions and cook 1 minute longer.

4 Tip the broccoli into the pot with the spaghetti. Add the red pepper flakes, lemon juice, and season with salt and pepper to taste. Toss lightly over gentle heat. Serve immediately with a sprinkling of grated cheese.

In this tasty supper dish, the broccoli is cooked for slightly longer than usual, and then mashed. The addition of lemon and chile really lifts the flavors of this common brassica.

Marinated lamb chops
with chile broccoli

Serves 4 • **Prep** 5 mins, plus marinating • **Cooking** 30 mins

INGREDIENTS

4 lean lamb loin chops, fat
    trimmed
sea salt and freshly ground
    black pepper
handful of fresh rosemary
    sprigs
12oz (300g) broccoli florets
    and stems, chopped
    fairly small
juice of 1 lemon
pinch of crushed hot red
    pepper flakes
mint jelly, to serve

For the marinade
2 tbsp sherry vinegar, cider
    vinegar, or white
    wine vinegar
pinch of sugar
splash of soy sauce

METHOD

1 Preheat the oven to 400°F (200°C). First, prepare the marinade. Mix together the vinegar, sugar, and soy sauce, then pour over the lamb. Leave to marinate for 5 minutes, or longer if time permits. Pat dry.

2 Place the lamb chops into a shallow roasting pan, season well with salt and black pepper, and throw in the rosemary sprigs. Roast in the oven for 20–30 minutes until cooked to your liking.

3 While the lamb is cooking, put the broccoli in a pot of boiling salted water, and cook for about 10 minutes until just soft. Drain, keeping the broccoli in the pot, then mash very gently with a fork. Squeeze over the lemon juice, and add the pepper flakes, a pinch of salt, and some black pepper. Put a lid on the pan, and give it a shake. Serve immediately with the roasted lamb chops, and offer mint jelly on the side.

If you have the patience to grow broccoli, you'll want to do something special with it when it finally arrives. This Asian-style dish is a great accompaniment to stir-fried meat or seafood.

Stir-fried broccoli
with sesame seeds

Serves 4 • **Prep** 5 mins • **Cooking** 6 mins

INGREDIENTS

1 tbsp sesame seeds

1 tbsp vegetable oil

1 tbsp soy sauce

pinch of crushed hot red
  pepper flakes

1$\frac{1}{2}$lb (675g) broccoli florets
  and stems, peeled and sliced
  diagonally

$\frac{1}{4}$ cup vegetable stock
  or water

sea salt and freshly ground
  black pepper

METHOD

1 Heat a large nonstick frying pan or wok. Add the sesame seeds and toast them, shaking the pan constantly for 1–2 minutes, or until the seeds turn golden. Transfer to a plate.

2 Add the oil, soy sauce, and pepper flakes to the pan, and stir to combine. Add the broccoli and cook, stirring and tossing, for 2 minutes.

3 Pour in the stock and cover the pan. Cook for 1–2 minutes, or until the broccoli is crisp-tender. Stir in the sesame seeds and season to taste with salt and freshly ground pepper before serving.

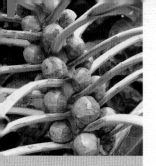

BRUSSELS SPROUTS

When to pick
Harvest these tiny brassicas from the bottom of the plant upwards, when they are no bigger than a walnut, and the leaves are tight and firm. Pick as required, leaving the upper buds to mature on the plant.

Eat and store fresh
Shred and eat tiny sprouts raw. Store larger ones in the fridge for 3–5 days. To prepare, peel the outer leaves and cut a cross in the base to allow equal cooking of the stem and leaves.

Freezing options
Trim and blanch for 2–3 minutes, cool, and freeze for up to 12 months.

Although many people dislike Brussels sprouts, it is hard to find someone who doesn't like them when treated in this manner. A perfect foil to a Thanksgiving or Christmas meal.

Brussels sprouts with chestnuts and pancetta

Serves 4 • **Prep** 10 mins • **Cooking** 10 mins

INGREDIENTS

1lb (450g) Brussels sprouts, trimmed, halved if large
1 tbsp butter
4oz (100g) pancetta, diced
4oz (100g)chestnuts, cooked, peeled, and coarsely chopped
1 tsp finely grated lemon zest
sea salt and freshly ground black pepper

METHOD

1 Boil the Brussels sprouts in plenty of salted water for 5–7 minutes, depending on their size, until they are just tender, but not overcooked. Drain well.

2 Melt the butter in a large frying pan or wok. Add the pancetta and cook for 3–4 minutes, stirring often, until crispy. Add the Brussels sprouts, chestnuts, and lemon zest, and continue to cook for 2 minutes, stirring, until heated through.

3 Season well with black pepper and a little salt, to taste; you may not need much as the pancetta can be very salty.

When to pick
Pick Asian leaves small for eating raw in salads, or leave to grow a little larger for stir-fries. With spicy varieties, the larger the leaves, the hotter they will taste. Pick bok choy when the base bulb is swollen and firm.

Eat and store fresh
Eat baby leaves as soon as possible after picking if using raw. Wash and dry larger leaves, and store in a plastic bag in the fridge for up to 2 days. Store bok choy whole.

Freezing options
Blanch leaves for 1–2 minutes, cool, then freeze in freezer pots or bags. Depending on the greens, you may need to separate stalks from leaves and blanch stalks separately, for longer. Keeps for 9 months.

A selection of the finest greens your garden has to offer can be used to make this recipe. Try any combination of spinach, chard, green beans, peas, Asian greens, or spring onions.

Asian greens
with chiles, garlic, and soy

Serves 4 • **Prep** 15 mins • **Cooking** 15 mins

INGREDIENTS

handful of shelled hazelnuts

1 tbsp sesame oil,
    or vegetable oil

2 fresh medium-hot green chile
    peppers, seeded and finely
    chopped

3 garlic cloves, thinly sliced

1 tbsp soy sauce

1 tbsp Chinese rice wine or
    white vermouth

1–2 heads bok choy, quartered
    lengthwise

handful of spinach leaves,
    or chard leaves,
    coarsely chopped

2 handsful of sugar snap peas,
    or snow peas, sliced
    into strips

salt and freshly ground
    black pepper

METHOD

1 Spread the hazelnuts on a baking sheet or in a shallow pan. Toast under a hot broiler until golden brown, turning them frequently and watching carefully to prevent burning. Put the hazelnuts in a clean kitchen towel, and rub the skins off. Chop coarsely, and set aside.

2 Heat the oil in a wok over medium-high heat, and swirl it around to coat the surface. Add the chiles and garlic, and cook for 10 seconds, then add the soy sauce and Chinese rice wine, and cook for a few seconds more.

3 Throw in the bok choy, and spinach or chard, and cook, stirring and tossing, for 1 minute. Add the sugar snap peas or snow peas, and stir-fry for 1 minute more. Toss, and season with salt and black pepper. Serve immediately with the toasted hazelnuts scattered over the top.

Asian greens are easy to grow and provide a good source of dark green leafy vegetables in the winter. Try them stir-fried with Asian aromatics, served with five-spice chicken.

Spicy honeyed chicken
with chile greens

Serves 4 • **Prep** 10 mins • **Cooking** 45 mins, plus marinating

INGREDIENTS

2 handsful of Chinese greens, such as bok choy, sliced

splash of soy sauce

1in (2.5cm) piece of fresh ginger, grated

pinch of crushed hot red pepper flakes

salt and freshly ground black pepper

1–2 tbsp honey

juice of 2 limes

3 tbsp extra virgin olive oil

2 tbsp five-spice paste, or 1 tsp five-spice powder mixed with 1 tbsp Asian sesame oil

8 chicken pieces (a mixture of thighs and drumsticks), skin on

METHOD

1 Preheat the oven to 400°F (200°C). Put the greens in a large bowl. Add the soy sauce, ginger, and pepper flakes, and season well. Set aside.

2 In another bowl, mix together the honey, lime juice, 1 tbsp of the oil, and the five-spice paste, until well combined. Spread over the chicken, and season well. Cover and leave to marinate in the fridge for at least 20 minutes.

3 Heat another tablespoon of the oil in a large frying pan over medium-high heat. Working in batches, add the chicken pieces, skin-side down, and cook for 5–8 minutes on each side until golden and crispy, then transfer to a roasting pan. Roast in the oven for about 30–40 minutes, or until cooked throughout on the inside and beginning to char on the outside.

4 Meanwhile, wipe the frying pan with paper towels, reduce the heat slightly, and add the greens. Drizzle over the remaining tablespoon of oil, and cook, stirring and tossing, for about 5 minutes until beginning to wilt. Serve hot with the crispy-skinned chicken.

This Asian-inspired recipe is a quick yet luxurious way to serve beef with bok choy from your garden. It is important to use the best quality meat you can, since it is simply spiced and cooked.

Wasabi beef
with bok choy

Serves 4 • **Prep** 10 mins • **Cooking** 10 mins

INGREDIENTS

2 tbsp extra virgin olive oil

2 tsp wasabi paste

4 beef sirloin steaks,
    about 7oz (200g) each

7oz (200g) bok choy, cut
    lengthwise into 8 pieces

5 garlic cloves, grated or finely
    chopped

1 tbsp soy sauce

salt and freshly ground
    black pepper

METHOD

1 Heat a ridged grill pan until hot. Mix 1 tablespoon of the olive oil with the wasabi paste. Use to coat the sirloin steaks, ensuring a thin, even covering.

2 Add the steaks to the hot grill pan and cook over high heat for 3 minutes on each side. Remove to a plate, and leave to rest in a warm place for 5 minutes. Keep the grill pan hot.

3 Meanwhile, in a bowl, toss the bok choy in the remaining olive oil with the garlic and soy sauce. Working in batches if necessary, cook on the grill pan for 2–3 minutes, or until charred and just wilted. To serve, cut the steak diagonally into $\frac{1}{2}$in (1cm) slices, season, and serve with the grilled bok choy.

Note This can also be cooked on an outdoor grill.

Asian greens are perfect in stir-fries, adding color and a fresh flavor to the finished dish. The rice noodles used here are quite delicate, so be careful not to overcook them.

Thai noodle stir-fry

Serves 4 • **Prep** 15 mins • **Cooking** 20 mins

INGREDIENTS

6oz (175g) thin rice noodles

3 tbsp peanut oil or vegetable oil

3 skinless, boneless chicken breast halves, cut into narrow strips

1 onion, sliced

1 stalk of lemon grass, outer leaves removed, woody end trimmed, and finely chopped

1 orange or red bell pepper, seeded and sliced

4oz (115g) fresh shiitake mushrooms, stemmed and sliced

1 fresh hot red chile pepper, seeded and finely chopped

1 tsp finely grated fresh ginger

2 heads of bok choy, shredded

2 tbsp soy sauce

1 tbsp Thai fish sauce (nam pla)

1 tsp sweet chili sauce

METHOD

1 Soak the noodles in a bowl of boiling water until softened, or as directed on the package. Drain and set aside.

2 Heat 2 tbsp of the oil in a wok and cook the chicken over high heat, stirring and tossing, for 2–3 minutes, or until lightly browned. Remove from the pan and set aside.

3 Reduce the heat to medium, add the remaining oil, and stir-fry the onion for 2 minutes. Add the lemon grass, bell pepper, mushrooms, chile, and ginger, and stir-fry for 2 minutes.

4 Add the bok choy and stir-fry for another 2 minutes, then return the chicken to the pan and add the noodles. Pour in the soy sauce, fish sauce, and chili sauce, and toss everything together over the heat for 2–3 minutes, or until piping hot and the chicken is cooked through. Serve at once.

Cavolo nero, or Tuscan kale, is an extremely tasty, dark leafed kale and one of the hardiest sources of greens in the garden. Its strong flavors work well with smoked fish and garlic.

Portuguese-style kale
and haddock soup

Serves 4 • **Prep** 20 mins • **Cooking** 25 mins

INGREDIENTS

2 tbsp extra virgin olive oil

1 onion, finely chopped

3 garlic cloves, crushed through
   a press

1 large waxy potato, peeled
   and diced

1 cup whole or low-fat milk

salt and freshly ground
   black pepper

10oz (300g) cavolo nero or
   curly kale, ribs removed and
   leaves thinly sliced

10oz (300g) smoked haddock
   fillet, skinned and flaked

METHOD

1 Heat the oil in a large sauté pan or saucepan over medium heat; add the onion and cook, stirring, for 4–5 minutes, until softened. Stir in the garlic and cook 1 minute longer.

2 Add the potato and milk, then pour in enough water to cover everything by $3/4$–$1^1/4$in (2–3cm). Season generously, bring to a simmer and cook for 5 minutes, then add the kale and continue cooking for 10–15 minutes until the vegetables are tender.

3 Stir in the haddock and simmer for 1 minute, then take off the heat and cover. Leave to stand for 5 minutes to blend flavors before serving.

KALE

When to pick
Harvest this valuable source of winter greens as needed. Pick the biggest leaves first, leaving the smaller ones to mature on the plant, unless you want to eat them raw in salads.

Eat and store fresh
Eat the baby leaves raw. Trim the central rib out of larger leaves, since they can be a bit tough. Wash, dry, and store larger leaves in a plastic bag in the fridge for up to 3 days.

Freezing options
Remove any tough stalks, slice, then blanch for 2 minutes and leave to cool before freezing in freezer pots or bags. Keeps for 6 months.

This extremely tasty and economical dish, based on a traditional Tuscan soup, is my Monday night supper. To make your own store of navy beans, leave French beans to dry on the stalk.

Monday night "ribollita"

Serves 4 • **Prep** 10 mins, plus soaking • **Cooking** 2 hours 20 mins

INGREDIENTS

1 leftover roasted chicken
　　carcass
2 sticks celery, 1 roughly
　　chopped and 1 finely diced
2 carrots, 1 roughly chopped
　　and 1 finely diced
2 small onions, 1 roughly
　　chopped and 1 finely diced
1 bay leaf
1 bouquet garni
sea salt and freshly ground
　　black pepper
$1/2$ cup dried navy beans,
　　soaked overnight
2 tbsp extra virgin olive oil
2oz (50g) pancetta, diced
2 garlic cloves, crushed
2 sprigs of fresh thyme
2 handfuls shredded kale
　　leaves, or 4oz (100g) kale,
　　tough center stalks
　　removed, leaves shredded
$1/4$ cup freshly grated Parmesan

METHOD

1 Put the chicken carcass and roughly chopped celery, carrot, and onion into a large saucepan, along with the bay leaf, bouquet garni, seasoning, and 12 cups water. Bring to the boil and simmer for $1^1/2$ hours until the carcass has broken down completely. Strain the stock into another pan, reserving the carcass until cool enough to handle, then prise out all the bits of cooked meat and add them back to the stock. Clean the pan and return it to the stovetop.

2 Meanwhile, rinse the soaked beans and place in a pan with plenty of cold water. Bring to the boil, skim the top, and turn down the heat to a simmer. Cook the beans for about 1 hour, until softened. Drain and set aside.

3 Heat the olive oil in the large saucepan and add the pancetta. Cook for 2–3 minutes on medium heat, until crispy. Add the diced onion, carrot, and celery. Then add the garlic and thyme. Continue to cook for a further 2–3 minutes, until the vegetables are soft. Pour in the chicken stock and add the drained beans. Simmer the stew, uncovered, for 30–40 minutes, until the beans are soft.

4 Add the kale, cover, and cook for 5 minutes until wilted. Season to taste, add the Parmesan, and serve with bread.

CABBAGES

When to pick
Pick cabbages when the heads are tight, firm, and heavy for their size. Winter cabbages are frost-hardy, so they can be left on the plant and harvested as needed.

Eat and store fresh
Eat young fresh cabbage raw in salads and coleslaws. Store large cabbages in a cool, dark place for several weeks, or in the fridge for up to 1 week.

How to preserve
Cabbage is often salted to make sauerkraut (see pages 330–1), and is used in relishes and pickles.

Freezing options
Wash, chop, and blanch for 2 minutes. Then cool and freeze for up to 6 months.

A traditional country soup, this dish takes minutes to prepare and makes a substantial lunch or supper, served alongside some fresh crusty bread. For a vegetarian option, leave out the bacon.

French cabbage soup

Serves 4 • **Prep** 15 mins • **Cooking** 30 mins

INGREDIENTS

1 tbsp extra virgin olive oil

4oz (100g) diced bacon

1 onion, finely chopped

1 garlic clove, crushed through a press

1 large Savoy cabbage, halved, cored, and leaves cut into shreds

sea salt and freshly ground black pepper

3 sprigs of fresh parsley

METHOD

1 Heat the oil in a large flameproof casserole over medium heat. Add the bacon, setting aside 2 tbsp to finish. Stir in the onion and garlic. Cook, stirring frequently, for 3–4 minutes or until the onion and garlic start to brown. Add the shredded cabbage, reserving a handful to finish. Stir well and season lightly with sea salt, and generously with pepper. Continue cooking for 2–3 minutes, stirring occasionally.

2 Pour $3^1/_2$ cups boiling water over the vegetables and bacon, stir well, and add the parsley. Cover, lower the heat a little, and simmer gently for about 20 minutes, stirring occasionally.

3 Meanwhile, place a nonstick frying pan over medium heat. Add the reserved bacon and cook until crisp and golden. Add the reserved cabbage shreds and cook until they wilt, stirring frequently. Season with a little pepper.

4 Taste the soup and adjust the seasoning. Lift out and discard the parsley sprigs. Ladle into 4 bowls and scatter over the fried bacon and cabbage mixture.

Note The soup will freeze for up to 3 months without the bacon garnish.

This is a simpler version of the Thai salad *som tam*, which has a wonderful sweet and sour, salty, and hot dressing. Eat it just as it is, or add some cooled rice noodles to turn it into a main course.

Thai vegetable salad
with cabbage and peanuts

Serves 4 • **Prep** 15 mins

INGREDIENTS

2 eating apples

4 carrots, grated

1 small white cabbage, cored
   and shredded

handful of shelled sunflower
   seeds

handful of salted, or dry-
   roasted peanuts

For the dressing

1 tbsp soy sauce

1 tbsp Thai fish sauce (nam pla)

1 fresh green chile pepper,
   seeded and finely chopped

1 garlic clove, finely chopped

juice of 2 limes

1–2 tsp granulated sugar

handful of finely chopped
   cilantro

salt and freshly ground
   black pepper

METHOD

1 First, make the dressing. Put all the dressing ingredients in a small bowl, and mix thoroughly until the sugar has dissolved. Taste, and season with salt and black pepper as needed, then check the seasoning again. If it needs sweetening, add more sugar, and if it needs saltiness, add a little more fish sauce.

2 Quarter and core the apples, then chop into bite-sized pieces. Put in a bowl with the carrots, cabbage, and sunflower seeds. Toss well. Drizzle over the dressing, and toss together so that everything is well mixed. Transfer to a serving dish, and scatter over the peanuts.

In this dish, the slow braising of the guinea fowl allows the tender cabbage to soak up the rich flavors of the stock, transforming the humble Savoy into something really special.

Pot-roasted guinea fowl
with cabbage and walnuts

Serves 4 • **Prep** 20 mins • **Cooking** 1 hour

INGREDIENTS

2 guinea fowl, about
2³/₄lb (1.25kg) each
salt and freshly ground
black pepper
2 tbsp butter
2 tbsp extra virgin olive oil
1 small onion, finely chopped
1 leek, thinly sliced
2 celery sticks, sliced
4oz (100g) bacon, diced
³/₄ cup walnut halves
and pieces
1 small Savoy cabbage,
about 14oz (400g)
¹/₂ cup hot chicken stock

METHOD

1 Preheat the oven to 400°F (200°C). Season the guinea fowl with salt and freshly ground pepper.

2 Heat the butter with half the oil in a large, deep, flameproof casserole, and cook the guinea fowl over medium heat for 10 minutes, turning to brown on all sides. Remove from the heat and lift out the birds.

3 Add the remaining oil to the casserole with the onion, leek, celery, and bacon, and cook, stirring for 2–3 minutes, or until lightly colored. Add the walnuts, then place the guinea fowl back on top of the vegetables.

4 Cut the cabbage into 8 wedges. Tuck them into the casserole. Pour over the stock and season lightly. Bring to a boil, then cover and cook in the preheated oven for 45 minutes, or until the vegetables are tender and the guinea fowl juices run clear when pierced with a skewer.

5 Let stand 10 minutes before serving. To serve, remove the guinea fowl and cut each one in half. Arrange on plates and serve with the vegetables and cooking juices.

This traditional Christmas recipe belonged to my great and great-great grandmothers, a cheroot-smoking, poker-playing mother and daughter team who ran a restaurant in southern Sweden.

Slow-cooked Swedish
red cabbage

Serves 8 as a side dish • **Prep** 20 mins • **Cooking** 2 hours 20 mins

INGREDIENTS

4 tbsp butter

2 tbsp granulated sugar

1 tsp salt

6 tbsp unseasoned rice wine
   vinegar or wine vinegar

1 red cabbage, approx. 2$\frac{1}{4}$lb
   (1kg), cored and finely
   shredded

2 apples, peeled, cored, and
   coarsely grated

2 heaping tbsp red currant jelly

METHOD

1 Preheat the oven to 300°F (150°C). In a large, heavy, flameproof casserole, heat together the butter, sugar, salt, 6 tablespoons of water, and vinegar. Bring to a boil and simmer for 1 minute.

2 Fold the cabbage into the liquid to coat, and return to a boil. Remove the casserole from the heat and cover tightly with a double layer of foil. Fit the lid on snugly over the foil and cook in the oven for 1$\frac{1}{2}$ hours.

3 Remove from the oven and add the grated apples and red currant jelly, stirring well. Add a little more water if it looks dry. Replace the foil and the lid, and return the cabbage to the oven for another 30 minutes. Serve warm.

Salt vegetables

Preserving certain vegetables in salt relies on their natural lactic bacteria reacting with the salt and fermenting. Known as lacto-fermentation, the lactic acid produced preserves the vegetables. Lactic acid can help digestion by promoting the growth of healthy flora in the gut. The best vegetables to salt are cabbages, cucumbers, radishes, green beans, and runner beans. To calculate the salt needed, weigh the prepared vegetables and use about $^1/_4$ cup of salt for every 5$^1/_2$lb (2.5kg).

1 **Calculate the salt** Weigh the shredded cabbage and calculate the amount of salt needed. Place the cabbage in a bowl and sprinkle over the salt. Leave for a few minutes.

2 **Pack in large jar** Pack cabbage in 2in (5cm) layers; scatter caraway seeds between. Leave 3in (7.5cm) space at top. Add bowl juices and extra cold brine to cover.

Recipe Sauerkraut

Makes approx. 3lb (1.35kg) or 2 medium preserving jars • **Prep** 30–45 mins, plus fermentation
Keeps 1–2 months, refrigerated

INGREDIENTS

$5^{1}/_{2}$–$6^{1}/_{2}$lb (2.5–3kg) hard white or red cabbage, or half red and half white cabbage, shredded

approx. $^{1}/_{4}$ cup coarse sea or kosher salt

1 tbsp caraway seeds

cold brine, to cover, made from $1^{1}/_{2}$ tbsp fine sea salt to 4 cups boiled water

Successful fermentation

The ideal temperature for fermentation is 68–72°F (20–22°C). At this temperature the sauerkraut is ready in 3–4 weeks. It takes less time if it is warmer, and longer if it is colder.

If your sauerkraut develops a pinkish hue, goes dark, or is very soft and mushy, it has not fermented properly and shouldn't be eaten. You may have used too little salt, left air pockets in the jar, the cabbage was not completely submerged, it was stored too long, or the temperature was too high.

3 **Ferment cabbage** Cover with muslin, a plate, and a weighted jar. Leave at room temperature. Check daily that the cabbage is submerged. Remove scum and replace muslin.

4 **Bottle and seal** Fermentation is complete when all the bubbling has ceased. Bottle up into sterilized jars, seal, and store in the fridge.

LEEKS

When to pick
Pick leeks young for a more delicate flavor. Larger leeks should be harvested when tall and firm, and before the centre starts to harden and bolt.

Eat and store fresh
Eat baby leeks within 2 days of picking. Leave larger leeks in the ground until needed, and then store cleaned but untrimmed in the fridge for up to 1 week.

How to preserve
Leeks can be used in chutneys and pickles. Baby leeks can be grilled and preserved in oil (see pages 38–9).

Alliums are not often used as a main ingredient, but they sometimes deserve to be given a starring role. Served like this, baby leeks make a delicious starter or side dish.

Roasted baby leeks
with tomato dressing

Serves 4 • **Prep** 10 mins • **Cooking** 12 mins

INGREDIENTS

1 tbsp oil-packed sun-dried tomatoes, finely chopped

3 tbsp extra virgin olive oil, plus extra for coating the leeks

1 tbsp red wine vinegar

1 tbsp black and green olives, very finely chopped

1 tbsp fresh basil, finely chopped

sea salt and freshly ground black pepper

8 baby leeks, rinsed and trimmed

METHOD

1 Preheat the oven to 400°F (200°C)). In a bowl, mix the tomatoes with a little of their oil, the olive oil, vinegar, olives, and basil. Season with salt and pepper to taste.

2 Put the leeks into a pot of boiling water and cook over high heat for 2 minutes. Drain well.

3 Place the leeks in a roasting pan and drizzle with olive oil; toss gently to coat. Roast in the oven for 10 minutes until golden and tender. Spoon the dressing over to serve.

This is an easy way to make soup, using a potato masher rather than a blender to reduce the cooked potatoes to a rough purée. The finished soup has an interesting texture and hearty flavor.

Leek and potato soup

Serves 4 • **Prep** 15–20 mins • **Cooking** 1 hour

INGREDIENTS

2¼lb (1kg) small russet potatoes, peeled but left whole

1lb (450g) leeks, trimmed, and chopped

1 large onion, chopped

6 cups vegetable stock

4 tbsp butter

salt and freshly ground black pepper

METHOD

1 Put the potatoes, leeks, onion, and stock in a soup pot or large saucepan. Season lightly. Bring to a boil, reduce the heat, cover, and simmer for 30 minutes.

2 Using a slotted spoon, lift the potatoes out of the pot and mash with the butter. Return the mashed potatoes to the pot, stir thoroughly, and simmer for a further 25–30 minutes, stirring occasionally. If the soup gets too thick, simply add a little extra water to thin down to the required consistency. Taste and season again with salt, if necessary. Ladle into warm bowls and add a good grinding of black pepper to serve.

BELGIAN ENDIVE

When to pick
Harvest endive when young to eat raw in salads. Leave to grow larger for cooking.

Eat and store fresh
Eat salad varieties as soon as possible, or store in the fridge, unwashed, for up to 3 days. Eat radicchio raw, or char-grilled with pasta dishes. Endives can be cooked or eaten raw.

This elegant soup is best served well chilled. The subtle flavor of Belgian endive combines perfectly with orange to make a delicate and refreshing start to a meal.

Belgian endive gazpacho

Serves 4 • **Prep** 15 mins, plus chilling

INGREDIENTS

1 large orange

2 heads Belgian endive (white chicory)

2 slices bread, crusts removed, torn into large pieces

1 garlic clove, chopped coarsely

4 scallions, chopped coarsely

1 large beefsteak tomato, peeled, quartered, and seeded

2 cups cold vegetable stock

2 tbsp extra virgin olive oil, plus extra for garnish

2 tbsp white balsamic vinegar

4 large fresh basil leaves

salt and freshly ground black pepper

METHOD

1 Thinly pare the zest of half the orange. Cut it into narrow strips and cook in boiling water for 1 minute. Drain, rinse with cold water, and drain again. Set aside for garnish. Grate the remaining half of the orange zest finely, squeeze the juice, and set it aside.

2 Cut a cone shape out of the base of each head of endive and discard. Separate the heads into leaves. Reserve 4 of the smallest for garnishing. Chop the remainder coarsely.

3 Soak bread in about $1/2$ cup of water for 2 minutes. Squeeze out some moisture, then put it in a blender or food processor with the chopped endive, garlic, scallions, tomato, stock, olive oil, balsamic, basil, and the reserved orange juice and finely grated zest. Working in batches if necessary, purée and season to taste. Transfer to a bowl and refrigerate, covered, until ready to serve.

4 Ladle into 4 shallow soup bowls, and drizzle with a little olive oil. Garnish each with a tiny endive spear and a few strands of the blanched orange zest. Serve cold.

Note The soup can be frozen for up to 3 months.

The slight bitterness of the endive in this salad works well with the sweetness of the pears and the strong mustard dressing. This is delicious served with a barbecued fillet of beef.

Endive salad
with spinach and pears

Serves 6 • **Prep** 10 mins

INGREDIENTS

7–8oz (200–225g) baby
   spinach leaves

2 heads Belgian endive (white
   chicory), cores removed and
   leaves separated

2 firm, ripe pears, peeled
   and sliced

3 shallots, thinly sliced

For the vinaigrette

2 tbsp red wine vinegar

1 tbsp honey

$\frac{1}{2}$ tbsp Dijon mustard

6 tbsp extra virgin olive oil

salt and freshly ground
   black pepper

METHOD

1 To make the vinaigrette, place the vinegar, honey, mustard and oil in a screw-top jar and shake well. Season to taste with salt and pepper. Alternatively, whisk the ingredients together in a bowl.

2 Place the spinach, endive, sliced pears, and shallots in a salad bowl. Drizzle the vinaigrette over the salad, gently toss, and serve.

CELERY ROOT

When to pick
Harvest these knobbly roots when they reach the size of a tennis ball or bigger. Do not let them get too big, as they can become tough and woody.

Eat and store fresh
Store celery root for 1 week unwashed in the fridge. Alternatively, leave them in the soil until hard frosts appear, or store in the same way as potatoes (see pages 140–1).

How to preserve
Use celery root in pickles, or cooked and preserved in oil.

Freezing options
Griddle slices and open freeze on trays, or freeze as a cooked purée, for up to 9 months.

This classic French bistro dish is traditionally served with cold meats or fish. The light and tangy mustard dressing works well with the celery root and the dish is a good alternative to coleslaw.

Celery root rémoulade

Serves 6 as a side dish • **Prep** 15 mins

INGREDIENTS

2 shallots, finely chopped

2 tbsp chopped flat-leaf parsley

2 tbsp chopped fresh tarragon leaves

2 tbsp Dijon mustard

1 tbsp capers, rinsed, gently dried, and chopped

4 pickles, chopped

5 tbsp mayonnaise

1 celery root, approx. 1lb (500g), peeled

juice of 1 lemon

salt and freshly ground black pepper

METHOD

1 In a small bowl, mix together the shallots, parsley, tarragon, mustard, capers, pickles, and mayonnaise. Season to taste.

2 Coarsely grate the celery root, add the lemon juice and mix well to coat.

3 Add the mayonnaise mixture, then mix again. Adjust the seasoning and chill until required.

Celery root combines the mild taste of celery with the texture of potato to produce the perfect vegetable for soup. Any white-rinded soft cheese could be used in place of Camembert.

Camembert and celery root
soup with cranberry swirl

Serves 4 • **Prep** 10 mins • **Cooking** 25 mins

INGREDIENTS

1 1/2 tbsp of butter

1 onion, chopped

1/2 small celery root (celeriac), peeled and coarsely chopped (about 8oz (225g) prepared weight)

2 cups chicken or vegetable stock

1 bouquet garni

salt and freshly ground black pepper

2 cups whole milk

4oz (115g) ripe Camembert cheese, diced

1/4 cup heavy cream

4 tsp prepared cranberry sauce

4 tsp orange or cranberry juice

4 tsp sunflower or vegetable oil

METHOD

1 Melt butter in a large saucepan. Add onion and cook over low heat, stirring, for 3-5 minutes, or until softened but not browned. Add celery root, stock, bouquet garni, and a little salt and pepper. Bring to a boil, reduce the heat, cover and simmer gently for 15 minutes, or until celery root is tender. Discard bouquet garni.

2 Purée, using a hand-held blender or let cool slightly and transfer to a blender or food processor. Working in batches, if necessary, process in milk and cheese until well blended. Return soup to rinsed-out saucepan, stir in cream and reheat gently. Taste and adjust the seasoning.

3 Meanwhile, whisk cranberry sauce with juice and oil until blended. Ladle soup into warm soup bowls. Whisk the cranberry mixture and, using a teaspoon, swirl a little into the center of each bowl and quickly draw a wooden skewer or toothpick from the center to the edge all round to form a decorative design. Serve immediately.

A hearty, warming pie that you could also make using parsnips or Jerusalem artichokes instead of celery root. The deep, earthy flavors work particularly well with whole grain pastry.

Celery root soufflé pie

Serves 4 • **Prep** 40 mins, plus chilling • **Cooking** 50 mins

INGREDIENTS

For the pastry

1¼ cups whole wheat or
    spelt flour
a large pinch of salt
1 tbsp caraway seeds
5 tbsp cold butter, diced
3oz (85g) farmhouse Cheddar
    cheese, shredded (¾ cup)
1 egg, separated

For the filling

1 celery root, about 1lb (450g),
    peeled and cut into chunks
4 tbsp butter
¼ cup whole milk
4 thick bacon slices, diced
2 eggs, separated
2 tbsp minced chives
freshly ground black pepper

METHOD

1 Mix flour and salt in a bowl, add seeds, and rub in butter until crumbly. Stir in cheese. Mix 3 tbsp cold water with egg yolk, and stir into the flour mixture to form a firm dough, adding water if necessary. Reserve egg white for filling. Knead dough gently on floured surface, cover in plastic wrap and chill 30 minutes.

2 Meanwhile, cook celery root in salted boiling water until tender. Drain and cook briefly, stirring until dry. Add butter and milk, and mash. In a dry frying pan, cook bacon until crisp. Add bacon to celery root mixture, with bacon fat. Beat in 2 egg yolks and chives. Season.

3 Preheat oven to 400°F (200°C). Roll out the pastry and line an 8in (20cm) flan tin. Line with parchment, fill with baking beans, and bake 10 minutes. Remove paper and beans and cook 5 more minutes. Remove from oven.

4 In a large bowl, combine the 1 reserved egg white with the 2 remaining whites. Whisk the whites into stiff peaks. Mix 1 tbsp of beaten whites into celery root mixture. Fold in remaining whipped whites with a rubber spatula. Spoon into the pastry shell and bake 25 minutes until set, puffed, and golden. Serve hot.

JERUSALEM ARTICHOKES

When to pick
Harvest once the foliage has collapsed. In the colder months, leave in the ground and dig up as needed. If the ground is likely to freeze, they can be harvested and cold stored.

Eat and store fresh
Eat roasted or puréed, in stews, as soups, or in gratins. Jerusalem artichokes last up to 1 week in the fridge.

Freezing options
Jerusalem artichokes can be frozen once they have been cooked and puréed (see page 342).

These flavorsome, nutty roots seem to spring up everywhere once planted. They can be difficult to prepare, although new varieties with smoother surfaces make the process easier.

Jerusalem artichoke
soup with saffron and thyme

Serves 4–6 • Prep 15 mins • Cooking 35–45 mins

INGREDIENTS

2 tbsp virgin grapeseed oil, or extra virgin olive oil, plus extra to garnish

2 medium onions, chopped

3 garlic cloves, chopped

12oz (350g) Jerusalem artichokes (sunchokes), peeled or well scrubbed, and coarsely chopped

12oz (350g) carrots, trimmed and coarsely chopped

sea salt

5 cups hot vegetable stock

1 tbsp chopped fresh thyme leaves, or 1½ tsp dried thyme

large pinch (about 30 strands) of saffron

juice of ½ lemon

freshly ground black pepper

METHOD

1 Heat the oil in a large pan over medium heat, add the onions, and cook for 5–10 minutes, or until soft and translucent. Add the garlic and cook for 30 seconds or until fragrant. Stir in the artichokes, carrots, and a little salt, then cover with a lid and cook over low heat, stirring frequently, for 10–15 minutes or until the vegetables are softened.

2 Add the stock, thyme, and saffron, bring to a boil, then lower the heat to a simmer and cook for 20 minutes, or until the vegetables are soft.

3 Cool briefly, then purée until smooth using a hand-held blender or by transferring to a food processor or blender, in batches if necessary. Stir in the lemon juice and season to taste with salt and pepper. Serve in warm bowls, with a drizzle of grapeseed or olive oil on top.

Making a purée is one of the best ways to store Jerusalem artichokes. This tastes sublime served with roasted meat or game, baked with eggs and cream, or thinned as a soup.

Jerusalem artichoke
freezer purée

Makes approx. 2^1/$_4$lb (1kg) • **Prep** 10 mins • **Cooking** 30 mins

INGREDIENTS

1 tbsp fresh lemon juice
2^1/$_4$lb (1kg) Jerusalem
    artichokes (sunchokes)
^{1}/$_3$ cup heavy cream
4 tbsp butter, cut into pieces
splash of whole milk
salt and freshly ground
    black pepper
pinch of grated nutmeg

METHOD

1 Stir the lemon juice into a large bowl of cold water. Peel the artichokes as thinly as possible, removing only the thin skin, or just leave the skins on and scrub the vegetables well if you don't mind a discolored purée. Cut them into pieces roughly the same size, and immediately put them into the lemon water as you work.

2 Drain, place in a large saucepan, and cover with fresh water. Bring to a boil, reduce the heat slightly, and simmer for about 25 minutes or until very tender. Drain and return to the pan. Heat gently, stirring, to dry out.

3 Put the artichokes through a ricer or food mill, purée with a blender, food processor, or mash thoroughly with a potato masher. Beat in the cream, butter, and milk, and season to taste with salt, black pepper, and the nutmeg.

4 Leave to cool, then pack in small portion-sized freezer containers with lids, or plastic freezer bags. Seal, label, and freeze. Thaw before reheating.

Note Keeps for 6 months in the freezer unopened.

Home-grown rutabagas tend to be smaller and sweeter than store-bought ones. This versatile vegetable purée is absolutely delicious and can be served in place of mashed potatoes.

Creamed rutabagas

Serves 4–5 • **Prep** 10 mins • **Cooking** 25 mins

INGREDIENTS

2½lb (1.1kg) rutabagas, peeled and cut into chunks

salt and freshly ground black pepper

4 tbsp butter, cut into pieces

2–3 tbsp heavy cream

pinch of grated nutmeg

METHOD

1 Place the rutabagas in a large saucepan. Add enough cold water to cover, and a pinch of salt. Bring to a boil, cover, reduce the heat, and simmer for 20 minutes, or until tender. Drain well.

2 Return the drained rutabagas to the saucepan and place over very low heat to dry out. Add the butter, mash well, then add the cream and grated nutmeg. Season to taste with salt and pepper, and mash again until smooth.

Note To save time when planning a big meal, this purée can be made up to 2 days in advance. Refrigerate until needed and reheat just before serving

RUTABAGAS

When to pick
Young rutabagas have a sweet taste and can be picked from tennis-ball-size upwards. Rutabagas may be left in the soil to grow larger, although they can become woody.

Eat and store fresh
Eat smaller rutabagas soon after harvesting. Store larger ones in the fridge for 1 week, or in a clamp for longer (see pages 140–1).

Freezing options
Freeze as a cooked purée and keep for up to 9 months.

TURNIPS

When to pick
Early turnips are delicious when picked at golf ball size. Leave other varieties to grow larger and they will have a stronger taste, and can turn woody.

Eat and store fresh
Eat baby turnips as soon as possible. Store larger ones in the fridge for 1 week, leave in the ground until the first frosts, or harvest and cold store (clamp).

How to preserve
Turnips can be used in pickles and chutneys.

Freezing options
Freeze as a cooked purée and keep for up to 9 months.

343

Turnips are often overlooked, but you won't be disappointed with this light, colorful soup with a chile kick. Larger turnips have a stronger flavor and are perfect for using in this recipe.

Turnip noodle soup
with pimento and chile

Serves 4–6 • Prep 10 mins • Cooking 30 mins

INGREDIENTS

4 scallions, chopped

2 large turnips, peeled and diced

½ tsp crushed hot red pepper flakes

1 fresh green jalapeño chile pepper, seeded and cut into thin rings

2 star anise

2 tsp tomato purée

4 cups hot vegetable stock, or light chicken stock

4oz (125g) dried, thin Chinese egg noodles

1 canned or bottled pimento, drained and chopped

soy sauce, to taste

freshly ground black pepper

small handful of fresh cilantro leaves, torn

METHOD

1 Put the scallions, turnips, pepper flakes, chile, star anise, tomato purée, and stock in a soup pot or large saucepan and bring to a boil. Lower the heat, partially-cover, and simmer gently for 30 minutes or until the turnips are very tender. Discard the star anise.

2 Meanwhile, put the noodles in a bowl, cover with boiling water, and leave to stand for 5 minutes, stirring to loosen, then drain. Stir the noodles into the soup, along with the pimento. Season to taste with soy sauce and pepper, then stir in half the cilantro. Ladle into warm soup bowls, top with the remaining cilantro, and serve.

As winter approaches you may have enormous parsnips left on your plot. This warming soup is an ideal use for them. Their natural sweetness is balanced by a mild curry flavor.

Curried parsnip
and apple soup

Serves 4 • **Prep** 20 mins • **Cooking** 30 mins

INGREDIENTS

1 tbsp extra virgin olive oil

1 1/2 tsp butter

1/2 cup finely chopped onion

1 garlic clove, crushed

2 tsp mild curry powder

2 1/4 lb (1kg) parsnips, chopped

sea salt and freshly ground
    black pepper

1 large Granny Smith or
    Bramley apple, peeled,
    cored, and chopped

4 cups hot vegetable stock, or
    chicken stock

6 tbsp half-and-half

2 tbsp fresh lemon juice

METHOD

1 Heat the oil and butter in a large sauté pan over low heat. Add the onion, garlic, and curry powder, and cook gently, stirring frequently, for 2–3 minutes or until the onion has softened. Add the parsnips and season lightly with salt and pepper. Turn the heat up a little and cook, stirring frequently, for 5 minutes or until the parsnips are golden.

2 Add the apple, stir for 1 minute, then pour in the stock and bring to a boil. Lower the heat and simmer for 10–12 minutes or until the parsnips are tender. Take off the heat and leave to cool for several minutes, then transfer to a blender or food processor, and process until smooth and creamy. (Alternatively, use a hand-held blender to purée the mixture.)

3 Pass the soup through a sieve placed over the sauté pan, then rinse out the blender with 1/2 cup hot water and stir this into the soup. Reheat gently, then stir in the cream and lemon juice. Adjust the seasoning and serve piping hot.

PARSNIPS

When to eat
Pick baby parsnips as required. Larger parsnips are ready to be picked when the leaves die back, but will have a sweeter flavor if picked after the first frosts.

Eat and store fresh
Store in the fridge for up to 1 week, or in a cool, dry place for up to 2 weeks. Parsnips can also be stored in the soil in boxes (see pages 268–9), or cold stored (clamped) until needed (see pages 140–1).

How to preserve
Use parsnips for home brewing or as an ingredient in chutneys.

Freezing options
Freeze as a cooked purée and keep for up to 9 months.

INDEX

Page numbers in **bold** indicate main treatment of, and techniques for dealing with, each type of crop. Page numbers in *italics* indicate recipes.

INDEX

ACKNOWLEDGMENTS

Picture credits

All images © Dorling Kindersley.
For further information see www.dkimages.com.
Except: 270 (tl), 272–3: © Rough Guides; 53, 55, 56:
Foodcollection RF © Getty

Dorling Kindersley would like to thank

Luis Peral for his art direction at the photoshoot, Jane Lawrie for her food styling, and Sue Rowlands for her props styling; Tessa Bindloss and Nicola Erdpresser for design help; Claire Bowers and Romaine Werblow for picture research; Anna Burges-Lumsden and Jan Fullwood for recipe testing; Sue Morony for proofreading; Liz Cook for indexing.

Caroline Bretherton's acknowledgments

My thanks go to all at Dorling Kindersley, for giving me such a joy of a project. To my parents, at whose respective knees I learnt the gentle arts of gardening and cooking. Also, to my husband, who has tirelessly consumed and appreciated almost everything I've ever cooked, as well as being a source of much encouragement. To Gabriel and Isaac, who are learning to eat most of what we grow with little fuss. Finally, thanks must go to the Acton Gardening Association, whose gift of an allotment has given me untold pleasure over the years.